PETER SCHARF
ARNOLD BINDER

THE
BADGE
AND THE
BULLET

POLICE USE
OF DEADLY FORCE

PRAEGER

PRAEGER SPECIAL STUDIES • PRAEGER SCIENTIFIC

Library of Congress Cataloging in Publication Data

Scharf, Peter, 1945-
  The badge and the bullet.

  Bibliography: p.
  Includes index.
  1. Police shootings—United States. I. Binder,
Arnold. II. Title.
HV8141.S29 1983   363.2'32   83-4106
ISBN 0-03-062963-2
ISBN 0-03-062964-0 [pbk.]

Published in 1983 by Praeger Publishers
CBS Educational and Professional Publishing
a Division of CBS Inc.
521 Fifth Avenue, New York, NY 10175 USA
©Praeger Publishing

Printed in the United States of America
on acid-free paper

THE
BADGE
AND THE
BULLET

To Doris, Adria, Sage, Razi, and Tessa,
and to Virginia, Andrea, Jeffrey, and Jennifer

Acknowledgments

Much of the substance of this book came from ideas developed while the writers were principal investigators of a research project funded by the National Institute of Justice, U.S. Department of Justice. The research was aimed at evaluating the use of deadly force by police officers on a national basis from the perspectives of social forces on the police, psychological characteristics of individual officers, and the problems of management and control. The project manager for the research was Shirley Melnicoe, a person as competent as she is genial and helpful.

All ideas expressed in this book are the authors', and do not necessarily reflect any position or opinion of the National Institute of Justice or its parent organization, the U.S. Department of Justice.

Our most intense investigations were in the police departments of Birmingham, Miami, Newark, and Oakland. The line officers, supervisors, administrative officers, and, most particularly, the chiefs in those cities were cooperative to a degree that most critics of the police would find unbelievable. Our deepest gratitude is therefore directed to the police in those cities—and most especially to Chiefs Bill Myers, Ken Harms, Hubert Williams, and George Hart.

Critical in helping us get the research underway and in carrying it through to a successful conclusion were David Schetter, Doris McBride, Shirley Hoberman, Debbie Dunkle, and Marti Dennis of the Public Policy Research Organization at the University of California, Irvine. Ray Galvin joined our research team early as a coworker and remained as our expert on police management and practices who would never let us drift too far into the world of fuzzy thinking. Gil Geis worked as a team member at various points in the project, while being at all times a close, helpful friend.

Other police professionals who contributed significantly to the research effort directly and to this book indirectly are Jack Kenney, James Fisk, George Tielsch, George Dicksheid, Ed Lingo, Sister Roberta Derby, and Lee Hitchcock.

And we exaggerate not one bit when we point out that the book would have been impossible without the devoted assistance of Carol Wyatt.

PETER SCHARF
ARNOLD BINDER

Contents

THE
BADGE
AND THE
BULLET

1 Violence—American Style

SHOOTING IN THE GHETTO

In the summer of 1980, one of us had the opportunity to ride along as an observer with a tactical patrol unit (Target Red) in the central ward of the city of Newark. Newark is, as almost everyone knows, one of the more violent cities in the United States. In July, more than 25 citizens died at the hands of other human beings. A three-month-old baby was killed in a revenge slaying. A respected black community leader was killed as he mildly reprimanded two young robbers who were holding up his store. Another shopkeeper was killed as he delivered his money to his attackers. An elderly man was killed because he had but a few dollars to give his attackers.

At every turn the city gives evidence of the price exacted by urban violence. Many of the stores and buildings are abandoned, long torched by arsonists. Interestingly, one finds an ethnic history in many scorched stores: Goldstein's Tailor Shop, Marcutti's Radio Store, Sullivan's Meat Market. A bent sign hangs outside a Safeway store: "To our customers: We will open soon. Signed A. Guzzi, Manager, July 1967." Many of the stores still in business are guarded by armed security guards. Tellingly, in an ice-cream parlor, a strawberry ice-cream cone is retrieved through a slot behind a bulletproof glass protecting the clerks.

As the tactical team begins its Saturday night patrol, several of the most hardened veterans speculate that even for Newark this night will be special. "Something," one of them says, "is surely going to go down tonight." No more than ten minutes after the car leaves the tactical patrol headquarters, the officers see a young, tall, black man offering plastic bags of heroin to the mostly white passersby in their cars. The officers jump from the car and frisk, search, and handcuff the man. A dark woman runs up to the car just as the police officers arrest the man, screaming:

> Don't let them take him, I'm pregnant. We just got married. I only have had him three months. Don't let them take him. It's my husband. Don't take him away. We just got married a week ago. Don't hurt him. He didn't do nothing wrong. Don't do it.

As the police officers move the man toward the car, a small crowd hostilely gathers in front of the police car. One man in Black Muslim garb menaces the officers: "Where are you taking that man?" As the car starts to drive away, the man's wife suddenly throws herself on the car, screaming again and again, "Don't do it . . . don't do it." The prisoner shakes noticeably. "It ain't right," he moans. "Please, mister, don't do it." The crowd thickens. Finally, the Black Muslim grabs the woman and tells her, "They're just doing their job, honey. You'll see him again." The officers relax in the car and drive the man to the station. A warrant check indicates that he is wanted for robbery in two states and for murder in another.

The booking precinct turned out to be almost as bizarre as the world the officers had left on the streets. As the officers were writing their reports, a young man came into the station requesting a patrol car to aid his mother, who, according to him, was being attacked on an upper floor of a housing project across the street from the police station.

> *Young Man:* Please, sir, come quick, my mother is being attacked.
> *Police Sergeant:* Where is she?
> *Young Man:* On the seventh floor of the Hays Project, Apartment 702.
> *Police Sergeant:* Why didn't you call 733-6000?
> *Young Man:* It's always busy. Are you going to send someone?
> *Police Sergeant:* I don't have a single car to send.
> *Young Man:* What about these guys [looking at us]?
> *Police Sergeant:* They're busy. Look, son, it's a rough town.

The young man left in disgust. A few minutes later a cab driver staggered into the precinct bleeding from a wound below the neck.

"This whore took me to the Club 666. Said she's give me a blow job free and then these guys came out from the bar and took my money and shot me. . . ." Several minutes later, the woman herself entered the station with a friend, complaining that "this cab driver" had stolen her house keys. The woman was arrested; the cab driver was taken to the hospital.

Minutes later another car brought in a man, mercilessly beaten about the face. "He might die," one of the officers offered prophetically. The officer went on to observe that "this guy was a hit man who tried to stiff out a dealer twice his size with a .25. He hit the guy in the shoulder and then the bigger guy did this to him with his gun. Tragic, ain't it?" The sergeant, at this point, chimed in with some additional news to add to the lore of the evening: "Guess what; they hit Sully, the dealer that owns the Lucky Star. 357 car found him; $1,600 cash in his pants, keys to his El Dorado. I guess they weren't trying to rob him."

As the tactical team finally left the station, its prisoner at last incarcerated in a cell, the officers heard the following dispatch: "455 officer needs assistance. Shots fired. Special Officer 235 Seymour Ave." As they reached the address, the officers saw a young security guard waving frantically at them with a shotgun.

> *Italian Security Guard:* They came up to me and tried to get my gun—like this [demonstrates].
> *Black Tactical Officer:* How many of them were there?
> *Italian Security Guard:* A dozen; I kicked one of them out and they all came back trying to get me.
> *Black Man on Street:* He could have hit some children. There were children down the street.
> *Another Black Man on Street:* He was wrong. That's how you get riots by doing shit like this. Good thing he didn't hit no one or there be lots of buildings burning tonight.
> *Italian Security Guard:* [Talking rapidly to the black police officer.] What do you do when a nigger tries to take your gun? He was just like this [demonstrates].
> *Black Tactical Officer:* A what?

A few minutes later, while patrolling in a known red-light district, the team stopped to chat with a few other officers. "Look over there," said one officer. "There are some shitum, dragging another one into that lot." "I guess that's one less shitum," the other officer nonchalantly replied. While continuing their discussion, the officers received a call to assist on a person-shot call. The officers sped to a dark side street in the south end of town and found a man lying on the ground bleeding from a gunshot wound in the leg.

Officer: Who shot you?

Man: These guys from Springfield.

Officer: Let me talk with the detectives [turns on portable radio]. [To the radio.] Hey, there is this guy on Tenth Street who's been shot by three guys who he said robbed him. What do you want me to do with him?

Radio: Does he know who shot him?

Officer: Do you know their names? Where they live?

Man: Oh, it hurts. Not truthfully. I think they hang out up on Seventeenth and Springfield, I think.

Officer: [Into the radio.] No!

Radio: Take the guy to the hospital, write the report, and routine it.

Officer: Routine it?

Radio: Yah, routine it. We're busy here.

The tactical team car rode on. A few blocks later they passed a group of 15 or 20 young men hovering over a heated game of dice.

Officer One: You see that guy cover up?

Officer Two: Yup. You want to do 'em?

Officer One: Why the fuck not?

As the young officers approached the dice game, most of the participants automatically scattered into the streets. Two men were singled out and halted. One of the men was the young man whom the officers had noticed before. As he spread-eagled on the wall, the officer whistled, "Look what we found here, a .32 with six, nine, no, thirteen bullets. My, my." The apparent owner of the gun was placed in the car and began to chatter: "It wasn't mine. This guy gave it to me. He said he was going down to Eighteenth and for me to hold it. My weekend's all fucked up. Can you imagine two years in jail for a lousy favor? I'm going to get that motherfucker when I get out. You can motherfucking believe that. Hey, you guys got some dope I can smoke? I really need some herb. . . ."

After booking the man with the gun in the precinct, the officers returned to the street. Less than a block from the precinct they received a call to investigate a shot-fired call involving a shotgun in a Spanish billiard parlor in a high-crime zone. The glass window of the billiard parlor was totally shattered by the blast. A short black man stood, obviously shaken, next to a rather large woman—his mother.

Mother: God damn Norman, he's gone too far.
Police Officer: Who's Norman?
Mother: He's my son's cousin, my nephew. He lives with me sometimes.
Police Officer: Where is Norman now?
Mother: Well, he'll be at 177 Chestnut at about midnight. I know he'll
be there, and I know he'll have the shotgun.

Apparently the blast was the work of Norman. The team hid behind a wall in front of 177 Chestnut Street. Some children approached them: "Hey, are you police officers?" An older teenager laughingly approached the front of the house. "Hey, you guys want some broads?" He laughed and walked on. Another young man approached the officers kneeling with their shotguns.

Man: Hey, someone just broke into my house.
Police Officer: Can't you see we're busy?
Man: You guys don't do shit! You are never fucking there when anyone
needs you.

Finally, after waiting more than an hour, the officers saw a man dancing down the middle of Chestnut Street. It is the son, who presumably was a target of assassination an hour earlier. He obviously was drunk. "Hey, guess what?" he calls to his friends on the sidewalks. "The police are going to shoot Norman. The police are out there with shotguns and are going to kill Norman." The tactical officers sullenly resheathed their shotguns and returned to the car.

Driving back toward the center of town, the officers stopped to talk with a "snitch" watching a group of nearly 50 black bikers contentedly drinking beer and chatting on their parked motorcycles. "It's been quiet here," offered the snitch. "I don't know about the rest of the area." All of a sudden the patrol car radio began spewing forth a series of "in-progress" reports that highlighted life at its worst in Newark:

●   Shots fired, Club 666; persons hit; check to see if there is someone who knows about a baby left in a baby carriage. One of the victims was its mother.
●   Shots fired; tavern; amphetamine robbery; several persons; roll both a unit and two ambulances to the location; looks like same guys on job before; check license 790 *L*ove *V*ictor *U*tah, New York; four black males; older model Olds or Ford.

Finally:

• Car 127 has observed a car matching that description; Eighth and Avon; three or four males seem to be inside; they are in pursuit; all cars please assist.

In the tactical car, the officers advise the observer to "hold on." As they speed toward Eighth and Avon, barely missing several cars. one officer whistles, "I wish I had my lollipop, I wish I had it now," obviously to relieve the tension. Suddenly, there appeared before the speeding tactical car the flashing red lights of Car 127 less than one block in front of them. Just ahead of the tactical car was a white Ford with New York plates weaving chaotically. Later, an official report would describe the events that transpired as follows:

> 0010 hrs P/O M. along with P/O C. L. in unit 127 were fired upon by three suspects in an auto that they had been following which committed several traffic violations. These officers while following a 1965, Ford reg. 790 LVU with 3/B/M, attempted to pull this suspect auto over to check same out. This auto tried to elude these officers and suspects fired twice at P/O A. and L. Officer L. then returned this fire by firing four times at these suspects. This auto continued to elude these officers but were finally apprehended at 108 Sherman ave with all occupants by unit 516 P/O J. and P/O M.
>
> Driver of this auto M. W. of 30 Gillette Pl. was found to have been shot in the rt. shoulder upon apprehension. This suspect was taken to College Hospital where he was detained for gunshot wound of the rt. shoulder.

At the sound of each shot, the officers picked up speed. Finally, the white Ford stopped, with officers from 516, 127, and our car pulling three men from the vehicle—one man was bleeding profusely from an arm wound—which now sat double-parked (almost innocently) at an intersection with a busy tavern on one corner filled with happy drinkers. Several dozen men and women from the bar poured out onto the street to see what had happened. An unmarked car carrying the tactical team commander, a lieutenant, also arrived on the street corner:

Lieutenant: What happened? Is everyone alright? You okay? You sure?
Officer: I'm okay! [He pulls nervously and in pain at his right trigger finger as if he had hurt it in his hurried firing.]
Lieutenant: Now, what happened?
Officer: The cocksuckers shot at me, that's all; the cocksucker shot at me.

By now, the rather drunk spectators became bolder. One man announced in a loud belligerent voice, not directed, however, at anyone in particular: "Why don't you poleece go shoot people in your own neighborhood? Why did you go shoot this poor nigger in the car? It happens all the time; the police shoot at us poor niggers. I'm tired of this shit!" The man in the car lay writhing in pain. "Ooh," he screamed, "get me a doctor." A man who was riding in Tac Car 127 (a prisoner in custody due to a child support warrant) fended off an angry police officer who glared at him, almost pleading, "I didn't have nothing to do with this. I'm here for something else."

The shooting of the man in the car would be the fifteenth police use of deadly force incident in Newark during 1980. It was but one of the almost 2,000 incidents in the United States during that year in which experts estimate a police bullet would hit a human being. The remainder of this volume will present a perspective on the police officer's decision to use or withhold deadly force. What are the social factors that determine whether a police officer will use deadly force in an encounter with a citizen? What types of police use of deadly force are avertable? What strategies exist to control unnecessary police use of deadly force and to prevent further violence following a controversial police shooting?

In Chapter Two, "The Dilemmas of Police Deadly Force," we use four illustrations of actual deadly force encounters with different outcomes to demonstrate the many facets of police decision making where shooting is a potential or actual outcome. In Chapter Three, "A Tool of the Trade," we will describe the cultural marriage of the gun with policing and the gun as a "psychological identity tool" of many police officers. We will suggest that guns for police officers serve a variety of symbolic purposes in addition to the obvious protective one. We will also describe the importance of police weapons in contexts where no shot at a human being might even plausibly be fired, illustrating the variety of purposes guns serve in different police activities.

In Chapter Four, "Barrel to Barrel," we will describe the variety of armed confrontations faced by police officers, emphasizing situational differences in the opponents faced by police officers. The type of opponent, whether an "instrument" criminal or an insane person, creates very different dilemmas for the police officer. Similarly, we will suggest the importance of the mode of contact (off-duty, regular patrol, or planned apprehension), the numbers of officers present, and "space and light" in determining the decision to use deadly force and the outcome of an armed confrontation.

Chapter Five, "We Pay Them to Make Decisions," will analyze some of the differences in confrontations that result in shots being fired against an opponent with those in which deadly force is averted. We will analyze in depth two cases involving very similar circumstances but very different outcomes. In one incident a woman armed with a knife is killed by two police officers. In the other incident, a woman similarly armed is arrested without injury to her or to the police officer. We will also suggest that one key to understanding the differences between the two types of incidents is to focus upon decisions made by police officers early in the confrontation. Finally, we will analyze the social influences that shape police officer decisions at each phase of the encounter.

In Chapter Six, "Police Officers Are Human Like the Rest of Us," we will analyze the psychological competencies required for an officer to cope effectively with armed confrontations. We will describe the personality profiles of some officers who have shot numerous times, contrasting them with officers who have rarely fired in scores of armed confrontations. We will, for example, explore the role of human emotions, ability to recognize reality accurately in armed confrontations, interpersonal and physical skills, and moral judgment as they affect the police officer's ability to cope with armed confrontations.

In Chapter Seven, "Administrative Control," we will analyze the impact of police administrative policies and procedures upon decisions to use deadly force: How does formal police administrative policy affect a typical police officer's decision process in armed confrontations? What influence, similarly, do shooting guidelines, training, operational rules, and shooting review exert upon the rate of police deadly force?

The final chapter is an overview of some of the remedies that follow from the analysis. How might police departments control unnecessary use of deadly force and ameliorate the consequences of those incidents that do occur?

It is our goal to describe, as faithfully as we are able, the complex world of the police officer as decision maker. The extent of our success will depend upon our ability to isolate those forces that influence police decisions to use deadly force and to understand the world of the police officer without either undeserved praise or condemnation.

2 The Dilemmas of Police Deadly Force

Few cities are as violent as Newark in terms of the frequency and intensity of expression in citizen-to-citizen encounters. Nevertheless, more generally, violence is almost as centrally associated with the American image in the 1980s as apple pie and McDonald's hamburgers. Concrete support for the appropriateness of that association is readily available in the crime statistics provided by the Federal Bureau of Investigation in its Uniform Crime Reports. And the police throughout the United States cannot avoid that violence any more than the police in Newark can. Indeed, the shooting of the man in the car, as described in Chapter One, was one of possibly 2,000 incidents in 1980 that resulted in a police officer wounding or killing a citizen with a gun.

Although that shooting in Newark was not at all controversial, conceptual questions regarding the officer's decision to use deadly force are still relevant. What tactics by the officers preceded the shooting? Could these have been changed? Why did the officer fire at the car rather than break off the pursuit? What enabled him to remain calm enough to hit the driver of the car in the midst of a relatively high-speed pursuit?

It is also important to understand the impact of the shooting on both the officers involved and the community. How do officers understand their decision to use deadly force? What is the long-term impact of a use of deadly force upon their lives? How do perceptions of community members of such incidents differ from those of police officers? What is the relationship of such differences in perceptions to further disorder and violence?

Finally, there are questions as to how the rights of citizens and police officers are to be balanced in a manner consistent with the ideals of fairness implicit in a democratic society? What risks should constitute a sufficient threat to warrant the use of deadly force by a police officer? How might policies be developed to protect simultaneously the safety of police officers and of citizens who are threatened by criminal activity? What policies might be encouraged to reduce the chance of injury or death to both police officers and citizens?

The following inquiry is important for political and moral, as well as very immediate practical, reasons. Many communities have been literally torn asunder following a perceived abuse of police force. The Miami and Chattanooga riots of 1980 and 1982 as well as 84 of 136 of the major urban riots of the 1960s, were precipitated by perceived abuses of police force.[1] Other major cities have experienced profound political unrest over the issues of the police control of deadly force. At the same time, minority citizens have charged the police with abusing their power in the use of deadly force, and police officer unions have argued that overly restrictive shooting policies have hampered their officers' effectiveness and ignored the safety of their lives. It might be added that the deadly force issue has often polarized blacks and whites, liberals and conservatives, and police officers and civilians.

Obviously, the issue of police deadly force poses some difficult moral issues for a constitutional democracy. It reflects, in very real terms, Weber's observation that the idea of the nation state implies by definition a monopoly of legitimate force in the hands of the state.[2] The very concept of the state thus implies a capacity to defend its interests by force, including lethal force. On the other hand, a democratic society demands that any use of force be bounded by firm rules. Also, the ideals of the U.S. Constitution imply that force in our society be minimized and used in only the most extreme situations. Viewed in this context, the issue of police deadly force reflects the symbolic issue of the moral limits of the power of the state.

In terms of human cost, the problem of police deadly force is far from an insignificant problem. This year, at least 300, and possibly 600 people, according to Sherman and Langworthy, will be killed by police officers.[3] Many more will be wounded (some permanently) by police bullets. Additionally, about 100 police officers will be killed by citizens and more than 400 police officers assaulted by deadly weapons. In many thousands of incidents, armed police officers will confront citizens who actually (or are believed to) possess deadly weapons.

The terrain to be covered in this inquiry clearly will be extremely broad, involving concepts from many fields. We hope to describe to the readers, as faithfully as we can, the world of police officers faced with armed confrontations. We will present in the final chapter some remedies we believe essential to control police deadly force. More importantly, however, we hope to present a novel and coherent perspective toward the problem of police use of deadly force. This perspective views the police officer as a decision maker faced with violent human interactions and not much time for thought. As illustrated by the case described earlier, the reasons an officer shoots or doesn't shoot result from complex immediate and long-range circumstances. We will attempt to understand police decisions to use deadly force in a complex matrix of social forces (such as a police department, legal context, and larger social culture). These forces, we will argue, both influence and help interpret the decision to use deadly force in armed confrontations with citizens.

FOUR ARMED CONFRONTATIONS

To introduce the major conceptual dilemmas of police use of deadly force, we will briefly describe four armed confrontations faced by police officers in four different circumstances. Each officer, facing a unique set of circumstances, made a decision as to whether or not to fire his gun and possibly take a human life. In two of these confrontations, the officers fired shots that killed people; in the other two encounters, no shot was fired by a police officer.

The Man with the Ax on Market Street

In some confrontations, a use of deadly force almost certainly saves the officer's or another person's life. Officers P. and W. were on foot patrol at a main intersection of a business district in one of the most crime-ridden and violent cities in the United States. The officers were enjoying a quiet moment in a rather busy day when they saw an older officer across the street. One of the officers described the moments leading up to the confrontation:

> We were walking along the street and we see Sid directing traffic. Sid was a real nice old man and we just were about to wave when we see this man run across the street and hit Sid across the back with a long-handled ax maybe two feet long. We were stunned, but we just run across the street to help, cutting through the cars, trucks, and buses.

As the officers rushed across the street, they saw the badly wounded officer limp away from his assailant, with the ax, bizarrely, still stuck between his shoulder blades. The black male who was attacking the officer attempted forcefully to wrest his ax from the wounded officer but had difficulty as the ax stuck in the cloth of the heavy jacket the officer was wearing. After he finally freed the ax from the bleeding man, he pulled the ax up, ready to strike his victim again. An official report described the incident up to this point:

> The officers immediately started across the street to assist the wounded officer, weaving their way thru traffic. Officer H., wounded and moving away from the assailant, talking to him and attempting to draw his revolver. In the seconds it took P. and W. to cross the intersection, the assailant had tripped, got up, and started pursuing Officer H., who was still moving and had reached a point at the northesast corner in front of 786 Broad St. As Officers W. and P. arrived, the assailant was standing in the street in front of 776 Broad St., facing Officer H. (who was wounded and leaning on a parked auto), with the ax raised to strike him a second blow.

In the moments that followed, Officer W. rushed to protect the badly wounded policeman; Officer P. faced the man and, in his own words, "Tried to get the guy's attention, you know, have him get me. I said something like 'how about me?' Come get someone your own size. Something like that."

Eventually, the man came toward Officer P.; however, Officer P. was unable to fire at the man immediately, because a crowd of almost 800 people had gathered to watch in horror the bizzare events occurring at 11:41 A.M., on one of the busiest intersections of the city. Carefully, Officer P. maneuvered the man toward him but circled so that he was facing the wall of a bank and the crazed man with the ax facing the street. Still, the officer held his fire demanding that the man drop his weapon; the man came ever closer with the ax raised over his head. Officer P., now less than four feet from him and kneeling by the curb, finally fired his gun. The first shot had, according to the officer, almost no effect. "It was like it just didn't bother him. He was coming towards me with his ax in his hand. I fired again. He suddenly got this strange look in his eyes and blood came out of his mouth and he fell down." An official report, recommending the officers for medals, described the final moments as follows:

> He [the assailant] turned towards the officers and backed onto the sidewalk making a semicircle. He then came back into the street, this time facing P/O P. and shouted, "You're next, motherfucker!" and started towards P. with the ax raised to strike. P/O P. again told him to drop the ax, and when his commands were ignored by the assailant and when the assailant took another step in his direction screaming, "You're next!" P. fired a round from his service revolver. When this failed to stop the assailant, P. fired a second shot, also striking the man in the chest. This time the assailant fell to the ground fatally wounded.

This case provides an illustration of the type of imminent threat that is characteristic of many, if not most, incidents where police officers use deadly force. In other confrontations, the threat to the police officer is far more ambiguous, as illustrated by this next incident.

"They Shot the Wrong Woman"

The approbation that followed the shooting of the man with the ax by the police is certainly not a typical reaction to a police shooting. Often the reaction of the community is one of indifference, occasionally it is shock without animosity toward the police, and often it is outrage toward the police that may be so strong it leads to demonstrations (which may become violent). The last of these is most often associated with the killing or serious wounding of a member of a minority group.

The indifferent reaction is typically associated with a media report of the wounding or killing of a bank robber who was carrying a gun or of a young hoodlum in a shoot-out with the police or of a similarly dangerous criminal. Shock comes when the expectations of impeccable professionalism on the part of the police are upset, but there is no reason to believe that the shooting was more than an unfortunate mistake—for example, no reason to invoke a concept such as racial bigotry. In Newark, for instance, a young Guardian Angel was recently shot by a local police officer while he was responding to a report of a burglary. A female police officer in Nashville shot three people trapped during a holdup. And an off-duty New York police officer shot and killed two brothers who were pursuing a man who had just robbed them in their small bodega.

In contrast, the case of the killing of Bonita Carter provides a dramatic illustration of a police shooting that led to outrage and to violent demonstration. The incident that led to the death of Bonita Carter began rather inauspiciously: On Friday, June 22, 1979, a man named Alger Pickett became embroiled in a dispute with Mike Avery, an employee of Jerry's Quik Mart (a 7–11 store) in Birmingham, Alabama.[4] The dispute began when Pickett objected to paying for gasoline before pumping; it became more and more intense, reaching a point of mutual punching. The fight was broken up by two other men. Pickett left the store and drove away but returned shortly thereafter. After parking on the 7–11 lot, he opened the car's trunk and removed a rifle. He shot from the parking lot into the store with that rifle, hitting Avery in the left shoulder with one of the bullets.

Employees from the store shot back at Pickett, including a double shotgun blast. Pickett ran away, crossing a street and leaving his car behind. From his distant position he called out a request to have his car driven off the parking lot to his present location.

A young woman by the name of Bonita Carter responded to his request; she got into his car and started driving it off the lot. She was a rather tall girl who was wearing a cap that concealed her hair. As Carter was pulling away, the manager of the store ran after the car with a pistol in hand. The manager, Ray Jenkins, had been sleeping in a rear storage area and, when awakened by the earlier shots, guessed that a robbery had taken place. He assumed, as he ran after the car driven by Carter, that he was chasing a robber who shot his friend Avery.

Two Birmingham police officers were arriving in the 7–11 parking lot for a refreshment stop when they heard a radio dispatch stating that there was a robbery in progress at the store. The dispatch in that form came about because Jenkins had earlier triggered a robbery alarm when he came into the store proper from the storage area. The officers stopped their car abruptly and, with guns drawn, went toward the car driven by Carter, which by this time had stopped in response to shouted orders from Jenkins. As the officers approached the car, Jenkins stated, "That is the car. They have got a shotgun. They shot Mike."[5] Officer Hollingsworth approached the car from the rear on the driver's side and Officer Sands from the rear on the passenger's side. They called out a warning to Carter that they were police officers, but she was apparently petrified by the whole affair by this time and slumped down in a concealed fashion on the front seat.

Several witnesses to the events stated that they shouted to the officers that the driver was an innocent girl, not the man who shot into the store, but in all the excitement the officers apparently did not hear them. As the officers eased toward the car, a head with a light colored hat suddenly popped up. Officer Sands fired four times. Carter died a short time later.

The area of Birmingham in which the shooting took place is characteristic of many urban "zones in transition" in that it faces severe racial tensions and often violence. A reflection of the violent atmosphere in this area is evident in the testimony before the hearing committee called to investigate the case. Wayne Crusoe, another employee of the 7-11 store on duty on the night of the Carter shooting, testified before the committee as follows:

> Well, sir, while I was stocking, which I think was approximately about five minutes after I had been in the cooler, I first heard something go bam, which I thought was the cooler door opening and closing like somebody has just opened it and closed it. Then, I heard a series of bam, bam, and looked out and saw the customers scrambling for safety. A lady fell down in front of the cooler. I realized, when I heard the next bang, I figured somebody must be shooting, so I *got my pistol out out of my pocket* [italics added] and pushed the cooler door open.[6]

David Hallman, another store employee, testified:

> Q. When the shooting started and you got down behind the counter, did you do anything else at the time?
> A. Yes, sir. I shot at the man.
> Q. Did you have a weapon of some type down behind the counter?
> A. Yes, sir.
> Q. And did you go to the door and shoot or just tell me what you did when you shot?
> A. As I got over the counter—well, Mike Avery grabbed a shotgun and went out the door and shot at the guy. Then the guy came around the front of the car and shot at us and I shot at him.[7]

All this occurred with many bystanders in the area of the store, including young children.

Within a week there was major unrest in the black community protesting the Carter shooting. By the following weekend, the Kingston neighborhood (in which the Carter shooting had taken place) was the scene of a rock-throwing episode and tense police-citizen interactions. The windshields of the police cars were covered with canvas bags to protect them against rocks. The Southern Christian Leadership Conference demanded the firing of the officer in the shooting.

The next week, community leaders warned that riots would continue unless there was legal action taken against Officer Sands. While the parents of Bonita Carter urged citizens not to commit violent actions, they demanded official action in the case involving their daughter. In the following weeks, a citizens' panel was formed to provide a public forum for the controversy; it decided that the shots were fired "without sufficient justification." A police review panel had ruled the shootings were within departmental guidelines. Protagonists for the police as well as for black rights marched on the convenience store in Kingston. Black groups demanded the firing of the officer. White groups protested in sympathy with victims of violent crime. By midsummer, there were numerous scuffles between black and white groups.

At stake was the question of political control of the police. A use of deadly force by a police officer had become the most marked symbol of political power and control. Much as a tea tax or an obsolete battleship had become heated political symbols for earlier wars, Bonita Carter had become a volatile symbol in the political battle for political control of the cities of a changing urban South.

While the mayor of Birmingham, David Vann, refused to dismiss the officer who shot Carter, he was far from publicly unsympathetic toward those who suffered from the tragic event. (After the shooting he had visited Carter's parents for half an hour.) Still, events identified him with support for the police rather than the black cause (although he had previously been elected with black support). The election that followed between Vann and a black councilman named Richard Arrington focused largely on the issue of police shooting, particularly deadly force policy.

The Bonita Carter incident is, unfortunately, not an isolated incident. For many citizens, especially blacks, the image of police use of deadly force has become symbolic of the tension (and often hatred) between the police and the minority community. A New York psychotic man was shot 21 times by five police officers. A retarded boy in Seattle, looking for odd jobs, was killed by police officers. The controversy that followed resulted in a city referendum on police shooting guidelines and mandates for new training. In Los Angeles, a 30-year-old woman named Eulia Love was killed by two LAPD officers following a dispute over a bill with employees of the gas company. In Houston, a Chicano gang member was apparently murdered by police in the bayou. In San Jose, a male Chicano who pointed his finger at a police officer was fatally shot, causing major protests within the Hispanic community. In Columbus, a shooting of a black teenager fleeing from a store theft spurred demands for civilian review of the police. In Oakland, a black 15-year-old unarmed boy was shot by police officers who thought he had a hand gun. Shortly thereafter, the city initiated its first complaint review board. The political consequences of these incidents have been enormous. The aftermath to the killing of Arthur McDuffie in Miami provides perhaps the most extreme example of the political volatility of the deadly force issue. After a trial, which produced a verdict of innocent, Miami experienced a massive riot that saw a billion dollars worth of damage and 14 persons beaten or shot to death.

Officer Shot in the Hallway: Danger to the Police Officer

Death or injury may come, of course, not only to an innocent citizen but to a police officer as well. And during one 33-day period, no fewer than four police officers were shot in New York City. Shootings of police may have equally important political and psychological consequences. A rash of questionable shootings by the police followed the ambush deaths of two policemen in the lower east side of New York City in 1971. In Southern California a car (wrongly it turned out) suspected of being involved in the shooting death of a police officer was riddled with more than 55 bullets. (The driver of the car almost unbelievably escaped injury.) About 2:15 A.M. on November 8, 1980, according to a *New York Times* report,[8] a police officer was found "shot through the neck and bleeding to death in a ditch alongside his patrol car" in a black area of New Orleans. In the next five days, four blacks were shot to death by the police, three of them, including a woman in a bathtub, occurred in encounters where the police were seeking the police killer(s) with murder warrants. In other cities, the deaths of police officers have resulted in demands for more officers, higher velocity weapons, and fewer restrictions on police gun use. And the action on the part of the police may, in turn, lead to reactions from the minority community. For example, the New Orleans incident led directly to the resignation of the city's nationally famous police chief (James Parsons). The president of the local chapter of the NAACP stated, "We can't have the police acting as arresting officers, lawyers, prosecutors, judge and jury, and deny people all their civil rights."[9]

Research on shootings of police officers by Chapman[10] and Margarita[11] indicates that armed confrontations in which police officers are shot share much in common with those in which a citizen is shot. The following incident, in which an officer was nearly killed by an armed suspect wanted for murder, illustrates the unique peril faced by police officers forced to apprehend dangerous, armed, and violent persons. The officer involved was a detective in a large urban department noted for the danger of its duty and the poverty and violence of its citizens. The officer described the incident vividly, although it had occurred more than eight years before:

> We were looking for this guy, a real bad guy, wanted for at least two murders. We had sort of lost hope of finding the guy. I was with this state trooper trying to get more information on the guy. We had a photo of the guy and knew all about him. We decided to visit this woman who used to visit this guy in prison to see if she wanted to tell us where he was.

The two officers went to the neighborhood where the woman lived—an area that makes the South Bronx or the worst parts of Harlem almost enviable environments. The officers were told by a group of children that the woman they wanted to speak to was not there, that she "had gone to the store." Finally, a woman matching the description walked up the apartment steps. The detective said, "We followed her up and went to the door. We were expecting just to interview her. She comes out and we see this guy sitting on the couch just watching us."

The next few seconds were recalled with understandable horror by the officer:

> When we approached the door, we were thinking this was just going to be an information call; probably she wouldn't tell us nothing. What happened was that, as we stepped into the hallway of the apartment from the building corridor, we saw the woman and this guy sitting on the couch. We didn't know who it was. He just stands up and starts shooting at me. I retreated into the hallway. He escaped through the window. I fired but missed. They took me to the hospital.

The wounded detective was on the critical list for seven days and in the hospital for three months. After the incident he commented:

> It was like a dream. It was different from most police work. We were just reacting. There was no time to plan. It was all out of control. Maybe we were unprepared because we didn't know he was there. . . . Maybe I should have had her come to the apartment house corridor.

In other incidents, the outcome of an armed confrontation may be death, not injury, to the police officer. Often a slight lapse in attention, the disregard of warning signals, poor timing, or other unfortunate circumstances result in the death of a police officer.

In Reno, Nevada, a young narcotics officer is making a drug buy from a large-scale dealer. A new "microradio" in use for the first time breaks down. He loses contact with backups and is killed by the dealer. In New York, a much-decorated officer chases an opponent around a corner and is killed by the man, who is waiting for him as he passes the edge of the building. In Los Angeles, a young harbor patrol officer is killed by an insane man with a machete who virtually decapitates him after the officer hesitates when the man refuses to drop his knife. In Newark, New Jersey, a 58-year-old officer is first fatally shot and then pummeled by a group of bank robbers. An off-duty officer in New York heroically confronts a robbery team in a social club and is shot seven times. In Birmingham, Alabama, an officer stops to interrogate a young man about a reported robbery. The young man reaches into his shopping bag and then kills the police officer instantly. In a small California beach community, a young police officer responds to a medical call. He goes to an alley behind a local newspaper office and sees a man who is apparently holding his bandaged right arm with his left hand. As the officer approaches to give aid, he is killed with three bullets by the man, who is later sent to a hospital for the criminally insane.

These incidents should remind the reader that it is not always the criminal who is killed in an armed confrontation. About 100 police officers lose their lives yearly in armed confrontations with citizens.

"Christmas Eve in the Ghetto": An Averted Shooting

In a surprising number of armed confrontations, even those in which both police officer and opponent have drawn weapons, the situation is resolved without injury to either police officer or citizen and even more often without a shot being fired by either party.

Such "averted" shootings in armed confrontations have been only a recent concern to sociologists, largely because they are rarely recorded in anything but the most obscure police arrest records. Experienced officers in many hard-core areas report that such averted shootings are common, almost commonplace events. One officer commented: "There are lots of people I could have shot. Sometimes I don't even know why they are alive. You just bring them in.

Sometimes someone says something. Other times you just go out on the street."

In one such averted shooting a man with a high-powered rifle is lured to a doorway "to talk" and then disarmed by two tactical patrol officers. In another incident, an officer is attacked and cut by an insane woman with a knife but is able to disarm her without shooting her. A detective sees a man with a gun in a tavern involved in a gun deal hesitate when commanded to drop his gun. The man finally complies and is arrested. A man confronts a police officer from another department who is drunk and refuses to drop his gun when commanded; the drunk officer is finally disarmed. A tactical team surrounds a car with four robbers armed with two .38 pistols, a .45 automatic, and a shotgun. The robbers surrender without serious incident. An older man who has fired at his son-in-law with a rifle is arrested by a calm, older police officer. An off-duty officer sees a young woman stab a younger man to death with a long knife. The officer and a barber, who knows the woman, convince her to surrender. An insane woman, armed with a pistol, is convinced to surrender, rather than kill herself, by a young police officer. A man who has occupied a church tower in a midsized California town, armed with an M-1, is talked down by a courageous detective.

The following incident described by a veteran police officer saw him and his partner able to disarm a man armed with a gun who was robbing another man:

> It was last Christmas. What a day to work. We get a call to the Sudder homes, the worst part of the city. A domestic disturbance of some type. We walk up to the doorway and open these big steel doors. As we open it, we see this guy holding a gun on a young guy, looked like he was robbing him.

As the officers yelled, "police, halt," the robber pointed his gun at the police officers but, for some reason, did not shoot. Both officers and the robber and the victim stood frozen in what must have seemed to them an eternity. One officer said:

> It was weird like. We just barged through the door standing over them. First, he has the gun on the guy. We were surprised. We thought it was just going to be a domestic dispute. The dispatcher didn't know anything about it. The people didn't think we needed to know that.

The second officer commented that, but for the surprise, they might have shot the man:

> It happened so fast I just didn't have a mental set towards firing; by the time our gun got out, it was like here we were. There he was just standing there pointing a .25 at G's belly.

The first officer commented:

> It was like three, four seconds. We were all startled. We were just four feet away from each other. Us, the robber, and the guy on the floor. The only way I can explain it is that in those three seconds with us pointing guns at him and him at us, we didn't think he'd shoot. It was his eyes or something. Finally, we just pushed the gun away from him and arrested him.

After the incident, the officers were treated almost indifferently. "The desk lieutenant just read the report like it was nothing special and sent us out." Their sergeant told them, "The next time just plug the son of a bitch." The officers themselves just commented, eight months after the incident, "Hey, it's part of the job."

Although such outcomes are less dramatic than a shooting, wounding, or killing of either a police officer or a citizen, they are the most common result of a confrontation between an armed police officer and armed citizen. As we observed, such averted shootings are often difficult to identify, especially in high-contact districts where they are almost commonplace.

In reviewing each of these four incidents, one might ask certain questions. One series of questions is psychological in nature: What factors in the confrontation (the strategy employed by the officer or possibly the personality of the officer) influenced the outcome of the incident? Was the result of the shooting of the detective almost inevitable given the nature of the confrontation? Did the positioning of the police officer in the Bonita Carter incident contribute to the tragic outcome of the incident? What qualities in the officer, faced with the ax-wielding madman, might be related to his obviously heroic resolution of the incident?

Other questions are sociological: What role did police administrative policies play in the outcome of each incident? How might different training policies or tactical rules have altered the path the incident took? Would better departmental guidelines on tactical positions make less likely the tragic shootings of policemen? Could more effective training have reduced the likelihood of a death such as that of Bonita Carter? Also, it might be noted that all of the opponents described in this chapter were black. Blacks, according to Kobler,[12] although comprising only 19 percent of the population, account for well over 50 percent of the victims of police homicide. While this statistic may be surprising, it is commensurate with violent crime rates among blacks. This raises the question of the relationship of police use of deadly force to broader social dynamics, such as race, poverty, and violent behavior.

The most difficult issues, however, are conceptual. One issue involves the evaluation of police use of deadly force. How does one define which of the above cases were justified from either a legal or a moral point of view? We also must confront the problem of legal statutes and case law that regulate the use of deadly force, the problems of criminal and civil negligence as they apply to police uses of deadly force, and the moral position that respects the legitimate claims to life of both citizen and police officer. Obviously, this is not a simple intellectual task, but just as obviously, neither is it one society can avoid facing.

EVALUATING POLICE USE OF DEADLY FORCE: CORRECT VERSUS REASONABLE DECISIONS TO USE DEADLY FORCE

Perhaps it makes most sense to present a brief overview of the conceptual framework that will guide our approach. We will briefly present some thoughts on how one might evaluate police decisions to use deadly force as a framework to interpret some of the more systematic approaches to follow. In the four cases presented, two of the cases had seemingly salutary outcomes. In the first case, an officer's life was saved from certain death at the hands of an ax-wielding madman. In the last case, a life was saved due to the quick thinking (and perhaps luck) of the two officers faced with the bandit with a pistol. In the remaining two cases, the result was clearly tragic. In one case, an innocent woman was killed, triggering a major racial confrontation. In the other case, a police officer was almost killed.

A key premise in our analysis will be that, in virtually any armed confrontation (in which both citizen and police officer are armed), any one of these four outcomes is possible. By shooting, a life may be saved or lost. Similarly, by withholding fire, a life may be lost or saved. It is the balance of life, held often by an instant of circumstance, that makes the decision of the use of deadly force both bewildering in its complexity and awesome in its consequences.

These four logical possibilities are illustrated in Table 2.1, which conceptualizes two errors in the use of deadly force. This conception

TABLE 2.1 Correctness and Incorrectness in Police Uses of Deadly Force in Armed Confrontations

	Shot Fired	No Shot Fired
Correct decision	A person who is armed and dangerous and an immediate threat to life is prevented from harming the officer or another person by a use of fatal force.	A person who appears to be armed and dangerous is not shot by a police officer, and there are no unfortunate consequences.
Incorrect decision	A person presumed dangerous but, in fact, not actually armed or dangerous is killed by a police officer.	A police officer or citizen is killed because a police officer fails to shoot.

of errors in police use of deadly force is perhaps useful in clarifying the fundamental tension in any armed confrontation. The police officer in a very few seconds must assess the danger of a situation, facing the possibility that, if he fires in error, he may erroneously kill a human being. If he holds his fire when imminent danger exists (and he or another person could be saved by shooting), a human life will be lost unnecessarily.

This conception of shooting errors suffers, of course, in its over-simplicity, in several respects. First, police officers may shoot for reasons other than to save a human life. In some jurisdictions for example, police officers may shoot to kill in order to stop an armed felon or to stop a fleeing person suspected of being a felon. Also, it is not certain what proportion of armed confrontations involve a sufficient degree of threat to the police officer and simultaneously enable him to protect himself by shooting the opponent. It also is not certain if reducing the number of false positive errors—that is, citizens shot erroneously by police officers—will increase the risk of false negative errors—that is, police officers killed because they held fire in a critical moment in an armed confrontation with a dangerous citizen.

Finally, this conception of errors in police uses of deadly force ignores a critical distinction between correct and reasonable decisions to use deadly force. In commonsense usage, an error in any decision is judged simply by the outcome of a decision. Thus, a physician may decide to operate on an ill patient. If the patient dies due to complications resulting from the operation, the operation might be considered an error. Similarly, a businessman may invest all his working capital in a new line of ski equipment. If for the next two winters no snow falls and his company goes broke, the decision might be considered an error.

The reasonableness of a decision, in contrast, must be judged by the facts at the moment of decision. If the surgeon, for example, believed, given his tests of the patient, that his needed operation had 90 percent chance of success (that is, the patient would be significantly helped by the surgery) and only a 10 percent chance of lethal outcome for the patient, then his decision to operate might be considered reasonable, despite the outcome. So, too, the businessman's decision, given the weather and economic facts available to him, might have been considered reasonable, again despite the outcome.

We would argue that a police officer's decision making must be considered in terms of the criteria of reasonableness rather than of correctness of outcome. Thus, a use of deadly force must be evaluated by the extent to which the shooting decision is reasonable, judged not from the point of view of outcome but rather evaluated given the facts knowable at the moment of decision. Viewed in terms of the distinction between reasonable and correct decisions to use deadly force, a shooting may be incorrect (in terms of outcome), yet reasonable given the facts known at the time. The Bonita Carter shooting clearly was not a correct one. Carter, in fact, posed no life or death threat to the officer or anyone else. Yet the officer might have made a reasonable (even if regrettable or erroneous) choice judged in terms of circumstances and information at the critical point of decision making.

This conception of reasonableness in police decisions to use deadly force must be even further qualified by an awareness that a police decision to use deadly force is in reality an interconnected and interdependent sequence of decisions. From this perspective, a final decision to use deadly force may be reasonably judged as a single decision. However, the realities of this final frame are clearly functions of earlier decisions. This might be illustrated in the shooting of a black housewife (Eulia Love), armed with a knife, by two Los Angeles police officers (described more fully in Chapter Five). The final outcome, according to many observers of this incident, was largely determined by the early decision by one of the officers to place his gun in his strong right hand and his baton (which might have been used to disarm a 139-pound woman) in his left.

This discussion hopefully suggests a framework for viewing the four cases and a conceptual context for the analysis to follow. Some principles, useful in the evaluation of a decision to use deadly force, will be offered. First, it is suggested that one can only evaluate a use of deadly force on the basis of the facts known at the instant the decision is made. Thus, the decision to use deadly force by the officer in the Carter shooting and to withhold fire in the episode in which the detective was shot, clearly were wrong decisions judged in terms of outcome; they may not have been unreasonable decisions given the facts available at the time. (It may even be argued that, in the confrontation described earlier where the officer did not shoot, thus saving a life, a reasonable man would have fired.)

It is clear that any responsible deadly force policy must be based upon the realities of field encounters with an orientation toward the maximum safety of both citizens and police officers who might become involved in an armed confrontation. This point is worthy of emphasis because some of the major earlier treatments of police use of deadly force have assumed either an explicit or implicit police or citizen bias.[13-17] Put simply, these studies began with an assumption that either the problem of police deadly force is to prevent excessive citizen deaths or to protect police safety. As Fyfe suggests, the conclusions of this earlier research are suspect because the authors seek to document either a pro or anti police bias—too many citizens are killed vis-a-vis police officers or that too many police officers are killed relative to civilians.[18]

In these earlier studies, sympathies for the particular or potential victim of a shooting (either police or citizen) are often transparent. A "robber with a pistol," who was shot by police after he fired at them, is described in one account by a radical criminologist as a "victim of the police state." A police manual describes an unarmed woman, shot in error by a sheriff's deputy, as a "suspect" and later in the manual as a "potential offender." Tagaki, in his effort to show abuse of blacks on the part of police, observes that from 1962 to 1971, police shootings of citizens increased by a factor of 3—ignoring that police fatalities increased at an even greater rate.[19]

We argue, in contrast, that any responsible policy must be concerned with both the legitimate rights of citizens and those of police officers. It is essential to protect the rights of officers involved in dangerous contacts with citizens while at the same time ensuring the safety of citizens who may be wrongfully hurt by the police. Viewed from this perspective, an officer safety program, designed to save officer lives at a cost of undue risk to citizens, would be exceedingly unwise. Similarly, a gun lock program, designed to slow officer reactions in armed confrontations, thus placing them at greater risk, would be unwise. From our point of view, any reforms in the control of police deadly force must be concerned with more than saving either citizen or police lives. Rather, they must be concerned with establishing an equitable balance of risk protecting police officers (from being hurt by armed citizens) and citizens (from being erroneously shot, as in the case of Bonita Carter, by police officers).

A final implication of the perspective we have offered involves the sequential nature of decisions to use deadly force. From this perspective, each of the four cases must be viewed not only in terms of the final decision to fire or not but also in terms of the decisions that came earlier. Thus, for example, the officers' ability, in the first incident, to "turn" the man away from the crowd (of 800) permitted them to shoot the man without risk to any innocent persons; similarly, the decision to approach the car in a certain manner in the 7–11 parking lot in Birmingham obviously contributed to the tragic outcome of the Carter incident. This distinction as to the sequential nature of police decision making in armed confrontations has more than semantic importance. Research questions, given this perspective, might be properly directed at police behavior well before the actual decision. For example, what forces led to guns being first drawn or to a breakdown in communication between the police officer and the opponent?

NOTES

1. See Law Enforcement Assistance Administration, *Prevention and Control of Urban Disorders: Issues for the 1980's* (Washington, D.C.: University Research Corporation, 1980); and H. D. Graham and T. R. Gurr, *Violence in America: Historical and Comparative Perspectives*, vol. 2 (Washington, D.C.: U.S. Government Printing Office, 1969).

2. H. Garth and C. W. Mills, eds. *From Max Weber* (New York: Oxford University Press, 1948).

3. L. W. Sherman and R. H. Langworthy, "Measuring Homicide by Police Officers," *Journal of Criminal Law and Criminology* 70, no. 4 (Winter 1979): 546–60.

4. Hearing, "Blue Ribbon" Citizens Committee, *In Re: Bonita Carter* (Birmingham, Ala.: Office of the Mayor, 1979).

5. Ibid., p. 674.

6. Ibid., pp. 14, 15.

7. Ibid., pp. 111, 112.

8. *New York Times*, November 20, 1980, p. A18.

9. Ibid.

10. S. G. Chapman, *Shootings of Police Officers* (Norman: University of Oklahoma Press, 1972.

11. M. Margarita, "Killing the Police: Myths and Motives," *Annals of the American Academy of Political and Social Science* 452 (November 1980): 63–71.

12. A. L. Kobler, "Police Homicide in a Democracy," *Journal of Social Issues* 31, no. 1 (Winter 1975): 163–84.

13. C. H. Milton, J. W. Halleck, J. Lardner, and G. L. Abrecht, *Police Use of Deadly Force* (Washington, D.C.: Police Foundation, 1977).

14. Kobler, "Police Homicide in a Democracy."

15. R. W. Harding and R. P. Fahey, "Killings by Chicago Police, 1969–70: An Empirical Study," *Southern California Law Review* 46, no. 2 (March 1973): 284–315.

16. P. Takagi, "A Garrison State in 'Democratic' Society," *Crime and Social Justice*, no. 1 (Spring–Summer 1974): 27–32.

17. Southern Methodist Law School, "Report on Police Shootings," Unpublished report prepared for Dallas Police Department, 1974.

18. J. J. Fyfe, "Shots Fired: An Examination of New York City Police Firearms Discharges," Ph.D. dissertation, State University of New York at Albany, 1978.

19. Tagaki, "A Garrison State in 'Democratic' Society."

3 A Tool of the Trade

PROLOGUE:
A LOCKER ROOM CONVERSATION

It was 6:00 P.M. The tactical team would hit the street in less than an hour. It was three days after a riot in another city in which several people had been killed, and the officers were preparing for a night's tour in a tough tactical team in Newark.

> *Officer A:* Why do they give us these fucking 158 grain bullets when every motherfucker on the streets carries a .45 or 9mm. If we get into something, guess who's going to get his ass—us or them?
>
> *Officer B:* I guess they care more about the shitum getting shot than us. Hey T., pass me some shotgun shells. About six will do. Lou, wanna see me put nine of these pellets in one of the college motherfuckers who writes the rules around here?
>
> *Lieutenant:* Why the fuck do I care? When I retire next year and get 20, I'm going to go out and break the fucking law. I'm sick of keeping people from killing and raping each other. I want to break the fucking law myself for a while. . . . I need to love to come to work. I hate it now. I hate robbers, muggers, and almost everyone I meet. Go shoot whomever you want. I don't give a fuck. . . .

The officers slowly load their 00 buckshot into the regulation magazines. Then on go bullet-proof vests, all purchased by police welfare funds. Next, the automatic pistols are cleaned, emptied, reloaded, and checked. The clicks of the magazines are synchronized with a TV rerun of the "Streets of San Francisco." James Broderick is in a shoot-out with three robbers. The robbers run away. The officers barely notice. The subject turns to guns, a tool of the trade.

Officer A: Did you hear about Monty?

Officer B: What happened to that wacko now?

Officer A: They took away his gun.

Officer C: What the fuck for?

Officer A: I guess they thought that he shouldn't have shot into the bar without saying, "Hey, I'm a police officer, would you please stop robbing these people and drop your guns, Mr. Afro-American citizen." [Everyone laughs.]

Officer C: Next thing you know, they'll give us pillows to hit them with. They are fucking out to lunch. It's like I was talking to him, and it was almost a castration thing, like they cut off his balls. . . .

Officer B: Did you guys hear about the guy up in Plainfield? Some guys from the North were up doing training and there is a class of Plainfield rookies and there was this young kid who is sitting there playing with his gun, you know rubbing it like it was his pecker.

Officer D: Did the gun go off? [Everyone laughs again.]

Officer B: Now, seriously, a lot of cops shouldn't carry guns. There was this guy I knew in Philly when I worked there who once was so crazy he staged his own shootout. He fired into his own patrol car radiator just to make it look like he had been in a shooting. A cab driver saw it and called the station to say, "Hey, there is this cop shooting his own car."

Lieutenant: Sounds like he should work here!

Officer A: You know what they did to him?

Lieutenant: What?

Officer A: They sent him to a psychiatrist who said he was under stress and then sent him back to work. Now if that was me rather than a fucking sergeant, it would have been either jail or the unemployment line.

Sergeant: O.K. you guys, enough of this. Roll call: M., S., B. . . . Everyone pay attention. Now tonight we're going in on a gun deal up in the projects. Our snitch says that 30 guns may change hands; $400 Luger jobs. It will come down at about 9:45 P.M., on Springfield and Seventeenth. Be careful. Also, watch for the robbery gang that hits the buses. They come on the bus with a sawed-off shotgun, do everyone, ride two stops, and book. Try and get them off the bus before you take them. It's too dangerous to take them on the bus.

Officer A: What do we do if we see them, Sarge?

Sergeant: Careful, Al, just be careful.

Officer A: Be careful of what?

Lieutenant: Be careful of your piece and be careful of his. It's dangerous out there. We don't want no problem "I.A.'s" [Internal Affairs investigations], and no dead cops!

The final preshift rituals are being conducted as the officers clus-
ter solemnly in pairs talking softly. Each officer almost reflexively
unlocks the magazine of his automatic pistol and visibly inspects the
chamber. One officer helps his partner tie on his bullet-proof vest.
Two other officers finish seemingly desperate phone calls to wives or
girlfriends. The sergeant shows a huge pile of papers to an older officer. "All robberies, all fucking robberies; one guy was shot when he
only gave up $3; another guy was killed for pills."

Finally, without command the men walk toward the unmarked
police cars in the parking lot. One officer in each pair carries a shotgun, frontier style over his shoulder. When they reach the cars, they
place the shotguns in the trunk of the cars. "Let's do it," T. tells his
partner. . . . "Let's just hope nothing fucking happens, no shootings
or nothing." . . . "Tac/Car 357 on Broad and Main." . . . "10–4, Car
357."

As one might guess from this scenario, guns for most police officers serve a number of symbolic and real purposes. Here we will
describe some of the ways that deadly force might be considered a
core implement of the police officers' world. First, we will discuss
police deadly force as a psychological tool. We will describe the role
firearms play in the police officer's sense of professional identity,
focusing on such things as police humor, horseplay, and culture. We
will then turn to the role played by lethal weapons in a variety of
routine police activities. We will emphasize that the availability of
deadly force is important even when shots are not fired and the
police officer does not even consider firing. We hope to define the
role guns play in police work as a means of better understanding the
psychological and occupational contexts of police deadly force for
law enforcement officers.

POLICE DEADLY FORCE AS A PSYCHOLOGICAL TOOL: THE GUN AS A TOOL OF SELF-IDENTITY

Goffman speaks of a professional "identity kit" that establishes
the unique dimensions of a particular status or role.[1] A professor
may be sure to display conspicuously his Phi Beta Kappa pin, his

Harvard Club tie, or perhaps, if he is a professor of literature, his unabridged copy of *Finnegans Wake*. A construction worker may conspicuously leave a lug wrench sticking out of his back pocket or wear dungarees stained with grease. A doctor may carry a beeper in his suit pocket or have an identifiably obvious stethoscope wire dangle from his briefcase. A banker may similarly display her investment portfolio, an engineer his microcomputer, and even a prostitute may display garments that give psychological evidence of her profession. Tie manufacturers are well aware of the phenomenon, and so one sees the symbols of high-status professions emblazoned on neckwear.

Such identity equipment serves such purposes as establishing the person's self-worth, giving information to others about his or her interests and inclinations, and establishing a sense of status in the eyes of others. The gun for the police officer, we argue, has a variety of similar psychological functions. The gun for many is indeed the primary symbol of law enforcement. One officer with a large number of gunfights reported:

> I carry it wherever I go. It's always near me when I sleep. I take it to court and to the gym. I always know where I can get it. I know a guy on this department who got robbed when he was getting diapers for his kid. Not me. Any motherfucker comes at me, he gets this [his gun] up his asshole.

It should be noted, however, that some officers have markedly different attitudes toward the gun, regarding it almost as an unnecessary encumbrance. One suburban officer offered that he wasn't sure why he had to wear one. Another deputy chief stated, "I hate the goddamn things. I always have. I've been on the job for 17 years and have never shot it except at the range." For others the gun is almost a forgotten aspect of the job. One man said, "You know you put on your tie, your jockstrap, your watch, your badge goes in your pocket, and, oh, yah, don't forget your gun." While officers with negative or neutral attitudes toward guns can be found in any department, they are in the minority.

Some police officers show a completely opposite attitude in carrying multiple exotic weaponry. One officer carried no fewer than four ("second") guns with him at all times. A .25 is strapped to each leg, a derringer is kept in his coat pocket, and a fourth is in his belt. In addition, he carries his regulation piece. "All I need these for is that one time." Other officers prestigiously carry shotguns, "auto-burglar" guns, and antisniper pieces. For them, their guns are symbols of their power in the world as much as they are a method for coping with violence and physical threat on the streets. Although the emphasis is upon dealing with the violent world, the psychological overtones are blatantly apparent in this quote from Wambaugh's *Choir Boys:*

> "In addition to knowing your car you gotta know all your equipment," Roscoe continued, "like that pea-shooter you're carrying. I wish I could talk you into buying a magnum and carrying some good, gut ripping hollow points in it. I want a gun that'll stop some scrote when I need him stopped. After the prick's dead I'll worry about the ammunition being department approved. I ever tell you about the abba dabba burglar my partner shot when I used to work the Watts car? Ripping off a gas station when he set off the silent alarm. We were carrying those peashooters like you got. That sucker could run the hundred in ten flat till my partner shot him, and then he ran it in nine-nine. So I made a vow to get rid of this worthless ammo and get me some killing stuff. I made a study of velocity and shock."[2]

Another example of guns as an element in the policeman's self-identity may be found in Berkley's description of a particular St. Louis policeman: "He is a professional cop all the way. A riot gun stands locked in a frame near the front seat. Another part shows in his quality weapon. It's a .357 magnum, one of the most powerful guns made."[3]

Also, consider the advertising directed at police audiences. At police conferences the vast majority of exhibits are devoted to guns and their "softwear": holsters, paper targets, gun sights, ammunition, and the like. Bullets and revolvers are described in police magazines in terms of their "stopping," "hitting," and "penetration" powers. In magazine advertising pictures, opponents are depicted falling backward as they are hit with the powerful round being advertised. One videotape display showed a new "expansion round" hitting a blob of gelatin, fully demolishing it. "Look what the new '357' controlled expansion round can do to your target," droned the announcer.

Magazines like *The Police Chief, Police Product News,* and *Law and Order* devote many of their pages to types and models of weapons, the use of weapons, the concealment of weapons, and strategies of survival in gun encounters. Of course, the relevant articles and advertising do convey important information for the police officer who must rely upon his gun. But beyond that there is a distinct aura of religiosity about weapons in these various publications. To illustrate, the following quotes are from an article entitled "Putting the

Llama Commanche Through the Wringer" in the "Hot Lead" department of *Police Product News:*

> Gads, does time fly! While doing research for this article I was shocked
> to be reminded that the .44 Magnum cartridge is a quarter century old.
> During almost all of those 25 years, Smith & Wesson was the only com-
> pany in the world making a double action revolver to chamber this
> "most powerful" handgun cartridge. The .44 Magnum was the brain-
> child of the legendary Elmer Keith, and its popularity with the masses
> was assured for years to come by Clint Eastwood's portrayal of Inspec-
> tor Callahan in the movie *Dirty Harry*.
>
> It has only been during this past year that Smith & Wesson's monop-
> oly has been challenged with the entrance into the double-action market
> by such equally prestigious manufacturers as Sturm-Ruger, with their
> Redhawk .44 Magnum; and Dan Wesson with what probably is the most
> superb .44 Magnum double-action of them all.
>
> The blued finish and metal polish on the gun was nice, but I suspect
> the bluing wasn't too deep as there were signs of wear near the muzzle,
> apparently just from riding in the box. The side plate fit was sloppy just
> below the cylinder but, other than that, overall fit and appearance were
> very good. The heavy six-inch barrel sports a nice integral vented rib
> and extractor shroud.[4]

Police humor often involves guns, bullets and their consequences.
One officer in talking about the problems he was having with a real
estate broker announced to a group of fellow police officers that if
the man "charged any more commission, I might find it cheaper to
waste the motherfucker, but now that '9mm' ammo was so high,
I'm not really sure which was the most economical thing to do." In
police humor, targets of humor are routinely "wasted," "done in,"
"gutted," "dusted," or "blown away." It should be noted that in
such humor not only criminals are portrayed as the objects of lethal
force; superiors, wives, lawyers, judges, girlfriends, and politicians are
frequently mentioned as persons to be "hit."

Another interesting psychological use of the gun is found in
police horseplay. While doing an observational study in a hard-core
area on a Saturday night, one of us observed four police officers
approaching a locked precinct door. When the desk sergeant (known
to be a "good guy") did not open it fast enough, all four police
officers pulled their guns out and drew on him. The sergeant laughed
and drew back on them. At times such horseplay becomes even
bolder. One older detective described the following accident:

Some guys around here get carried away. Like there is this one guy—he is still here—who was fooling around. I was coming out of a diner checking on a "B and E" and he comes behind me and says, "Stick 'em up." I feel this derringer behind me. Now he did this kind of stuff all the time. This guy was weird. Once he brought a snake to work and left it on my seat. Anyway this time the gun goes off and hits me in the eye. I'm blinded in this eye. The union leaned on me not to prosecute so I lied and said it was just an accident, that we had taken this .22 off a hype and it went off.

A related aspect lies in the common police myth of the "macho" police officer who is fearless in the face of all bullets. This myth is presented in somewhat farcical terms in Wambaugh's portrayal of Bullets Bambarella in *The Black Marble:*

Rocco was called Bullets Bambarella after a gas station holdup in which a robber fired eight shots at him and missed. They found an outline of 9 mm bullet holes in the wall around Rocco Bambarella. It was only his slow reflexes that saved him. Any man with normal reaction time would have jumped left or right and been killed on the spot. Rocco Bambarella, who shot no worse than anyone else in combat situations, also emptied his gun, missed all six, but saved the day by throwing a full quart of 20W engine oil that coldcocked the bad guy and earned Rocco a commendation and something a policeman cherishes much more—a macho nickname. He was Bullets Bambarella forever.[5]

Other nicknames used to describe courageously masculine police officers include "Bullet Holes," "357," "Terror," "Rounds," and "Little Harry" (after Dirty Harry). And certain epithets used in reference to police officers are based upon the source of testosterone—the hormone highlighting hardness and toughness (masculinity) in contrast to its female hormone, estrogen, which highlights softness and tenderness (femininity). These include "Big Balls," "Steel Nuts," and "Iron Jock."

An incident observed by one of us is interesting in this respect. Following a fatality suffered by a member of a California sheriff's department, an officer (also shot in the same incident) was wheeled into the officer's public funeral still in critical care, an IV bottle strung above his mobile hospital bed. A week later the same officer left the hospital and went to dinner in a restaurant frequented by local police officers. The writer happened to be eating dinner at the same restaurant with a detective friend. As the police officer stumbled into the restaurant leaning on his cane, his arm in a sling, virtually half the restaurant stood up to applaud and cheer. The officer pretended not to notice and calmly found his seat.

It might be observed that there is much cultural support for the fusion of guns with the mythology of policework. The association is mediated by images of marshals dealing with gunfighters in the Old West and by G-men dealing with mobsters during the Prohibition era. Several critics have noted, however, that there is a certain irony in the mythology of the law enforcement officer as a gun toter. On the one hand, the central role of the gun in the life of the western law enforcement officer is emphasized in story after story. (In fact, the central role of the gun in the life of the Old West generally is so emphasized.) A reported interview with Wild Bill Hickok is illustrative of the gun-oriented descriptions of the wild, wild West.

> "I would like to see you shoot."
> "Would yer."
> "That sign is more than fifty yards away. I will put these six balls inside of a circle which isn't bigger than a man's heart."
>
> In an off-handed way, and without sighting the pistol with his eye he discharged the six shots of his revolver. I saw that all the six bullets had entered the circle.[6]

Prassel observes, however, that although some armed confrontations with desperadoes did occur, they were rare and as often involved petty theft, drunk, or loitering suspects as they did armed desperadoes:

> In the main, the crimes of the old West comprised primarily the same violations most common in modern America—drunkenness, disorderly conduct, and petty larceny. Most citizens lived peacefully and without great fear of personal attack. The cowboy's revolver, when worn, proved far more useful against snakes than rustlers. In many communities people rarely felt the need to put locks on their doors, while local saloons and gambling parlors made a sincere effort to exclude women and minors. Courts quickly appeared in most settlements, but the early judicial bodies rarely heard serious criminal charges.
>
> As a place of wild lawlessness the frontier's spectacular reputation is, therefore, largely without substantiation. It is true that a band of daring outlaws, enraged over "land theft" might sweep down from their mountain stronghold to terrorize an isolated village, take command of a courthouse, and shoot or capture local peace officers. But these events did not occur in the distant past, they took place in 1967. While a stage

passenger going through Nevada during the 1860s might certainly have been in some danger of hijacking, he probably enjoyed greater security than his counterpart flying over Florida in a jet airliner a century later. A pioneer of the old West surely may have had his property taken in the dead of night or even been physically assulted at noon on a main street, but these offenses also occur with appalling regularity in every modern American metropolitan area, usually with far less public attention than would have greeted a similar violation on the frontier.[7]

It has also been noted that the western states had often quite clear legal restrictions upon gun use, both for citizens and for police officers. Another irony is that in eastern jurisdictions, the police were largely unarmed until the latter part of the nineteenth century. Police in most urban areas more often carried a clapper (to rally citizens to his aid) rather than a pistol. The first citizen killed by an officer using a pistol in New York City was shot as late as 1859. In many cities, carrying a firearm was optional for a police officer as recently as World War I.

If the reality of nineteenth-century America was far less bloody than one would expect, its mythology is, of course, the opposite. Many of the legendary peace officers such as wild Bill Hickok found employment with traveling circuses and wild West shows in the East, perpetuating a conception of the wild West that was more fantasy than reality. In the 1930s a plethora of published "histories" of the West proliferated, picturing gun battles between courageous marshals and bold outlaws, authored by such men as Walter Noble Burns and Stuart N. Lake. Pulp novels portrayed the exploits of both fictional and actual western marshals. The rise of the cowboy movie, followed by radio and television depictions of the West ("Gunsmoke," "Maverick," "Hopalong Cassidy," and so on) build upon the mythical rendition of the Old West more directly, of course, than its reality. Urban police mythology similarly evolved as much on the basis of fiction as it did from real life. The depression era literary and film renditions of booze runners and mobsters versus G-men, for example, soon evolved into the contemporary television versions of "Starsky and Hutch," "Adam–12," and "Kojak" and such movies as *Bullitt* and *Dirty Harry*.

Acknowledging that the gun is central in police work, both psychologically and defensively, we argue, nevertheless, that art shapes reality more than reality shapes art. Although media producers will hire police officers (usually commanders) as technical consultants, their input into the content of shows may be far less important than is the impact of mythical literary and film conceptions of the "gun-happy" cop. Police officers exist in a powerful cultural milieu that presents them daily with media images of their profession.

And the forced mythology does have an impact upon real-life policing. It is thus quite common to observe police officers between arrests in the station glued to the latest account of the "Streets of San Francisco." What precise influence such information has upon police officers is something about which we can only speculate. What can be said with certainty, however, is that the role of the police officer exists in a culture in which a great premium is placed upon certain aspects of police work, most notably the use of force, particularly the deadly kind. Such an emphasis, it might be argued, may at least encourage or feed the natural police occupational hazard of obsession with weapons. What the impact of the media is upon actual police behavior in an armed confrontation is even more uncertain, but poses an extremely provocative research question.

A final factor related to the cultural marriage of deadly force and police work lies in the reality that force (its threat and actuality) is a culturally defined essence of police work. Indeed, police departments are widely referred to as police "forces." Bitner, for example, writes: "The capacity to use coercive force lends the unity to all police activity in the same sense in which, let us say, the capacity to cure illness lends unity to everything that is ordinarily done in the field of medicine."[8] Bitner argues that the police, while they may be involved in other actions (such as rendering medical attention), are possessed of a unique role in that they may legitimately use force when specific legal actions they initiate (for example, a legal arrest) are opposed. Deadly force is viewed from this perspective, not as an unnecessary or tangential aspect of the police role but, rather, as a logical extension of a social role that is centrally concerned with the implementation of coercive force under specific conditions. In this view, the police officer's concern with the gun is not an arbitrary cultural anomaly but rather reflects a core occupational reality: the legal right (and at times legal obligation) to exert force against those who may physically defy his legitimate demands and who may possess deadly force themselves.

In conclusion, it must be noted that it would be both unfair and misleading to portray all police officers as either "gun-happy" or even "gun-obsessed," as some critics have done. Even on television, some police officers—as in "Columbo" or "Barney Miller"—rarely, if ever, resort even to the threat of their guns. And, as stated above, for many police officers in many departments the gun is a necessary evil at best. One officer noted, for example, "That it's mostly the college motherfucker faggots who sit in an air-conditioned office who get all turned on at the range because they see the gun go 'bang bang.' That kind of shit doesn't turn on a real street cop like me. It's too real, when you've seen a ten-year-old with his stomach blown open by a .45."

At least some officers in private will admit that their attitudes toward deadly force confrontations and death are far closer to terror than bravado. In *The Onion Field*, Wambaugh describes a very honest, crusty patrolman's reaction to a department ruling that no police officer is ever to surrender his gun to an opponent. Such a surrender had resulted in the murder of a young Los Angeles police officer, Ian Campbell:

"I disagree with the whole damn thing." He lit a cigar and there wasn't a sound in the room. Not a sound. A baby-faced cop in the front row absently let a portion of bubblegum pop through his lips.

"I have been walking a beat down here pretty near as long as some of you kiddies been on this earth," the beat cop bagan, looking again right at the sergeant who dropped his eyes and began fiddling with something on his sleeve. "I think I maybe made as many good felony busts as anybody on the job. I think I had my share of back-alley brawls, and I even been in a shootin or two."

His voice, pervasive, enveloping, was trembling a little because he was not accustomed to making speeches. So he spoke with more force to control the trembling, and now he was growling. . . .

"Now I'm particularly pissed off about this order because once, a good many years ago, some asshole took my gun off me. He braced me and there I was point blank from this little prick and him with a .45 pointed right at my belly and not for one little minute did I even consider somethin as stupid as this crazy shit in this order. Sweet fuckin mother, can you imagine me rollin around on the ground like some big goddam walrus trying to knock him down, or yellin, 'Look out behind you, you little cumdrum.' Or tryin to grab that scrawny neck so I can shove a pencil through his crummy fuckin jugular? What the hell is goin on there these days? . . . Does this order make *me* a coward too? I'm wonderin if there's somebody in this room or even on that fuckin sixth floor who's got enough hangin between his legs to call *me* a coward too?"

"It's getting . . . getting . . . we're late. Let's relieve the watch," said the sergeant, walking quickly from the room.[9]

In private, many officers similarly will describe their fears of death, their abhorrence of the fake machismo of police work and what they consider a widespread unrealistic obsession with guns. One officer said: "When I got on, I got into the .357 this, waste that motherfucker that, all that shit. Now it's stupid, like a bunch of kids playing cowboys." A police officer's wife similarly observed: "The people who become cops are either bullies or the guys who *wanted* to be bullies but couldn't. That's what it's all about, guys still fixated on their junior year in high school fight in the parking lot."

An interesting question arises as to the relationship between the "tool of the trade" of the police officer and the concept of "police personality." One surely expects an interactive effect. That is, certain individuals choose to become police officers, and from that group a smaller group is chosen for recruit training in accordance with general selection criteria developed over the years. On this point, Lefkowitz argues, "It is difficult to believe . . . that the nature of the role and institution do not result in a significant degree of self-selection and organizational selection" in regard to important personality characteristics.[10] Thus, to illustrate, the central role of the gun might be enhanced by the selection from the general population of people for policing who are more likely to have authoritarian (militaristic) personality styles. It should be pointed out, however, that no evidence supports that sort of conjecture, as reasonable as it seems in casual consideration.

It may be—and some, like Niederhoffer,[11] argue forcefully in this direction—that commonality of behavior and attitudes in police officers comes from the powerful police socialization process rather than from unique personalities that make it through the selection process. The direction of operation of this process implies that police officers are socialized into glorification of the gun.

Certainly, everyone who has worked closely with the police will have noticed a related phenomenon—the badgering of a fellow officer who did not use his weapon when deadly force was fully justified under the circumstances. "Why didn't you blow the asshole away?" "I would have shot the son of a bitch full of holes." And, understandably, the comments become vastly more fierce if the decision against using deadly force endangered another officer, however remotely.

It seems to us that a function of that type of degradation (in addition to the obvious one of mutual protection) is to maintain an appropriate level of deadly force so that future users, in particular, those doing the badgering, do not stand out. Police officers are indeed very concerned, even intimidated, by the investigations of homicide, internal affairs, supervisory staff, district attorneys, and so on, that follow injuries and fatalities, as well as by the inevitable civil suits.

Returning to the concept of police personality, most observers of the police scene agree on two police traits: sensitivity to status and suspiciousness. The relationship of these two traits is expressed as follows: ". . . The use of force is called for when the policeman is treated in a derogatory fashion; when he is pushed around, spit at, and made a fool of, called a filthy name,"[12] and ". . . A young man may suggest that threat of violence to the policeman by his manner of walking or 'strutting,' the insolence in the demeanor being registered by the policeman as a possible preamble to later attack. Signs vary from area to area, but a youth dressed in a black leather jacket and motorcycle boots is sure to draw at least a suspicious glance from a policeman."[13]

The question of how the possession of a weapon affects the psychology of policing and policing encounters is of both research and practical interest. When the police officer confronts a surly gas station attendant, or an insolent juvenile robber, for example, how does the knowledge that he possesses deadly force affect the manner in which he approaches the encounter?

In describing the psychological uses of deadly force we must admit to posing more questions than answers. It appears from a range of evidence that the possession of deadly force exerts some impact upon at least some police officers. The precise impact of this reality and its effect on different officers are, of course, uncertain. We rather hope to alert the reader that for the police officer the availability of deadly force may serve psychological purposes beyond the obvious one (the protection of his life and those of others). What the precise consequences of these purposes are must remain an important topic of future research investigation.

DEADLY FORCE IN "ROUTINE" POLICE WORK

Another context for considering the police use of deadly force may be found in routine police actions where shots will almost certainly not be fired at a human being. We hope to demonstrate that in a variety of police activities the awareness of the availability of police deadly force is an important social reality in understanding police/citizen encounters, even those encounters in which shots being fired are not even plausible possibilities for either police officer or citizen.

It should be observed in this regard that actual firings of police weapons and hitting citizens are, using almost any basis of comparison, very rare events. In New York City, during 1979, for example, only 80 police officers fired shots that hit human beings. In 1980, there were more than 21,000 officers working for the New York Police Department. In Newark, New Jersey (one of the most crime-ridden and violent cities in the United States), in 1980 only nine of roughly 1,000 officers fired shots that hit human beings. In Buena Park, California (a city of 60,000 persons), only one officer of 93 fired a shot that hit a human being. Using another basis of comparison, the Washington State Patrol made 915,000 contacts with citizens. Of these contacts, shots were fired in only three cases. Similarly, the Los Angeles Police Department from 1974 to 1978 made roughly 220,000 felony arrests. Shots that hit human beings were fired in but 307 of these 220,000 incidents.

Of the 163 murders in Newark in 1980 only three homicides were caused by a Newark police officer. It might be further noted that of the approximately 300 murders in Atlanta, Georgia, in the same year fewer than ten were caused by police officers. Also, of the nearly eight million persons in New York City in 1979, 40 died at the hands of the police. Nationwide, using the most conservative (largest) estimates of the 300,000 police personnel, fewer than 600 will kill human beings. Of the 220 million persons in the United States, probably fewer than 2,000 persons will be shot at by police officers. Similarly, assuming that the average police officer works 200 days per year and handles eight assignments a shift (reasonable estimates) and fires his weapon on the average of once every nine years (Kobler's estimate[14]), the chances of his firing a shot on any particular assignment are roughly 14,400 to 1. Even in a city with a high rate of police use of deadly force, the chances of its use during assignments on any particular day will be very, very small, not very different from being involved in a serious auto accident or being beset by a serious illness.

Still, these average figures conceal the widely different probabilities in officers and assignments. During one shift in an inner city, one of the authors was "on scene" to two police shootings within a five-hour period. In that department, one officer used deadly force eleven times and another officer killed five people, even though most officers never used their weapons in the line of duty. And Fyfe observed in his study of police use of deadly force in New York City that there were many "sleepy hollows" in which police shooting was rare.[15] In other precincts, shootings were at times a weekly if not daily occurrence.

Specialized units such as tactical teams and antistreet crime units often face a markedly disproportionate risk of deadly force. Police officers in such units may directly face many opponents with weapons in the course of a single night, as well as other incidents in which challenge by an opponent with a weapon is highly likely. To illustrate this type of "high-risk" police activity, we offer selections from a log of activity from one of the authors' (Scharf) observational study with a tactical unit in Newark. During this study, all uses of guns and contacts were recorded that related to either police or citizen weapons (only one involving a shot fired by a police officer) during a three-day period. The area was hard core and the time of year, July, was particularly conducive to violence. Obviously, in other police contexts, deadly force (both its threat and reality) would be far less frequent.

> Thursday: Sergeant orders team to carry shotguns due to "sniper in project."
>> 11:00 a.m. D. and T. load extra shotgun shells in car.
>> 11:15 a.m. Sergeant gives briefing involving M.O. of suspect who is known to carry stolen .45 in boot. Tells us to be prepared.
>> 11:30 a.m. We are looking for armed robbery team known to have shot and possibly killed victims. Captain T. tells us to be careful.
>> 2:30 p.m. Raid of house on Sixteenth and Avon. We cover back. Everyone has guns drawn.
>> 2:50 p.m. Raid on apartment in Hays Projects. Guns drawn as we go upstairs. Everyone has guns trained as we go through door.
>> 3:30 p.m. Guns are still unholstered as we talk to suspects in apartment.
>> 4:00 p.m. Guns drawn as we approach suspects of beating on apartment steps. Sergeant apologizes to them for scaring them. They check out O.K.
>
> Friday: Shotgun shells again loaded.
>> 7:00 p.m. Captain reads speech about evidence following shots-fired incident.
>> 7:30 p.m. Shotguns are to be carried in car trunk from now on, drones the Sergeant. "Chief caught some guy with shotgun on 'B and E' call." Much shuffling of feet, mumbling.
>> 8:15 p.m. Drug raid on sellers on Seventh and Avon. T. has gun out. L. and B., not.
>> 8:30 p.m. Check on report of bomb in hospital.

8:45 p.m. Go to a "man with a gun" call. Call turns out to be an older man with a Spanish-American era gun he was trying to sell.

9:15 p.m. Raid on Belsinore Hotel.

9:20 p.m. Raid Room 402 looking for "Richard." Guns out as we force open door.

9:35 p.m. Raid on Room 414. Richard has moved. L. has gun pointed up at door from a crouch. B. points down at door knob.

9:50 p.m. Arrest man for suspicion of murder in Room 502. Find a toy pistol in his pocket.

10:40 p.m. Snitch tells us "drug house" on Orange Avenue. Tells us that there is a loaded .38 in Apartment 2; a .22 in Apartment 6.

11:20 p.m. Drug buy in apartment.

11:50 p.m. Raid on "house."

11:51 p.m. Woman surrenders .22 to officer W. She says she keeps it for "protection."

12:02 a.m. Man opens door of Apartment 3 with loaded gun. Officer G. is waiting. "Please, sir, don't do anything stupid," G. says as he grabs pistol out of man's hand.

12:40 a.m. Search of Room 8 produces third gun—another loaded .38.

Saturday (night)

5:25 p.m. No shotguns tonight. Snitch reports tell of big gun sale at 11:00 p.m. near projects.

6:55 p.m. Arrest woman on drug sales. Guns unholstered as we approach car.

7:20 p.m. N. and C. chase man down alley. They lose suspect. Snitch says they have two .45's and a .38. We back up.

7:55 p.m. Arrest older man and woman for erratic driving after leaving "drug handout." Guns out as N. approaches car.

8:17 p.m. Older man tells N. about whom he bought drugs from. We go to bar and arrest man. N. holds gun out as C. handcuffs him and puts him in car. Twenty people watch.

9:02 p.m. Big arrest of the night. A report comes in identifying car used in shotgun robbery and assault at bar. "Nine people robbed, three shot with pellets." We race to area. We see 1967 two-tone Eldorado/NY Plates 557 . . . . We follow car to project turn around. T. to D.: "Should we take them? We don't have a backup." D.: "We gotta. Those motherfuckers just did nine people." The backup approaches from the rear. Lights on. Both T. and D. exit. "GET YOUR HANDS ON WINDSHIELD." Finally the man complies. There is an orange towel covering his hands. He was cut in the robbery.

9:45 p.m. Dinner in Mike's Diner interrupted; "'455' officer needs assistance, White Castle at . . . ." We go. "Cannot find" reports D.

10:00 p.m. Off-duty officer arrests robber with gun. T. draws gun as man is placed in back of #316 car.

1:15 a.m. "'455.' Officer needs assistance." Officer locked in apartment with female. Husband outside with gun. We approach apartment with guns drawn. Woman refuses to let us in. She demands to see our faces. We refuse and storm out angrily into street.

2:50 a.m. Shots fired. Gang fight at . . . . We arrive with shotguns drawn. Nothing to be seen at location.

For this unit, the threat of police deadly force (guns being drawn, displayed, and aimed and the reality of citizens' guns) was a frequent experience. Although this unit's experience is unusual in terms of both the level of danger and the frequency of contact with violent criminals, it should be obvious that guns are an integral component of even their most routine police activities. Guns in other police environments are, of course, far less frequently used. However, in all but the most peaceful of suburban communities the implements of deadly force and the threat of their use do play at least some role in daily police work.

Although showing, drawing, or pointing weapons is a much rarer event in most units of most departments than is true of a Newark tactical squad, the majority of patrol officers will draw their weapons in at least some situations. In some hard-core areas of certain cities it is either standardard or informal police policy to draw one's weapon on specific types of jobs. One officer in a middle-sized urban police department offered: "Like there are specific calls in neighborhoods that make to expect trouble; so you have your gun out even before you hit the stairs. Like a 1017 [domestic disturbance] in the Jefferson Street area, that's almost automatic. Also any possible 'B and E' or a robbery you loosen the strap as you drive up and then your gun goes out as you leave the car." In other areas, the drawing of weapons is far rarer. One suburban officer, for example, noted that "(I) haven't had my gun out in months except to clean it. I can't really remember when I drew it last." Another officer in the same department described the role his gun played in police work as follows: "Let's just say it's there."

Officers will also use guns in contexts where firing is not a possibility. In some situations officers will draw their weapons to intimidate a disrespectful or apparently disrespectful citizen. One officer commented: "Like when we go deal with a bunch of youth gangs in the Sullivan Street area we will pull our shotgun out of the car. It's not like we are going to shoot someone at that point. It's more like we want their attention. To make them take heed."

The possession of the means to kill other human beings, many police officers believe, creates a certain "presence" that many citizens, subtly, but certainly, respond to. One officer, for example, said:

> It's like when you have a piece this gives you a certain edge in dealing with citizens. The gun may never come out, but it helps you in dealing with people, even those several inches taller. It's a myth, a hype, both for you and the citizen. You got to remember that 99.9 percent of all police work is showmanship.

In this view, the gun is a useful psychological tool that adds to the advantage possessed by the police officer in an encounter (presumably already established with his badge, training, and legal authority) with a citizen.

Police officers, it should be remembered, think about using their guns far more often than they face situations in which they possibly might use them. One veteran officer said:

> Like I'm always preparing you know mentally. Like what if that guy I see on the street mugs that old man on the street, how would I get position. What would I do? It affects how you even view driving home from work, always preparing for anything. I tell my wife what I'm thinking and she thinks I'm nuts.

Police officers will occasionally draw their weapons to "motivate" a citizen to obey a specific command. Often guns will be drawn in situations where they could not be legally used. This creates problems, some humorous, some more serious. A sergeant with 13 years' experience observed:

> Yah, most guys are draw happy for the first several years. I remember in the beginning I'd draw my gun for almost anything: drunks, juveniles. What cured me, and I guess other guys is the first guy who looks at your gun and tells you to go fuck yourself, like "Come shoot me motherfucker." They know better than you when you can shoot and when you can't. Your gun goes back in and soon you learn not to draw it if you're not going to use it.

It should be noted that the premature drawing of weapons may lead to an unnecessarily escalated confrontation and possibly a shooting. In a much publicized case involving an agitated woman, Eulia Love (this case is discussed in Chapter Five), the premature drawing of weapons seemed to be at least a contributing cause to a tragic episode. In other situations, officers with guns drawn have shot themselves while chasing felons or while grappling with citizens after they have prematurely unholstered their weapons. Also, unfortunately, many officers engaged in hand-to-hand fights with citizens have been shot by the citizen (often drunk or psychotic) with the weapons they unholstered prior to the physical altercation. Officers thus faced with the possibility of physical contact with a citizen are highly conscious of the "safety of the guns." One officer commented:

> Like let's say you are in a "415"—a family disturbance. There are lots of things you can't do because of your piece. Like you can't really sit back in a chair to let them feel comfortable because if you do, you can't get to your gun. Also, if you pat a guy on the arm you have to remember to keep your gun side free. While you are being all fatherly, he might grab your gun and kill you with it.

Chapman observes that a substantial percentage of all police officers killed by citizens are killed with their own (or a partner's) weapon. He writes, "Unfortunately, the very weapon the lawman carried for his own protection sometimes turned out to be his own worst liability . . . an officer must exert a titanic effort before allowing himself to be disarmed."[16]

The capacity both to possess and to use deadly force serves other purposes as well. One such purpose if that of identification. This is especially important for officers who are in plainclothes or off-duty status. Often, but not always, off-duty or plainclothes officers will wear their shirts out over their belts to conceal a gun placed in their belts. This is especially the case during the hot summer months. To an observant police officer (and possibly astute criminals) this bulge has significance. For example, one New York police officer stated:

> When I'm in a subway station or somewhere I can tell if there are other cops there, even if I don't know them by looking for a certain bulge under their shirts, under their jackets or by their ankle [as would be indicated by the increasingly popular ankle holster]. This tells me that there are probably friends near by and I can do things [like confront certain situations] which I wouldn't do otherwise.

Another purpose is for the use of warning shots. Such shots are permitted in some departments, although forbidden in most others. The forbidding departments assume that the potential gain is overwhelmed by risk to other citizens as well as additional risk to the officer by the resulting escalation. Some warning shots are fired when a shot aimed to kill would be acceptable. One officer, for example, pointed out:

> That when this older drunk guy with a .22 turned towards me kind of drunk like, I let go a warning and then ducked behind the car because I felt that I could still get him if he came around for real. Luckily the guy dropped the rifle and put his hands up when he heard the shot. He let go in his pants he was so scared.

Another officer described firing a warning shot at a "juvenile with a knife because frankly I didn't want the hassle of shooting a kid. If he's three years older, he's dead." Still another officer faced with a "wild family fight" in front of a grocery store fired a bullet into a "stop sign" near one of the main combatants' head to "alert" him to the seriousness of his actions. Another officer (an obviously excellent shot) reported firing a warning shot between the legs of a crazed man with a machete.

Other warning shots may be fired to startle a citizen or a group of citizens. One officer described the effect of a shot fired to "quiet" a bar brawl as follows: "Well, they were yelling and screaming and throwing bottles, so I fired a shot into the ground. A few seconds later it was like 10 A.M. in Sunday Mass it was so quiet."

Closely related to warning shots are shots fired for purposes of communication. One officer described how he fired a shot to attract the attention of other police officers when he was cornered by several angry residents of an all-black tenement house:

> I was in the back of this house in Springfield when these four blacks came running down the stairs. I had four of them in the bag but only one pair of handcuffs. I tried the radio but it wouldn't work in the stairwell, so I let a round go into the ceiling. That got half the tac team here in a hurry. We made four good arrests.

Gunshots, then, serve numerous purposes for the police officer; some of these are far from those one might presume from a casual observation of the police. It also should be noted that some of these uses of deadly force are either not encouraged or are actually prohibited by the police department. It is obvious that in some departments warning shots are either not reported or are reported as "misses" (even by officers who are obviously expert shots).

We have argued that in a variety of police contexts, deadly force plays a number of discrete, identifiable, important, and also surprising purposes other than to kill human beings. The actual use of deadly force by police officers is very rare, and the use with actual injury resulting far rarer. The frequency with which a police officer will use deadly force, of course, depends greatly upon the city in which he is located and his assignment within that city. In some cities, for some officers (for example, the tactical patrol team described earlier) the gun plays a central role in many (if not most) citizen encounters. In other less perilous settings, the role of deadly force recedes to far less importance.

LEGAL AND ADMINISTRATIVE CONTROL OF DEADLY FORCE

The first level of control of deadly force is state statute, the second is law court decisions, and the third is administrative policy of the particular department.

The oldest of state statutes is English common law where the use of deadly force in law enforcement was considered justified against a fleeing felon but not against a fleeing misdemeanant. The California statute, Penal Code Section 196, is typical of direct derivatives from the common law:

California Penal Code Section 196, Justifiable Homicide by Public Officers. Homicide is justifiable when committed by public officers and those acting by their command in their aid and assistance:
1. In obedience to any judgment of a competent court; or
2. When necessarily committed in overcoming actual resistance to the execution of some legal process, or in the discharge of any other legal duty; or
3. When necessarily committed in retaking felons who have been rescued or have escaped, or when necessarily committed in arresting persons charged with felony, and who are fleeing from justice or resisting such arrest.

More recently enacted codes (the California code dates from 1872), are likely to contain elements relevant to the modern American scene rather than "Olde" England. Thus, Karp, surveying statutory provisions authorizing deadly force, found 37 such laws for purposes of effecting an arrest.[17] But, while 19 of these 37 laws stipulate that deadly force may be used if the arrest is for a felony, 15 stipulate that deadly force may be used only if the felony involved the use of a weapon, a threat of serious injury, or some variation thereof. Two stipulate an additional requirement of substantial risk that failure to arrest will lead to injury or death.

It is worth mentioning in this context that a felony is not the same in the United States of the twentieth century as it was in England when the common law was being developed. In those days, capital punishment was authorized for all felonies; today, a felony can be so relatively trivial an offense as driving someone else's car on a joyride without approval. That difference was acknowledged in a court decision in California that ruled, apparently contrary to the state's Penal Code Section 196, that a police officer is *not* justified in using deadly force against a fleeing felon unless the felony was violent or there is reasonable fear that escape may lead to future death or serious injury on the part of the officer or another citizen.[18] The California ruling provides an example of the control of deadly force at the second level, by court decision.[19]

At the third level of control, virtually every major department, and most minor departments, have written policy statements regarding the use of deadly force. Policy statements serve to provide more specific guidelines for the police officer in deciding upon the use of deadly force and are generally more restrictive than state and court law. For example, the "Firearms Policy" of the San Diego police Department (dated March 14, 1979) lists the conditions under which weapons are authorized in three major categories: (1) to protect themselves from death or serious bodily injury; (2) to protect another officer or any other person from death or serious bodily injury; and (3) to apprehend a fleeing felon "reasonably known" to be armed with a "deadly weapon" for a felony involving great bodily injury or the threat of great bodily injury. And the overall bias of the policy is well expressed in its preamble:

> Contemporary society, the legislature, the judiciary, and the Department place a greater value on the preservation of life than on the apprehension of criminal offenders. For this reason, the Department considers firearms to be defensive weapons, to be used only when necessary to protect human life, or to prevent bodily injury.

That, clearly, is not the type of bias that was expressed in common law justification.

Such legal and administrative definitions are critical to the police officer who will try to establish early in an encounter what the legal and policy options are. To illustrate the point, one experienced officer said: "When you get into something, the officer wants to know what's possible. What is the crime? How do you know? Did you see it? This tells you whether you can use your piece." And differences in adjacent jurisdictions can be surprisingly large, as illustrated in the following comment by a police officer:

> There was this guy in Sparks [Nevada], where they can shoot you for running away with anything worth more than $100, who was running from one of their officers with his gun drawn. The guy ran across the street which is the border to Reno where we don't do that kind of stuff. The guy turned to the officer and yelled out, "Too bad, sucker," and took off into a parking lot.

The legal and administrative controls of the use of deadly force provide what has been called the "circumference" of police decision making to use (or not to use) deadly force. The variations of actual use within the circumference are indeed great. In Los Angeles, a man who had virtually decapitated and killed a harbor patrol officer was killed (although he posed no immediate threat to the officers who had him contained) as he ran through a vacant lot armed with a machete. Another man was similarly killed as he attempted to flee from the scene of a violent rape.

Even self-defense shootings may be surprisingly varied. In some uses of deadly force, the mere possession (or apparent possession) of a gun may provide the motivation for shooting. In other incidents, the opponent may point a weapon at the officer; in still others, a shot may be fired by the opponent prior to a shot being fired by a police officer. In other self-defense shootings, no lethal weapon may be present. The opponent may physically attack the officer with his hands. In one recent incident the provocation was a typewriter thrown at the officer by a crazed man.

Overall, our collective observations and formal research indicate that officers use their weapons at a far lower rate than authorization allows. The relatively few times that officers shoot in an inappropriate or "out of policy" or illegal manner are highlighted by the considerable public attention directed at them. But the many times greater number of situations where restraint is shown, even though law and policy permitted expression, go unnoticed, except, perhaps, by an award for "commendable restraint" that is quietly made in many departments.

The factors leading an officer to a decision to use deadly force will be the central topic in the next three chapters. In these chapters we will focus upon shooting risk in police-citizen armed confrontations (Chapter Four), the nature of police decision making (Chapter Five), and officer competencies and skills (Chapter Six). In Chapter Four, we begin our inquiry by focusing on the relative risk of different types of armed confrontations. We will be specifically concerned with the factors (opponents, assignments, partners and citizens present, and space and light) that make police officers more likely to shoot in one type of confrontation than in another.

NOTES

1. E. Goffman, *Behavior in Everyday Places* (Garden City, N.Y.: Anchor Books, 1962).

2. J. Wambaugh, *The Choirboys* (New York: Dell, 1981), pp. 49, 50.

3. G. E. Berkley, *The Democratic Policeman* (Boston: Beacon Press, 1969), p. 34.

4. A. Pickles, "Putting the Llama Commanche Through the Wringer," *Police Product News* 5, no. 5 (May 1981): 16–18.

5. J. Wambaugh, *The Black Marble* (New York: Delacorte Press, 1978), p. 181.

6. F. R. Prassel, *The Western Peace Officer* (Norman: University of Oklahoma Press, 1972), p. 245.

7. Ibid., pp. 23, 24.

8. E. Bitner, "Capacity to Use Force as the Core of the Police Role," in J. H. Skolnick and T. C. Gray, eds., *Policing in America* (Boston: Little, Brown, 1975).

9. J. Wambaugh, *The Onion Field* (New York: Dell, 1973), pp. 244, 245.

10. J. Lefkowitz, "Psychological Attributes of Policemen: A Review of Research and Opinion," *Journal of Social Issues* 31, no. 1 (Winter 1975): 3–26.

11. A. Niederhoffer, *Behind the Shield: The Police in Urban Society* (Garden City, N.Y.: Anchor Books, 1969).

12. W. A. Westley, *Violence and the Police: A Sociological Study of Law, Custom, and Morality* (Cambridge, Mass.: MIT Press, 1970), p. 126.

13. J. H. Skolnick, *Justice Without Trial: Law Enforcement in Democratic Society* (New York: Wiley, 1966), pp. 46, 47.

14. A. L. Kobler, "Police Homicide in a Democracy," *Journal of Social Issues* 31, no. 1 (Winter 1975): 163–84.

15. J. J. Fyfe, "Shots Fired: An Examination of New York City Police Firearms Discharges," Ph.D. dissertation, State University of New York at Albany, 1978.

16. S. G. Chapman, *Police Murders and Effective Countermeasures* (Santa Cruz, Calif.: Davis Press, 1976), p. 62.

17. D. J. Karp, "Statutory Regulation of Police Use of Deadly Force," report submitted to Ronald Gainer, deputy assistant attorney general, U.S. Department of Justice, December 13, 1979.

18. *Kortum* v. *Alkire*, 69 Cal. App. 3d 325 (1977).

19. Further analysis of the role of court decisions in controlling deadly force may be found in A. Binder and P. Scharf, "Deadly Force in Law Enforcement," *Crime & Delinquency* 28, no. 1 (January 1982): 1–23; and in W. A. Geller and K. J. Karales, *Split-Second Decisions: Shootings of and by Chicago Police* (Chicago: Chicago Law Enforcement Study Group, 1981).

4 Barrel to Barrel

PROLOGUE

A. Two Lucky Cops and a Lucky Criminal

Cars 347, 348, and 349 proceed to Avon and Seventh. Informant has called station saying that car matching description of car in tavern robbery was seen at that location. Use extreme caution. Suspects are believed to be armed with shotguns. Tavern robbery involved shots fired at victims. Car is two-tone American style coupe, about 1970, red and white. Repeat, two-tone coupe, red and white, License 943 *Victor Victor Boy*. Consider suspects armed and dangerous.

The tactical officers placed the magnetic red light on top of the car, did a wide U-turn in traffic, and sped through several intersections.

Officer A: Probably a big fucking nothing, but if we see them, stay down Doc. The police director don't want to lose you.

Officer B: What street goes into Seventh?

Officer A: Carlton.

Officer B: Let's swing up it then so we can come up behind him. Hold on now.

Officer A: There's a two-tone car up there parked up on Seventh at the corner. Think that's him?

An older two-tone car with a single driver suddenly started driving down Seventh Street. The car moved too slowly to be an unconcerned motorist. Even before the officers could read the license plate, they knew they had their car. Slowly the tactical car moved through the traffic in back of the suspect's car. A young black man was driving, holding an orange towel over the steering wheel. He nervously looked backward at the police car, as if in disbelief.

Officer A: Let's flash the lights; see if he'll stop.

The suspect car started to move more quickly onto Springfield Avenue, onto a bridge, then over toward the large, crime-filled housing projects. All police officers in the city knew that to lose a suspect in the projects meant probably losing him permanently. Police officers, except in large force, would rarely go above the third floor of the large red buildings, with most of the windows broken and violence filling every floor. Finally, the car stopped in a loop in front of the housing projects. The door on the driver's side was slightly ajar.

Officer A: Should we wait for backup? He may have a shotgun.
Officer B: This motherfucker done robbed nine people and shot three; we gotta do it. Stay down Doc.

Just then, another tactical car approached from the back. A white officer jumped from the car with a shotgun aimed right at the car. The second officer in the car jumped out with a search light illuminating the suspect's car but also blinding the two police officers with their guns pointed at the windshield of the two-tone Ford.

Officer A: FREEZE, POLICE! PUT YOUR HANDS ON THE WHEEL! PUT YOUR HANDS ON THE WHEEL! PUT YOUR HANDS ON THE WHEEL WHERE WE CAN SEE THEM! SLOW!

The man almost deliberately with an unnerving sullenness slowly placed his hands on the wheel; however, he still clutched his orange towel.

Officer A: Now drop that fucking towel.

The man slowly complied. With great speed, Officer B. reached into the driver's side of the car and grabbed the man by his forearms.

A young, very sullen black man, who appeared very stoned and was wearing dungarees and a white undershirt, spread himself on the car.

> *Officer C:* Where were you at 5:00 P.M., tonight? Some of your friends say you were shooting some people in front of Brown's Tavern. Looks like you got hit yourself.
>
> *Man:* It wasn't like that. It was a private beef. I swear man.
>
> *Officer D:* Lookey here [he pulls a shotgun from the back seat of the car]. Bingo, just like the gun that was used in the robbery, and look what we got in his pockets [he digs roughly into the man's pants], shotgun shells. Nice guy we got here.

On the way to the precinct, the observer asked Officers A. and B. about how they handled the incident. "How did you find the car?"

"Just fucking luck," came quickly the response of Officer B. "Just fucking lucky."

"It never happens like this. Usually you are three hours late. It's 'cause the snitch called the station house—that's how we got here so quick. Otherwise, if they called communications, we would have been in bed and so would he (pointing at the prisoner in the rear seat) before the call came in."

"How come you didn't shoot him?" the observer continued, ignoring the prisoner listening through his amphetamine haze with obvious interest. "How come you didn't shoot him when you saw the towel come up? You didn't know if there was a gun there or not."

"Don't know," was the response of Officer A. "To be truthful, the lights of C.'s car [the other tactical officer] were so bright, I couldn't see what was happening. Given what I saw, which wasn't that clear, I didn't feel I had to," Officer B. added. "Just put it this way, we were motherfucking lucky to catch him. He is goddamn lucky to be alive. It's as simple as that. Hey, A., call headquarters and get an arrest number for this motherfucker. I bet he has so many fucking warrants we won't eat till midnight."

B. High Noon

"Frank Miller has been released from jail" is the message to Gary Cooper, who plays a marshal, Will Kane, in one of the most popular Westerns of all time, *High Noon*. His plans at the time of that notification were to leave his job as marshal in a small western town and settle in another town to take up storekeeping. He had just married his Quaker girlfriend Amy (played by Grace Kelly). Kane had been instrumental in sending Miller to the penitentiary, and Miller, with the aid of three other desperadoes, intends to kill Kane in revenge. The three cohorts meet Miller when he arrives on the noon train, and all four set out for the main street of the town to confront Kane. As one observer says, "Blood will surely be shed." All of the townsmen who the marshal had hoped would aid him in confronting Miller and his gang refused his pleas for help; cowardice was the obvious motivation. The marshal must meet Frank Miller and his three armed henchmen alone.

"Do not forsake me, oh my darling, on this our wedding day. . . ."

As Miller and his men approach the town on foot, the brave marshal, armed with two six shooters, sees them coming and positions himself with an admixture of fear, frustration, and tension. He had been urged to leave town, but his sense of duty made it necessary for him to stay.

The four desperadoes draw. Marshal Kane fires first; one desperado falls dead on the street. A chase begins that finds the courageous Marshal Kane cornered in a barn. Miller sets fire to the barn, but Kane escapes while riding protectively under the belly of a horse. Kane shoots and kills another desperado during the barn scene. In the next scene, Kane, now wounded, is in a store, where he is threatened by Miller and the one other remaining bandit. But, then, Amy kills one of the bandits, overcoming her Quaker principles, because of the need of her husband, who had been deserted by everyone else. That leads to Miller finding her in a hiding place and taking her hostage. "Come out," he yells to the marshal. The marshal walks out from his cover into the street, apparently to certain death. Now Amy scratches Miller's face, disabling him for an instant. Will Kane fires four times, killing Miller. "Do not forsake me, oh my darling, on this our wedding day. . . ."

We placed the two types of armed confrontation between law enforcement and citizen—real life in Prologue A and fictional in Prologue B—to highlight the complexity and uncertainty of the former as opposed to the frequent simplistic predictability of the latter. In Hollywood encounters, particularly, the armed confrontation resembles a stylized ballet with the law enforcement agent first ordering the bandit to "drop it," the bandit refusing, the law enforcement officer drawing last, and almost inevitably the bandit lying dead in the street.

In this chapter, we will directly face the complexity and unpredictability of real-life confrontation. After defining the term armed confrontation, we will describe some of the different types of armed confrontation commonly faced by police officers. We will also discuss the concept of risk and how it affects the likelihood of an officer's firing a shot in an encounter.

POLICE-CITIZEN ARMED CONFRONTATION:
A UNIT OF ANALYSIS

One way to think about the types of armed confrontations faced by police officers is to consider them as a subclass of all police encounters. Fatal shootings, hits, and shots fired, in turn, may be conceptualized as possible, but not necessary, outcomes of armed confrontations. Suppose, in a hypothetical precinct in a particular year, police officers make 50,000 contacts of all types with citizens. Of these 50,000 contacts, perhaps 2,000 might be considered high-risk contacts in that the citizen has committed a dangerous felony (for example, armed robbery), or there are other reasons to believe the person to be dangerous. In a far smaller number of such contacts, say 500, the citizen will display such resistance to a legal request of a police officer (for example, refuse to leave a tavern, resist arrest, and so on) that a confrontation might be said to exist between the police officer and citizen. In an even smaller number of incidents (perhaps 50), the citizen will have a dangerous weapon and threaten to use it, or the officer will have other reasons to believe that it will be necessary to use his gun.

This type of confrontation is an armed confrontation, the topic of this and the next two chapters. As we shall observe, situational, episodic, and officer characteristics will determine the outcome of a particular armed confrontation. In some armed confrontations, no shot will be fired by the police officer, nor by the opponent; in others, a shot or shots may be fired, missing, hitting, or killing an opponent or a police officer.

The summary below, with hypothetical but realistic numbers, drawn from an active police precinct, illustrates the relationship of armed confrontations to other police-citizen contacts and outcomes:

In 1982 the X Precinct

1. Responded to roughly 100,000 "calls for service": a dispatch to a

specific circumstance-person incident where there is need of medical help, suspicious person, domestic squabble, and so on.

2. Of these 100,000 calls for service, 50,000 persons were actually contacted (questioned, arrested, and so forth).
3. Of these 50,000 contacts, 2,000 are classified as high risk due to the nature of the call or the citizen.
4. Of these 2,000 high-risk contacts, 500 result in a confrontation in which there is resistance to a legal request by the law enforcement officer.
5. Of these 500 contacts, 50 will result in armed confrontation.
6. Of these 50 armed confrontations, 40 result in no shots being fired by the police officer.
7. In the remaining ten armed confrontations, where shots are fired, the officer misses in eight.
8. In the remaining two confrontations, one officer hits but does not kill an opponent; in the other, the opponent is killed.

The above illustrates the relationship of armed confrontations to other police-citizen contacts and also to outcomes of police shootings, misses, hits, and kills. As one can see, armed confrontations are relatively rare in terms of all police contacts; however, it should further be noted that a shot being fired by the police officer is but one possible rare outcome of an armed confrontation. In our definition, an armed confrontation will signify an encounter between citizen(s) and police officer(s) in which all of the following conditions are present:

1. Firearms are available to one or more of the parties involved.
2. There is the threat of force by the citizen or the fear of the threat of force by the officer.
3. There is the mental awareness on the part of the police officer or citizen that he or she might require the use of deadly force to resolve the encounter.

Based on these specifications, an armed confrontation clearly need not result in an injury or death; indeed, in an armed confrontation a weapon might not even be used. An example (a perhaps typical one) of an armed confrontation is found in the encounter described to us by one urban police officer:

My partner and I were on general patrol when we got this call that there was a robbery in progress. When we encountered the suspect [a hostage taken and then released in the robbery identified him], he walked real calm down the street. I don't think he saw us. When we confronted him, he hesitated. He kept fiddling in his pockets, saying nothing. We hollered again for him to put his hands up. He looked around for an escape route. Finally he pulls a gun out and fires at us three times. Luckily he missed and luckily we got him before he shot us.

In this confrontation, both parties were armed and both recognized the situation as potentially involving a need to shoot; it occurred in an open street, and the citizen was a felon. In other armed confrontations, however, only the police officer may be armed. In some situations the citizen may appear to be armed but in reality not be armed at all or not even pose a plausible threat to the officer. An example of that situation in the following:

> A good samaritan who was mistaken for a beating suspect in West Hollywood Saturday night was shot and killed by a Los Angeles sheriff's deputy just after the man had helped the beating victim and called police.
> As [Deputy Jimenez] was jogging toward the rear of the staircase, suddenly and without warning, Mr. Steven Conger emerged from the phone booth behind the stairway. Mr. Conger came out quickly, in a slightly crouched position, empty handed and moving toward Deputy Jiminez. Deputy Jimenez immediately thought Mr. Conger was the suspect they were looking for and that he had been flushed out of hiding by Deputy McHenry. Deputy Jimenez instantly concluded that he was about to be attacked by the assault suspect who was supposed to be armed with a gun. He did not notice whether Mr. Conger had anything in either hand. In a reflex action, Deputy Jimenez raised his gun and fired one round at [Mr. Conger].[1]

In this example, the basis for specifying an armed confrontation was unilateral; only the deputy sheriff was armed, as only the deputy (apparently) anticipated a use of force.

Incidents in which there is definitional ambiguity as to the status of a confrontation reminds us of the methodological caution first suggested by the symbolic interactionalist school of sociology in its argument that common social encounters may be defined quite differently by different social actors. Thus, as in the case of a man on a bus who falls in love with a fellow passenger, whereas she regards him as a total nonentity, social reality may appear quite differently to particular social actors. Similarly, as with the shooting of Steven Conger, only one party in police-citizen encounters apparently conceived of the encounter as directly threatening. This lack of symbolic consensus as to the meaning of the encounter may be seen in police armed confrontations with dazed, psychotic, or drunk civilians who define their actions very differently than does the police officer.

VARIETIES OF RISK IN ENCOUNTERS
BETWEEN POLICE AND CITIZENS

Armed confrontations are extremely varied social events. For example, in one city the following armed confrontations were recorded during one six-month interval. It should be noted that the averted shootings among the armed confrontations listed were, of course, only those that came to the attention of police administration (probably overrepresented were types in which officers were recommended for medals or where the arrests were especially glamorous).

January 2   Patrol officer, face down, disarms armed robber in liquor store.

January 4   Off-duty patrolman wrestles pistol away from armed robber who placed gun in officer's stomach during armed robbery.

January 12   Patrol officer disarms juvenile armed with zip gun after short struggle.

January 16   Officer fires shot at car escaping from armed robbery.

January 18   Two officers disarm boy fourteen who shot three children in junior high school. Boy waved gun at officers, but no shots were fired by officers.

January 18   Two officers fire four shots at stolen and escaping oil truck.

January 20   Officer aims at fleeing bank robber; holds fire.

January 23   Officer wounds man threatening him with screwdriver, in alley, following pursuit of driver of stolen car.

January 30   Detectives disarm man behind on child support, armed with knife.

January 30   Tactical patrol arrests man armed with pistol wanted for murder.

February 14   Officer wounds two "B and E" suspects who had assaulted him while he was searching a building with other officers.

February 19   Decoy patrol arrests armed robbery team in store without shots fired.

February 26   Officer fires shot at car which attempted to run him down.

February 27   Off-duty officer disarms armed robber in tavern without shots fired.

March 1   Two officers disarm man attacking police officer with knife [no shots fired].

March 8   Armed robber confronted by patrol team. No shots fired.

March 10   Burglar with pistol disarmed by patrol officer.

March 15   Two officers shoot at but miss two street robbers caught in act of robbing older citizen on street.

March 16   Insane man with .22 pistol disarmed by SWAT team.

March 17   Officers fire shots at fleeing vehicle.

March 23   Narcotics squad raids drug dealer's house. Man threatens officers with machete but is disarmed.

April 1   Three officers fire shots at man with shotgun, escaping from liquor store holdup.

April 16   Off-duty officer is killed while interdicting armed robbery in tavern.

April 17   Woman with broken bottle attacks police officer but is disarmed.

April 17   Man fires shot and is disarmed by police officer.

April 25   Man with nephew as hostage holds SWAT team at bay for six hours. Finally surrenders without shots being fired.

April 27   Warning shots fired by single off-duty officer at fleeing larceny suspect.

April 30   Armed robbers in car disarmed by detective team.

May 23   Officer in decoy operation fires single shot at robbery suspect.

May 27   Traffic officer disarms man stopped for traffic violation and pulled gun on officer.

June 16   Officer arrests [without shooting] fleeing rapist who turns and confronts him with knife.

June 24   Officer arrests insane man holed up in hospital waiting room with gun.

June 28   Police officer disarms young woman who threatens boss with loaded pistol.

June 29   Officer wounds combative man after intervening to "quiet" fight in tavern.

June 30   Juvenile officer disarms at gunpoint two juvenile gang members armed with small caliber weapons. One juvenile then turns and escapes.

Obviously, each of these armed confrontations is unique in terms of many dimensions—type of opponent, duration of the encounter, number of officers present, spatial arrangements, and justification. One dimension used frequently for classification is that of preceding event; Table 4.1 illustrates its use in four studies. It is important to point out in considering these studies that the respective researchers focused not (as we will) on armed confrontation but on police shots fired (for example, Fyfe[2]) or shots that hit opponents (for example, Milton et al.[3]) or fatal shots fired (for example, Robin[4]).

In this context, it is worth noting that the event leading to the use of deadly force depends upon social, political, and administrative conditions; types of confrontation differ from city to city, precinct to precinct, and even month to month. Some police departments report high rates of armed confrontation with juveniles crazed by PCP; other jurisdictions may have virtually no such contacts with

TABLE 4.1 Events Preceding Police Use of Deadly Force

	Study Findings[a]							
	Robin, 1963 (N = 32)		Kobler, 1975b (N = 911)		Milton et al., 1977 (N = 320)		Fyfe, 1978 (N = 5111)	
	%	Rank	%	Rank	%	Rank	%	Rank
Disturbance calls Family quarrels Disturbed persons Fights Assaults "Man with a gun"	31	(2)	17	(4)	32	(1)	25	(2)
Robbery In progress Pursuit of suspect	28	(3)	20	(3)	21	(2)	39	(1)
Burglary In progress Larceny Tampering with auto Pursuit of suspects	37	(1)	27	(2)	20	(3)	7	(4)
Traffic offenses Pursuits Vehicle stops	3	(4)	30[b]	(1)	8	(5)	12	(3)
Officer personal business Dispute Horseplay Accident	?	(−)	?	(−)	4	(6.5)	?	(−)
Stakeout/decoy	?	(−)	?	(−)	4	(6.5)	?	(−)
Other	0	(5)	6	(5)	11	(4)	6	(5)

[a] Percentages may not total 100 due to rounding.
[b] Includes other misdemeanors not listed above.
Source: L. W. Sherman and R. H. Langworthy, "Measuring Homicide by Police Officers," *Journal of Criminal Law and Criminology* 70, no. 4 (Winter 1979).

"dusted-out" adolescents but commonly experience confrontations with armed bank robbers. It may be that administrative policy contributes to the incidence of particular types of confrontation faced by a police department. For example, a rule restricting high-speed chases might make less likely confrontations with joyriding juveniles. Similar, a rapid response capacity for in-progress robberies may encourage frequent confrontations with armed robbers.

More recent research has focused upon the actions of the opponent prior to the use of deadly force by a police officer as another dimension for classification. Myer, for example, analyzed over a five-year period the reported actions of opponents immediately prior to a shot being fired by a police officer in his recent audit of shots fired by the Los Angeles Police Department.[5] A summary of his relevant data is contained in Table 4.2.

Although such classifications are extremely useful, focusing solely upon incidents where police officers shoot necessarily omits critical information. For example, in how many cases in which a Hispanic

TABLE 4.2 Suspect's Actions Precipitating Shootings, by Race or Descent, 1974-78
(in percent)

	Black	Hispanic	White
Suspect using weapon	22	23	28
Suspect threatening use of weapon	39	45	43
Suspect displaying weapon	5	6	5
Suspect without weapon assaulting officer or civilian	5	9	6
Suspect appearing to reach for weapon	12	6	9
Suspect disobeying command to halt	15	9	9
Other (including accidental shootings at suspects)	1	3	1
Total	100	100	100
(Number)	(321)	(126)	(131)

Note: Disobeying command to halt or appearing to reach for weapon were coded only if no assault took place, and there was no use, threat, or display of a weapon in the period immediately preceding the shooting. Assault was coded only if there was no use, threat, or display of a weapon. For each person shot at, only one precipitating event was coded—the most life endangering.

Source: M. W. Myer, "Police Shootings at Minorities: The Case of Los Angeles," *Annals of the American Academy of Political and Social Science* 452 (November 1980): 104.

citizen threatened a police officer was deadly force avoided? It also is important, as we have suggested, to develop classifications based upon more dynamic aspects of armed confrontations. This type of thematic portrayal of armed confrontation could give some insight as to the risks of particular types of armed confrontation and how these risks are interpreted by the police officer himself. Police officers perceive an off-duty incident with a "wacko" (a psychotic person) in a dark alley very differently than they do an on-duty confrontation with a bank robber faced with a team of officers during broad daylight.

Other questions that our analyses will attempt to answer include the following:

1. Which types of confrontation present the greatest risk?
2. What are the most common types of opponents faced by police officers in armed confrontations?
3. Of the total number of types of armed confrontation, which particular types most frequently result in a shot being fired by a police officer?
4. What types of training are most appropriate to particular types of confrontation?
5. Is it possible to develop special training methods to avert particular types of shootings?
6. Are there interactions among types of incidents (for example, an apparently insane opponent in an off-duty confrontation) that make a particular type of confrontation inordinately risky?

THE CONCEPT OF RISK
IN POLICE–CITIZEN ENCOUNTERS

Key in responding to these queries is our ability to identify which types of confrontation possess the greatest hazard for police officers. Simply knowing the relative proportion of incidents that result in a fatality or a wounding by a police officer will not be very helpful. Knowing the proportion of hits or fatalities associated with a particular incident tells us little about the relative hazard of such incidents. For example, knowing that 25 percent of all New York City shots fired evolved from "disturbance" calls (see Table 4.1) does not yield any useful information about the relative danger of such calls. Such information is similar in kind to knowing that in a certain city, 25 percent of all deaths were related to influenza, whereas only 1 percent were related to the always fatal myasthenia gravis (or Lou Gehrig's disease). From such information one might, wrongly, conclude that influenza was more hazardous than is myasthenia gravis. In reality, myasthenia gravis is infinitely more hazardous; however, it is also far rarer. The lower proportion of deaths from myasthenia gravis is attributable to its rareness, not its benignity; similarly, influenza causes many deaths because it is an extremely common, if only occasionally fatal, disease.

This analogy may seem obvious, but its essential implication is missed by police researchers who attempt to analyze police-citizen armed confrontations on the basis of police shots fired (or, even worse, hits or fatal shootings) without delineating the relationship of such events to all armed confrontations. Thus, if one wishes to know the relative hazard of a particular type of confrontation, one must know not only how frequently shots were fired in this type of incident but also how many confrontations of this type were encountered by police officers. Consider, for example, the finding by Milton et al. that 32 percent of police uses of deadly force (in their seven-city study) evolved from disturbance calls and only 21 percent evolved from robbery calls (see Table 4.1). To establish the relative risk of each of these types of calls, one must establish the total frequency of each call, the frequency of armed confrontation that evolve from such calls, and the frequency with which each of these armed confrontations results in a shot being fired.

For example, consider the following hypothetical relationships: In City X there are 4,000 robbery calls. Arrests are made in 2,000 of these cases. In 200 incidents there was an armed confrontation between the police officer and the citizen. In 10 confrontations, the opponent was shot at by a police officer. Shooting thus occurred at rates as follows: .25 percent of robbery calls, .50 percent of robbery arrests, 5.0 percent of robbery armed confrontations. In the same city there were 50,000 "disturbance" calls. In 500 of these, there occurred an armed confrontation resulting in 14 shots fired incidents by police officers. Shooting thus occurred at rates as follows: .028 percent of disturbance calls, 2.8 percent of disturbance armed confrontations. These data, in summary, state that the risk of a shooting in a robbery call is 1 in 400, whereas the risk in a disturbance call is 1 in 3,571. Similarly, they show that the risk of an armed confrontation is 1 in 20 in the case of robbery and 1 in 100 in the case of a disturbance call.

Judging from these hypothetical data it is obvious that, although representing a smaller porportion of total calls, robberies have a significantly higher risk than do disturbance calls, both in terms of likelihood of armed confrontation and of shooting. Thus, these data should illustrate that the concept of risk requires knowledge about baseline frequencies.

To further our understanding of risk in police-citizen encounters, we will turn to consideration of various factors that are linked to relative risk, subjectively as well as objectively evaluated.

THE POLICE OFFICER AS A RESPONDING HUMAN BEING

Perceived Hazard in Police-Citizen Encounters

Clearly encounters of varying types pose to officers rather different levels of hazard of physical injury. In some encounters, the immediate peril may be minimal, as when the officer confronts a person fleeing from a crime and the person disposes of his weapon. For example, one officer described the following incident: "He came right over with his gun to these guys who were warming themselves over a fire in a trash can and shoots one of them. I rode up and yelled for him to freeze and drop it. He throws his gun up on a snow pile and then runs. I fired but missed him." In other situations the hazard may be immediate and imminent: "All of a sudden, in the middle of this crowd, this one guy comes over me with a crowbar. I thought he was trying to kill me. I shot him right before he came down with it."

Frequently, the hazard may appear greater to the officer than is actually the case. At times the officer may infer hazard from the context of the confrontation or the behavior of the opponent, which, while not factually accurate, is believed to be true in the psychological context of the encounter.

The Control of Options

Another factor that determines the risk of an armed confrontation or a shooting is the degree of control that an officer possesses (or feels he possesses) in the encounter. In some encounters an opponent's behavior may be so unpredictable as to make the officer feel that nothing he might do would have any impact on the opponent. Two officers, for example, found an insane man in a motel room who had just killed his sister and was apparently cannibalizing her. On being confronted by the officers and being told to remain still, the man persisted in moving toward a back room, where police officers believed there was a loaded weapon. In another situation, a police officer working as a hospital security guard was called to an emergency room, where a man was repeatedly stabbing his brother. Despite the repeated commands of the officers, the young man repeatedly stabbed at the brother, never even acknowledging the presence of the officer.

Other aspects of perceived control relate to the actual options of the police officer himself. In some confrontations, where cover is available, the officer may at any point choose either to fire or not fire at an opponent without risking his immediate physical safety. In other circumstances, where there is no cover available, the possibility of retreat or even holding fire may be virtually impossible. Consider, for example, the following description of an incident by an officer: "I walked up to this guy to arrest him, but before I got there he turns and sees me and suddenly starts to draw. Luckily his gun caught on his coat pocket. I had no choice; no cover or nothing. If I was somewhere else I might have waited." In such incidents, the officer possesses few options other than to fire. Protection, cover, dialogue, backup support, and even flight are all implausible (if not impossible) options.

Time Frame and Officer Preparation

Another factor affecting risk in encounters lies in the degree of preparation available to the officer and the time frame of the encounter. Armed confrontations last from many minutes (or even hours) to a few seconds. A description of a rather long (roughly six-minute) armed confrontation follows:

I was on patrol with Officer S. We were advised, by radio, to assist with a stolen motorhome involving a 245B [assault on a police officer]; the motorhome was involved in numerous accidents. The assault clearly was intentional. Approximately one minute later we saw suspects approaching on the median divider which is 12 to 15 feet wide. We started gaining speed to follow the pursuit. The motorhome was riding approximately six inches from the fence. The suspects were approaching at 70 mph. We heard what appeared to be gunfire at this time [later investigation proved that these shots came from Los Angeles deputy sheriffs]. Two sheriff's deputies were in front of us in the pursuit. We were in the third car. Traffic seemed to slow. Suspect was weaving between the number one and number three lanes. As he went through the lanes he intentionally rammed several cars. When all three lanes became blocked he returned to the median divider lane and plowed through several cars on either side. We continued in this fashion going between the number one and number three lanes. The suspect at this time proceeded to ram citizens' cars. There were numerous traffic crashes: approximately 37 collisions in four and a half miles. Soon one of the deputies in front of us got blocked in a slow lane. The other sheriff's deputies' car attempted to get on his side. He immediately was rammed and forced to slam on brakes and was knocked onto the dirt on the side of the road. We then found ourselves as the lead car directly behind the suspects.

We went directly behind the suspects' car, going wherever he went. At this point we began to talk among ourselves. "Watch out for this car, watch out for that one, oh, he hit another." At this point I suggested to Officer S. that we shoot out the tires. We observed one tire shred and flattened but as this was a dual tire on the back, it hardly mattered. Then we saw the motorhome ram a Honda Civic and literally demolish it. At this point we began discussing the possibility that the suspect was about to kill someone. We had seen numerous accidents and there was no way to terminate pursuit. After seeing the Honda demolished we saw him sideswipe another car and literally knock it into the dirt. At this point we contemplated shooting the driver. Officer S. said that he had been thinking about that and said it was necessary. . . . I said he's going to kill someone or already has. We thought of sideswiping him but didn't have the angle or power, even though we had a large Dodge, to knock him off the freeway. Officer S. agreed. Officer S. leaned out of the car with the shotgun, leveling it on his leg. The suspect drew back. I was watching his hands. He leaned forward and shifted his hands as if he was going to sideswipe us. At this point Officer S. fired one shotgun round, our only round left, striking the supect in the head.

These two officers faced an unusual decision in that there was considerable time to decide (and even discuss) whether shooting the driver of the recreational vehicle was justified. At several points during the pursuit the officers made conscious decisions: first, to continue the pursuit, then, to shoot at the car, and finally, to shoot the driver. Most police shootings, in contrast, occur during much shorter confrontations in which the time between first encountering the suspect and the decision to shoot may be less than a minute, perhaps only a few seconds, involving inevitably fewer identifiable decision points. In such situations, decision making is far less deliberate. In this type of confrontation, the decision to shoot becomes an almost reflexive response to a set of immediate circumstances. In a recent incident of this type, a police officer shot a man who suddenly pulled a shotgun from under his raincoat. The total time that elapsed from the officer encountering this citizen to his death was calculated at less than 15 seconds. One of the officers involved in the incident described it as follows:

> We were coming in in August, a few summers ago. It was right after we had had dinner in Mike's diner. All of a sudden my partner sees this guy with gloves, a trenchcoat, and a hat on, in *August*. My partner was coming in to call his wife, who was sick, to find out what was wrong and we were talking about that. All of a sudden he walks towards us and we see something sticking out of his coat. My partner says, "He's got a shotgun." First, I dove out of the car. He bailed out the driver's side. I fired six shots. So did my partner. Later we pulled the shotgun away from the guy. He had spasms; bled from the mouth; and finally died. He hit him just as he stepped in front of us. He never got to point his gun. It was .00 buckshot. It turned out the guy was a murderer who had escaped from Rahway [prison]. He didn't want to go back alone, I guess. He could have killed us, killed us in less than six seconds. That's what the whole thing took, six seconds.

The differences in the two incidents are, of course, enormous. In the first incident, the decision to shoot was deliberate, rationally justified prior to the action, and made with the support of another officer (his partner). It was a relatively long armed confrontation, although it lasted only six minutes. The officers were able to consider their options, their alternative actions, and the consequences to those alternatives prior to firing the fatal shot. In the second armed confrontation, the officers' behavior was almost reflexive; as the officer noted, the entire incident lasted perhaps less than six seconds from the moment they spotted the armed man to his death; the actual time frame between the officer deciding to shoot and actually firing may have been less than two seconds.

OPPONENTS AND RISK

The type of opponent may be said to affect directly the degree of hazard and control faced by the police officer in an encounter. Research by Fyfe,[6] Milton et al.,[7] Harding and Fahey,[8] and Myer[9] indicates that opponents in police armed confrontations are overwhelmingly male, young (aged 16 to 25), and black. Much has been made of the "overrepresentation" of blacks as victims of police homicide (see, for example, Tagaki,[10] Knoohuizen et al.,[11] and Kobler[12]). However, others have demonstrated (see, for example, Fyfe,[13] Harding and Fahey, [14] and Binder and Scharf[15]) that the number of black victims is roughly equal to the overall racial breakdown of persons arrested for violent felonies. For example, Harding and Fahey[16] found that blacks accounted for roughly 75 percent of the police homicide victims and 73 percent of violent arrests.

Buried within these aggregate racial and age statistics are some surprising variations in the types of opponents with whom police are likely to become involved in an armed confrontation. Moreover, different types of opponents will behave quite differently in the confrontation. Three types of opponents present unusual characteristics and are worth special attention.

Instrumental Opponents

One type of opponent is what might be called the instrumental criminal, who engages in a shooting exchange or physical conflict as a desperate means of escape. One such criminal was described as follows by a police officer: "Well, he was up for murder; he was going to do 99 years if we caught him. I guess he thought that if he shot us he couldn't add much to his time." Another officer similarly described a professional cat burglar who assaulted the officer in his effort to escape: "Well, he figured by knocking me over, he would avoid doing time." A narcotics dealer who was wounded by a narcotics officer was described as follows:

> It was a narco investigation. We had set it up for three weeks. We had a couple of sales on him. My partner went up for the final buy and we bashed in the door. We yelled police, but he went into his room, where we knew he had a gun. I guess he wanted to shoot his way out. He reaches for his gun in a closet. He thought he could hit the window and get out but didn't make it.

Instrumental opponents are, paradoxically, frequently preferred by police officers as opponents in armed confrontations. One police officer said, "They do their thing, we do ours. A professional criminal will shoot to get away but usually will not try to kill you." Another officer suggested, "Look, that guy just wants to be another black kid in sneakers. He is shooting, not to kill you but to escape. He won't try to kill you unless that's the only way out for him." A deputy sheriff similarly suggested, "If all he wants to do is get out of there, he is less likely to do something stupid. He is shooting to distract or stop you. He may kill you, but that's not the main thing he is trying to do." Another officer commented regarding the instrumental opponent. "Look, it's a big game out here. You try to get them. They try to get away. Shooting is just a part of the game—except it's when people get hurt."

Often, instrumental criminals are perceived as being emotionally calm, almost businesslike during the confrontation. One armed robber was described as "cool, almost like we had just a bit distracted him by busting in." Another escaped murderer reportedly smiled and waved at the police officer as he escaped over an alley fence. Another professional cat burglar was described as "icy cool. Like I caught him at work." At times, however, strong emotions reveal themselves in even the most hardened of professional criminals. An officer described killing an already wounded professional gunman with a sawed-off shotgun:

> I saw him running from the bar. He was hit with several shots and fell down. My partner ... said, "X. [the officer], kill the motherfucker, he's got a sawed-off shotgun." I didn't really see the gun. I shot as he wiggled the gun up and down at me. A burst of air comes out of the body. . . . He lay there, it seemed like a minute. I will always remember his expression. I guess he didn't want to go alone.

The Apparently Insane

A different type of opponent may be found in persons who are either temporarily or actually deranged (due to psychosis, drugs, or alcohol). The shooting of a biochemist, named Burkholder, provides a vivid example of such a confrontation with an insane person:

> [The officer, Sergeant Barz] was driving northbound on Hoover when he observed a male person without clothes jumping up and down in the middle of London Street close to Hoover. . . .
>
> Barz reported on the radio that the man was also psycho and requested code 2 (without delay) assistance. . . . Barz stated that at about the same time as he had made his second broadcast the man came off the signpost [upon which he had been swinging], ran toward the police vehicle and started banging on the right front passenger window and door of the car with his hands and fists. . . .
>
> Barz concluded the man was not an exhibitionist, he believed he was "high on something or psycho or something like that." For this reason, Barz "tried to be cool" and asked the man what was going on or words to that effect so as not to antagonize him.

The man advanced towards Barz making "kind of chopping-type motions" with both hands, the arms held out horizontally. The naked man stated, "I know Kung Fu" a couple of times.

Barz stepped back as the man kept advancing towards him. After stepping back four feet or so Barz decided to hit him with the baton to try and knock him down or injure his arm. . . . The man grabbed the baton with both hands. . . . They wrestled over the baton. . . . Barz realized he could not take the baton away from the man, "He was just too strong." All he could do was hang on to the baton, "and all during this time I saw his eyes and they were just totally psychopathic type eyes, you know." . . .

After another ten seconds of wrestling for the baton, Barz decided it was best to let go and step back. . . . The man had Barz' baton in hand when Barz took his gun out. They were at that time perhaps eight to ten feet apart.

Barz assumed a two-handed combat stance and told the man, "Stop or I'll shoot." The man said, "I don't care" or something to that effect and raised the baton over his shoulder. When the man threw the baton at Barz, Barz dodged and it missed by about three or four feet. . . .

Barz backed up, put his gun away and backed toward the police car, keeping an eye on the man. The man followed him with his slashing and chopping-type arm motions. . . .

When Barz reached the right rear of the police car, having almost made a complete circle, the man stopped at the front door of the passenger side, turned and ran off and was kind of jumping up and down in the middle of the street. Barz said to himself, "Thank God, he's gone."

All during this time Barz was waiting and hoping for a unit to get there.

The man returned to Barz. When he got to within about fifteen feet he started "going through these Kung Fu motions again with his right hand and left hand." Barz backed up. . . .

Barz took his gun out; the man continued to advance toward him. Barz held the gun to his side pointing it at the man and told him to stop. The man continued to advance. He struck at Barz. Barz partially evaded the blow so that he was hit by the man's extended forefingers on his left shoulder. This caused Barz to stumble. At the same time the man grabbed for the barrel of his gun. Barz, feeling himself to be falling and believing that his gun would be taken away from him and used against him, fired as fast as he could until he heard the click of an empty gun.[17]

Often confrontations with insane persons are the result of unprovoked attacks aimed at either the police officer or another citizen. The unpredictability of such confrontations is a common theme. One officer, for example, told of a man who was talking quietly to his partner when "suddenly the man started grabbing a beer bottle and started swinging it at both of us." One officer described a similar situation involving a female: "I was walking home from the convenience store and see this woman throwing Lysol at this other lady, again and again. I yelled, police, but she didn't hear me. Finally she sees me and fires a .22 at me." Another man described a case (which resulted in a fatal shooting) where, "I was on hospital duty and this guy comes in and starts stabbing his brother in front of us with a long knife. He stabbed him 26 times. He was so gone he didn't even care if I was there." At times, the intended victim of the deranged (and suicidal) opponent may initially be the person himself:

> At this time the deputy, who had previously identified himself and who was in uniform, ordered the victim to take his hands off the gun which was resting on the table, and to place them above his head. The victim replied that he would not, that the deputies would have to shoot him, and that he wanted to die. During this time the apartment house manager was directly behind the deputy. The deputy, on at least two occasions, clearly ordered the victim to take his hands off the gun and to place them above his head. The victim then pivoted toward the deputy and cocked the revolver. Fearing for his own safety as well as that of the apartment manager, the deputy fired two shots at the victim.

Alcohol as well as drugs contributes heavily to the behavior of a large number of apparently bizarre opponents in armed confrontations. One reported barroom armed confrontation is illustrative of a surprising number of off-duty shootings (Fyfe[18] and Milton et al.,[19] suggest such shootings may comprise roughly 20 percent of the total of shooting incidents) in which both the police officer and the citizen had been drinking.

> I was in a bar drinking and discussing national financial policy (of all things) with a friend. I was talking about the Big Board, when all of a sudden this guy comes over to me and says in a loud voice, "WHO ARE YOU CALLING BOY?" Everyone in this bar knows I'm a cop. I identified myself as a police officer and this guy yells out to everyone, "WELL, YOU GOT YOUR MOTHERFUCKING GUN, SO I'LL GET MINE, TOO."

Although the officer was able to disarm the man with only a warning shot into the ground, the incident illustrates the type of alcohol-related behavior that frequently contributes to an armed confrontation.

Such bizarre, unpredictable opponents are clearly not the opponents of choice for most police officers. One officer said, "Give me a good old bank robber anytime. At least you know what to expect." Another seasoned veteran exclaimed, "A nice church-going wacko can kill you much faster than a guy you know is a criminal. You will take chances with a crazy person you never would with a guy you know is a criminal." Another comment was offered by an officer who killed an insane man who had attacked his partner, "It was like nothing we said or did mattered. He was in his orbit and the only way we get him off it was to shoot him."

Juveniles

Another type of opponent, the juvenile, poses a unique hazard to the police officers: both psychological and legal. Such opponents are of special interest, as earlier studies suggest that more than 30 percent of all armed opponents may be under the age of 21.[20,21] And juveniles may be uniquely unpredictable. One officer found himself, for example, being charged at by a huge stolen truck being driven by a 13-year-old. Another officer, who was able to disarm a 14-year-old boy after he had shot two of his classmates in a junior high school, described the incident as follows:

> We got a "man-with-a-gun" call at a junior high school. There was a huge crowd in front of the school. We heard about five shots as we rode up the street. All of a sudden this tiny kid, must have been only 14, comes out and just stands there swinging the gun. We told him to drop it; finally he does. I didn't give a fuck if he was a juvenile. He could have killed me just as fast with that .38 if he was 10 or 110. When he got in the car he was real surly like, giving us all kind of shit, like he said, "if there wasn't two of you [that is, officers] I'd have tried it!"

Other problems develop from the legal status of the juvenile. In some departments, officers are forbidden from shooting at persons who could reasonably be believed to be juveniles, except in the most dire of circumstances. One officer, for example, when he realized that he had almost killed a 13-year-old commented, "It was like I understood the implications of my job. That I almost killed a child."

At times juvenile "mischief," adolescent energy, and officer misperceptions will result in shots being fired. The newspaper clipping cited below illustrates the reaction to the shooting of a 15-year-old boy who jumped into a house being guarded by Los Angeles police officers who were protecting a witness in a murder trial and tragically shot the young boy.

It was an apparent case of simple mischievousness which led to the shooting of 15-year-old Carlos Washington, a ninth grade quarterback on the Van Nuys Junior High School football team.

According to the family's attorney, Myrna Grayson, Washington and two friends, aged 13 and 14, wanted to participate in "Wednesday Night on Van Nuys Boulevard," a night when Valley teen-agers "cruise" up and down the heart of Van Nuys.

Mrs. Grayson said the boys had no car of their own so were "sneaking" a car which Mrs. Grayson said she confirmed as belonging to one of the boys' parents.

The three youths were pushing the car out of the parking lot of an apartment complex where one of them lived, when police spotted them.

"The boys got scared and started to run," said Mrs. Grayson. The shooting soon followed.

When asked why the boys ran, Washington's uncle, Eugene Singleton replied, "What would you do if you had just done something mischievous, and you're 13, 14 and 15 years old?"

"The family would like to know why deadly force was used against a 15-year-old boy who had done nothing. They can't understand it, and neither can I," said Mrs. Grayson.[22]

Juvenile opponents pose unique hazards to the police officer in both the types of expressive actions in which adolescents will engage and in the consequences to the officers who shoot and hit virtually any juvenile opponent. Adolescents will take risks, such as trying to outrun a police blockade, or attempt to shoot at police officers in situations where only the most desperate (or deranged) adults would act similarly. For the adolescent, such actions may be caused less from malice than from adolescent energy-expressing actions—truly dangerous, especially when viewed in the context of an armed and dangerous ghetto. Thus, officers typically will fear armed confrontations with juveniles, both because of the unpredictability of the juvenile's behavior and because of the emotional, administrative, and political consequences should a police officer shoot and hit an adolescent opponent inappropriately.

Although these examples present exaggerated pictures of the role of the opponent in determining the risk of armed confrontation or actual shooting, it is clear that risk varies, though perhaps more finely, over other types of opponents. And as important as the actual characteristics of opponents—irrational behavior, weapons carried, impulsiveness, and so forth—are the beliefs of the officer regarding the opponent. And the beliefs may be based upon statistical extrapolation from previous history or upon folklore. Thus, such belief systems as "crazy Puerto Ricans will cut you," or "Italian hoods carry guns," become important determiners of risk, independent of the reality of the statement. In this sense the attributions of risk (in the mind of the police officer) become what Robert Merton has called a self-fulfilling prophecy: A violent expectation on the part of the officer produces a general aura of danger that motivates the opponent toward violence.

ASSIGNMENTS

The time and preparation and degree of control an officer has in order to exert to resolve an armed confrontation are related to the type of assignment that brings him into contact with his opponent in the armed confrontation. In presenting this perspective we will discuss the unique dynamics of off-duty, police action, dispatched, and planned apprehension armed confrontations.

Off-Duty Armed Confrontations

Police officers commonly believe that the most unpredictable type of incident occurs in off-duty encounters. Often the officer is psychologically unprepared for an armed confrontation. The officer may be tired; have had a drink; be with children, girlfriend, or wife; and generally be in a leisurely rather than alert mood when the opponent is encountered. An extreme example of the psychological and tactical hazards of off-duty armed confrontations is found in the case below of an officer who engaged in a store parking lot gun battle with two armed robbers. The incident resulted in the death of the officer's three-year-old daughter.

> On Saturday, November 1979, at approximately 7 P.M., Los Angeles County Reserve Deputy Sheriff Gerald Douglas Slagle, accompanied by his daughter, Jennifer Slagle, age three, arrived at the Safeway Market in La Crescenta. . . .
> Slagle intended to do some grocery shopping. He was not working as a Reserve Deputy Sheriff at the time. He was, however, armed with a .38 caliber weapon issued to him by the Sheriff's Department.

Prior to entering the market, Slagle and Jennifer stopped at the mechanized pony ride located just outside the market, next to the west entry and exit doors of the market.

As Slagle started to lift Jennifer from the pony, he noticed two male individuals pushing an empty shopping cart past the east entry door towards his position. Slagle moved forward as the men walked past him. The two men entered the market through the west door with Slagle and Jennifer following them into the market. Slagle saw one of the individuals pull a ski mask over his face and pull out a blue steel revolver. The other individual pulled out a weapon described by witnesses as either a sawed-off shotgun or a rifle.

Following this, the two robbers came out of the west door together and walked towards Slagle's position. Slagle had Jennifer down on the ground near the right wheel of the vehicle Slagle was using for cover.

Slagle had his service revolver pointed across the trunk of the vehicle in a westerly direction. Slagle yelled to the two robbers, "Police, freeze!" The individual holding the weapon described as the shotgun or rifle yelled back, "Don't do it, don't do it!" This person is Manuel Castillo Perez. He is currently awaiting trial in Superior Court, Case No. 587995, charged with violations of Penal Code sections 187 and 211 in connection with his alleged participation in the robbery of the Safeway market and the fatal wounding of Jennifer Slagle.

Neither Perez nor his companion complied with Slagle's order. Perez, it is believed, pointed his weapon at Slagle and fired one round. Slagle immediately fired two rounds at Perez. One of Slagle's rounds, it is believed struck Perez, but Perez continued walking eastbound in the parking lot. His companion then separated from Perez and this person moved back to the front of the store and proceeded eastbound along the sidewalk, ultimately arriving at a getaway car parked in an alley located north of the market.

In the meantime, Perez had moved to a position almost directly south of Slagle's position. This put Slagle and Jennifer in a direct line of fire from Perez's weapon without benefit of the protection of cover. Slagle fired two more times at Perez. At this moment, Slagle became aware that Jennifer was standing up to the left of his field of gunfire. He yelled, "Jenny, get down!" Slagle glanced again at Jennifer and saw she was now down on the ground bleeding from a wound to her head. Slagle, believing his daughter was dead, stood up in disregard for his own safety and looked for Perez. He saw Perez at the front of the store. Slagle fired his two last rounds at Perez, missing him, both rounds hitting the concrete exterior portion of the front of the market.

Jennifer Slagle was taken to an emergency room at [a local hospital] where a medical team attempted unsuccessfully to save her life. Jennifer died at 7:53 P.M. The cause of death was a gunshot wound to the head.[23]

In an equally tragic incident, an officer, who was out on the town with friends, found himself accosted by a man with a gun who robbed the officer and his family and began fondling the breasts of the officer's wife. When the man threatened to "take this broad with him," the officer drew and fired his weapon. He missed the opponent but accidentally killed his wife. This incident (as the one involving the death of the young child) dramatizes the often tragic results associated with off-duty armed confrontations.

At times, off-duty police officers become involved in an armed confrontation when the officer's home or that of a companion is invaded by a criminal. An example of such a confrontation is the following:

> In the early morning hours of April 19, 1978, Deputy [T.] was *off-duty* and asleep with [M.M.] at her apartment when he was awakened by Ms. [M.]. They both observed an intruder inside the apartment.
>
> The intruder unlocked and exited the front door. Deputy [T.] immediately went into the front room and retrieved his weapon. At this time, he heard noises on the balcony outside the apartment and saw that the front door was moving open and closed. Deputy [T.] then went to the front door and as he attempted to open it, Mr. [D.] was pushing the door open. When the door was opened, Deputy [T.] saw [D.] with a *shiny object* in his hand. Before Deputy [T.] could say anything, Mr. [D.] jumped or moved quickly toward him and [the Deputy] fired twice.[24]

Off-duty shootings also pose difficulty for officers in terms of the rapidity with which the encounter occurs and the lack of partner backup support, as well as the lack of psychological preparation on the part of the officer. It should be pointed out, in addition, that officers who are in other than street assignments (such as office or communications work) may find themselves in a confrontation with their "street reflexes" dulled. One example was described to us by a police staff aide:

> I am coming to work. I see this guy eyeing these two young girls stuck in traffic. I jump out of the car and yell, "Freeze, don't move." The guy looks at me and sees my coat buttoned and realizes I can't get to it. He just runs. That never would have happened [this way] if I was day after day on the street.

Another off-duty officer (a communications computer specialist) chased a group of robbers (six of them) following a bank stickup; he pointed his gun at the robbers and pulled the trigger, only to find the gun was not loaded.

Police Actions

Similar in some ways to off-duty shootings are shootings that might be called personal assignments; these are actions that are initiated by officers who see suspicious actions or persons and become involved. Characteristic of armed confrontations of this type are poor support, a rapid time frame, and lack of preparation and information. The facts that precipitate officer action in such incidents may be highly ambiguous and even confusing.

Some police actions are initiated because the officer recognizes an armed and potentially dangerous person. Such reactive encounters are likely to provoke irrational behavior on the part of the opponent (often extremely dangerous persons):

> We stopped by the projects and see a guy holding a blanket (it turned out to be his girlfriend's kid). We recognized the guy as this man who is wanted for all kinds of stickups. We go over to him and won't let us hold the kid. He gets more and more agitated and finally just runs into the project with us holding the baby. _____ fired as he was going up the stairs. He died immediately. It was a panic thing on his part that got him killed. He just didn't expect anything at that point.

In other police actions, the officer may have very limited knowledge of the facts of a particular incident. One officer observed, for example:

> That on the streets you have to act fast often before you really know what's happening. If a woman screams, is it really a rape or is it just a lovers' thing? Lots of times you run in and she is delighted with him, but maybe just mad because he stepped out on her. Let's say you end up shooting the guy and it's no rape, what the fuck do you do then?

Police actions thus are often initiated by the most circumstantial facts. For example, consider the officers' descriptions of the different precipitating events that involved each of them in a use of deadly force:

> I was standing there on the corner with Nick and this guy comes up to another guy and stabs him with a machete—right through his heart.

I was coming into the station when I see this guy running away from X with a gun in his hand.

drove by my mother's house, while on patrol, and see this guy unloading three shotguns from his trunk.

I was driving in the _____ area when I see this pair of women's legs sticking out out of a doorway.

We passed Gino's Restaurant and I said to my partner, let's wave to Kathy, the waitress, and all of a sudden I see Kathy waving to us like there's trouble.

I'm driving to headquarters and I see this guy climbing up the wall of the hotel.

Obviously, such incidents, although occurring in the context of police duty, provide little information to basic sound tactical planning. Furthermore, these incidents usually are of such immediate importance that delay while awaiting backup is very nearly impossible. Thus, armed confrontations evolving from police actions lack the coordination and planning that mark confrontations evolving from dispatched assignments or "planned apprehensions."

Dispatched Assignments

A different type of incident is found where officers are on-duty and have at least some information about the incident prior to entering an armed confrontation. Typically, an incident will occur (for instance, an armed robbery) that is reported to the police. Officers approach the scene knowing, at least in general, the type of incident they will encounter. One policeman, for example, stated: "It's like at least you got something. You got the type of offense; based on this you know your options. If you are responding to an armed robbery, you know that there are certain ways that you can respond. Things you couldn't do in a petty theft." Another man similarly commented: "Also, you get your head into the incident. On the way to the situation you assess the information you have, the location of the call, what's been happening in the area. It helps you to mentally cope with the particular job at hand."

In such dispatched confrontations, officers have several advantages not present in off-duty shootings. First, they typically have an element of surprise in approaching an in-progress event. In many, but not all, dispatched encounters it is possible to call for backup support should the need arise. Also, because they are on duty, police officers come psychologically prepared to face an armed person. They are, additionally, often able to obtain position or cover prior to approaching the suspects. They have the benefits of teamwork, often a partner, radio communication, and possibly backup. Finally, they have some information regarding the opponents and incident prior to the actual confrontation.

This prior information advantage is greatest in encounters where the initial information given the officer accurately alerts the officer to the danger he will face. Often, this information allows the officer to take effective cover and to coordinate his efforts with a fellow officer: "We got a call that there was a 211 [armed robbery] in progress in a tavern. I told my backup car to park and then circle in the back. I went right up to the door and waited. When this guy walks out of the door he raises his hand with a bag in it without me saying nothing. It was easy."

Another officer described a dispatch rape encounter that resulted in a similarly effectively executed apprehension: "We get a call that there is a rape in progress in the East and the man is supposed to have an automatic and he is Spanish-speaking. I see the guy and approach the car with my gun drawn. The guy did something strange. He threw keys and gun out of car and rolled up window so we just sat there waiting for help."

Another advantage of dispatched encounters is the time available to the officer immediately prior to entry on the scene. During one confrontation with a group of armed robbers (of a tavern) while sitting in a car on a residential street, one of us overheard the following conversation between two experienced tactical officers:

Officer A: What's the street look like?
Officer B: Trees on both sides. A guy once took off on me through the alley. Lots of back alleys.
Officer A: Who lives there?
Officer B: Mostly working people; some shitum [crooks].
Officer A: How you want to do 'em?
Officer B: Tell George to come up on Seventh in case they see us and drive off.
Officer A: Sounds good. [Calls on radio to second car.] How about if we drive by 'em once to make 'em think we're not interested in them, then U-turn and come back.
Officer B: Let's do them.

The apprehension (of two men, both armed with guns) was made without incident.

There is also the advantage in dispatched armed confrontations of selection of position to minimize risk to other citizens (for example, to avoid shooting into an occupied house); also it is often possible to secure additional information on either the location or even the victim (for example, "Dispatcher, what is the name of the owner of the store involved in that robbery?"); finally there exists the possibility of disengaging from the confrontation if the risk factors appear too high in a particular encounter—for example, when a single police officer faces several armed persons at once ("We better back off. Call for SWAT").

Planned Apprehensions

A final assignment context in which armed confrontations take place is that in which police seek to apprehend a certain armed and dangerous felon. Some apprehensions are aimed at specified persons, as in a raid. Others are aimed at an unknown suspect such as a decoy operation in which the police officer will pose as a "victim" of the opponent. One officer described such a decoy operation as follows:

> We were in this oil truck waiting for it to get robbed when finally this guy comes up and points a gun at Tom. There had been a series of robberies on the oil truck, so I just hid in the back of the truck. I was just waiting. This guy comes up to the truck and sticks a gun in Tom's face, just like we planned. I yelled for him to "drop it," and he just put his hands up, just like that.

Accurate information is a crucial element in a planned apprehension. During an observation of a Newark police tactical unit (Target Red), the following notes were transcribed from a successful raid on a large drug-dealing operation that resulted in the arrest of several persons and the confiscation of large quantities of drugs and two loaded pistols:

> 11:00 Snitch comes in car and tells O.W. about large-scale drug sale in apartment house on Orange Avenue. Explains that he is going to grand jury and wants W. to help him. Draws map of house. Explains where gun is; how to get in the house through locked door; "Knock to get in like this. It's a Muslim knock. Two taps real quick.

11:30 Four cars meet under bridge. Sergeant goes through plan three times. "Paul [a black officer] will make the buy with Tommie backing up. Pete will hit Apartment 8; George the one on the left. Tommie the one on the right. Eddie will cover the back of the house.

11:45 The buy is made. We all meet again in the parking lot. Sergeant goes over plan again.

12:00 Raid on apartment house. I follow George. He stands by the door on the left. This is the apartment with the gun. There is shuffling heard from other apartments. Finally a peep hole opens and a huge black man emerges. "Don't do anything stupid," George commands, "Please sir, sit down!" A gun is pulled from the man's robe. White heroin powder covers the table. . . .

12:15 Woman in Apartment A surrenders second gun to Officer White.

12:45 Heroin (50 hits) found in Apartment 8. Man throws up on floor [early withdrawals].

1:00 E.L. and C. drive prisoners and evidence to North Precinct.

Often, planning will lead to rehearsal and discussion for hours or even days, and the outcome will surprise the planners. One officer, for example, commented:

There were these guys who were involved in an armed robbery thing on L. Street. We went over the thing again and again. Everyone had a specific position. I was to stand by a door to make sure they didn't come out of the back. Then they came out with a gun, but when he saw how many of us there were he just "gave it up."

At times, of course, even the best of preparations will not avoid a deadly exchange of gunfire. The Los Angeles narcotics search warrant raid described below is illustrative of an armed confrontation in which the police officers initiate the encounter and have prior (and often detailed) knowledge as to the danger of the opponent, but a use of deadly force still occurs.

At approximately 6 P.M., the deputies deployed around the apartment. . . . Deputy A. knocked . . . and announced in English, "Police officers, narcotic investigation; we have a search warrant, open the door." This was repeated three times, but the door remained closed. After waiting 20 seconds, both deputies kicked in the front door. A. entered the apartment first, going approximately three feet with his gun drawn. Deputy R. followed, standing slightly to the rear of Deputy A. Both deputies observed Hector Munoz run to a sofa and retrieve a shotgun. Munoz pointed the gun at the deputies. Both the deputies were yelling,

"Drop the gun, Sheriff's Department." At this point, Munoz fired one round at Deputies A. and R. Both men were hit by the blast. The deputies fired their service revolvers, and Munoz fired from his shotgun a second time. The deputies, injured and bleeding, were pulled outside.

Many officers have commented about the difference between behavior in what Reiss[25] refers to as "prepared" in contrast to "unprepared shooting" encounters. One officer, for example, who avoided shooting while on a narcotics raid team yet fired three times at cars driven by juveniles during patrol assignment, explained the difference in his reaction to the two types of confrontation:

> In one situation you could anticipate what would happen. You know like it is all planned out; we would spend five hours planning for the raid: you know you go here, I go here, you go there, that type of thing. In a street encounter it happens all at once. In one of those times I shot, all of a sudden I'm standing there, then the car like drives at me. I really thought I was dead. I really did, and I shot. I probably shouldn't have, but I did.

The risk of an armed confrontation, then, is clearly related to the mode of assignment that leads the police officer into the encounter. Both the degree of control an officer has over the situation and the time and information available to resolve it may be affected by the mode of assignment. In general, planned apprehensions and to some extent dispatched assignments allow for greater control and time than do off-duty and police-action armed confrontations. In this sense, it is hypothesized, personal actions and off-duty confrontations possess a higher risk than do confrontations evolving from either planned apprehensions or dispatched assignments (if the danger of the opponent is held constant). It might be interesting in this respect to compare the outcome of similar types of opponents (for example, armed robbers) who are encountered in different types of assignment contexts in terms of the likelihood of a police use of deadly force.

OTHER PERSONS: PARTNERS AND CITIZENS

Another factor determining the risk of a particular encounter relates to other persons (police officers or citizens) who may be present during the encounter. It might be suggested that the presence of others affects both the degree of control the officer (or officers) may exert and the degree of perceived hazard to the officer. The availability of partners may especially alter the risk in a particular encounter. One officer who fatally shot an escaping prisoner explained why he believed he shot and killed a man in this situation when in similar situations he had refrained from firing:

> I had faced this type of thing many times. We were chasing this guy down an alley and my partner left me to get another guy. He went one way and I went the other. All of a sudden I got caught in an alley alone with this guy. He turned and I shot. I'm not sure why I shot this time and not others. I keep thinking it was because we got separated.

A common phenomenon in police-citizen armed confrontations is what is referred to by military psychologists as "sympathetic firing." One veteran of the Vietnam War gave an example of this behavior: "When a rat kicks a can in front of the perimeter and one guy fires and then the whole squad, platoon, or even company starts opening up on it." In police-citizen gunfights such sympathetic firings are also common. In one incident, in New York, several officers fired 21 bullets into an emotionally deranged man who was attacking an officer with a pair of scissors. In describing an incident where eight officers fired at a man armed with a rifle, one officer observed, "It was like we had one gun. One guy fired and I swear I only heard one shot."

Partners may affect the decision to shoot in other ways. An attack on a partner may cause an officer to shoot even after the level of danger has been reduced. An illustration is found in a dramatic confrontation described by a detective who was badly wounded in the incident:

> He and I were partners for three years when this happened. Closer than friends. We were in this store and I thought I had this guy cornered, but he pulls out his gun and fires. He hit me five times. I was hit bad. T. (my partner) was behind me. I turned and fired back six times. I hit him once. He runs out the door. As I was going down, I said, "T., kill the motherfucker." He got him about a block away. Then he came back up to me in the car and drove me to the hospital. I was on the critical list for six months and in a coma for a week. Before I passed out I asked T. if he got him. He said he did and I went out knowing, at least, what happened.

An interesting issue in this respect involves the consequences and impact of "overmanned" and "undermanned" armed confrontations.

In some situations, literally dozens of officers may be on the scene for a single confrontation. One incident of this type was described by a seasoned police sergeant:

> Well, there was this guy with an M–1 in the church on Baker. Pretty soon he starts firing shots and it's like the whole P.D. responds. Another sergeant just drives up past a barricade and is shot by the guy. Pretty soon we have more than 60 guys on the scene all firing into the church. The biggest danger, of course, is them hitting each other in the crossfire. To be honest it was a panic situation. Someone should have blocked off the situation to control the number of cops on the scene, to keep them from killing each other.

In other situations, a single officer may find himself very alone. In one instance, a single officer responded to a robbery call in a jewelry store expecting one or possibly two opponents. No fewer than four opponents soon ran from the store, resulting in a shoot-out in which one robber was killed and the officer wounded. Similarly, the officer below describes an encounter in which he was able to hold six men at bay for more than ten minutes, winning a valor medal for his efforts.

> We had a series of "B and E's" in this factory on Springfield. Everyday I would go up on the roof and wait for a few minutes to see what was going to happen. This one day I hear noise downstairs. I creep down there and see a kid stripping one of the machines for parts to sell. I yell, "Stick 'em up!" As I move up on him I see another, then another. Soon I have six guys on the floor. One guy got up and started running but I fired a warning and he lay down. I was stupid going up there like that. If they had thought about it they could have rushed me and got my gun. I stopped working alone after that incident.

Citizens present may also greatly alter the risk of confrontation. At times, officers may hold fire (even when they are at risk) to avoid hitting an innocent citizen. One officer, for example, described the following incident:

> We go on this raid in the _____ area. We are supposed to cover the back, Paul and me. We go in a back room and see this little girl in there. All of a sudden this guy fires from behind the closet. We couldn't fire because of the girl. She was real young, maybe five years old. It wasn't worth it. The bullet lodged between us. We were no more than three feet apart. It makes you think.

Citizens may make officers feel more sympathetic or hostile toward an opponent. One experienced officer reported approaching a psychotic man after the man's mother begged him "not to hurt my son. He's sick." Conversely, another man shot at a fleeing strongman after the man had robbed and beaten a disabled man in a wheelchair. Another officer fired at and killed a drug addict after a man whom the drug addict had killed (in cold blood) was descended upon by a crowd to rip his pockets out to steal whatever money the man had. A black officer fired a shot at a Puerto Rican man whose friends had tormented him, calling him a "maricon nigger." Still another officer held fire at a man with a gun when another man yelled that the man was defending himself against another man who had just robbed him in the bar.

From these examples, it should be evident that the presence of either partners or of citizens can alter the risk of an encounter evolving into a shooting. The availability of partners can make the decision to use deadly force less likely by providing more control over the opponents and greater options for the officers. On the other hand, a decision by one officer to fire in the confrontation makes the firing of others more likely. Citizens may make a shooting less likely if they are exposed to fire; also, actions by citizens on the scene may influence the officer's perception of hazard and possibly his empathy toward the opponent.

SPACE AND LIGHT

Unlike the image conjured up by Gary Cooper's film battle in *High Noon*, police-citizen armed confrontations rarely take place in broad daylight on an uncluttered street. Far more common are confrontations in alleys, backs of stores, dark streetcorners, bushes, and staircases. Sometimes the spatial context, as in the following episode, is almost macabre:

> I was a young police officer when this happened. We caught guys in a building with a ringing alarm. It was one of those check-cashing operations. Real low rent. We look in and we see a hole in the ceiling. We went up the fire escape and saw a guy hiding in the hole. I go over to him with my partner and we all fall through about 11 feet. There are all three of us hurt, dazed together all lumped up in this hole. I turned to the guy and he says, "I'm hurt, I'm hurt." I look to see where G. (my partner) is and then I see the guy has a gun. I shot at him and he shoots at me. We were right on top of each other in the dark.

Another example highlighting space and light conditions is found in a case where an officer shot an unarmed burglar in the dark back room of a gas station:

Four months ago we responded at a truck repair place. I see a truck with a bunch of batteries in it. I think, What is a truck with North Dakota plates doing here? My partner walks around the back. I go inside. When I'm in the back room, it's totally dark. All of a sudden the door closes behind me and I feel this guy breathing behind me. I wheeled and fired; he fuckin' scared the motherfuckin' shit out of me. While he was lying there all wounded, I say, "What the fuck are you doing there in the dark?" If it was light I never would have reacted like that.

It should be noted that many shootings involve multiple settings during the encounter. For example, one confrontation of an armed rape suspect took place in the following different settings prior to the final capture of the suspect.

1. Officer sees victim and perpetrator in car.
2. Officer confronts perpetrator and he releases victim.
3. Perpetrator puts car in reverse and flees.
4. Officers pursue perpetrator (now joined by two other officers) over four miles.
5. Perpetrator crashes into parked car and flees through crowded Gino's Restaurant.
6. Perpetrator runs out of kitchen and fires at officers in back parking lot, fleeing through alley.
7. Perpetrator climbs over and hides in bushes of adjacent building.
8. Officer spots man; orders him to stop. Officer fires and misses.
9. Perpetrator runs from bushes, throws gun on ground, and runs down the street.
10. Perpetrator finally cornered in second alley; tries to escape over barbed wire fence and is finally captured without other shots being fired.

Although this episode involves a more complex series of multiple settings than is true of most armed confrontations, it graphically demonstrates that not all armed confrontations occur in a single setting under constant lighting conditions. The importance of the reality that many confrontations occur in multiple settings is that few training programs train officers to shoot in life-like environmental contexts; none anticipates the reality that a single confrontation may last several minutes and cover many miles, exhausting the officer in the process.

Space and light may alter the degree of control an officer can assert in the confrontation. Poor lighting may make more difficult an accurate assessment of the opponent's intentions. It also may shorten the time in which an officer must decide (in ambiguous circumstances) whether or not to use deadly force. Poor lighting may also increase the options of an opponent who, hiding in darkness, may feel (or actually be) in control of a life or death confrontation with a police officer. Space and light may alter the risk of a confrontation dramatically in terms of the police officer's psychological assessment of fear. A dark shadow in a dark warehouse may be far more frightening to the officer than would the same opponent confronted in another context.

CONCLUSIONS

In this chapter we have argued that different types of police-citizen encounters possess more or less risk of a shot being fired by an officer. Specifically, we suggested that the degree of perceived hazard and the degree of officer control and the time frame are related to the chances of an encounter evolving into an armed confrontation and eventual use of deadly force by a police officer. We also have demonstrated how the type of opponent, the mode of assignment, presence of other officers or citizens, and space and light affect the probability that deadly force will be used in an armed confrontation.

What, we might ask, are the implications of this view of armed confrontation and deadly force? How does it alter the administration of deadly force policy, police training, and the review of deadly force incidents?

Certain confrontations might be so risky that the police department should, through operational rules or policy, forbid or strongly discourage such confrontations. Off-duty confrontations by single officers, for example, might be discouraged unless the immediate peril to a citizen is extremely great. Similarly, other high-risk confrontations might be identified and made less likely through operational rules designed to reduce the probability of specific encounters.

Training might be altered to facilitate instruction and practice in both the most common and the most hazardous confrontations. Thus, simulations should be developed that correspond to those confrontations in which officers are most likely to be involved. Also, intensive instruction should be given to prepare officers to cope with the most risk-laden confrontations. Currently, most departments train officers in only dispatched armed confrontations. Often opponent type and time frame do not match the conditions officers will be likely to encounter on the streets. A training curriculum preparing officers in off-duty confrontations would be extremely useful, as the level of risk and decision making of these encounters are quite different from other types of police-citizen confrontations.

This approach we have taken has implications as well for the review of uses of deadly force. It may be that certain types of confrontation bear more hazard than do others. Through assignment, residence, or other factors, a particular officer may face more hazardous confrontations than do other officers. This information would be extremely useful to police administrators in both assessing the quality of an officer's decisions in an armed confrontation and in arranging assignments so that certain officers avoid the most risky of confrontations.

Most importantly, the move toward empirical validation of a risk typology would allow the law enforcement profession to understand better the risks and behavior of specific categories of police-citizen encounters. This step would move police management away from its ideological interpretations of police deadly force to a more predictive effort directed toward seeking and finding lawful behavioral relationships. Currently, police methodology is as crude as medicine was in the nineteenth century before medicine developed the concept of a syndrome (or type of disease), each with its own prognosis. Thus, just as a physician assumes that a particular type of strep throat carries a certain level of risk, so too different types of encounters might be assumed to have particular probability of injury to either police officer or citizen.

In Chapter Five we will continue our analysis of police-citizen encounters by describing police decision making in armed confrontations. We will suggest that very similar confrontations might be resolved in quite different ways. Given almost identical circumstances (opponent, assignment, setting, and so forth), some armed confrontations will result in shots being fired by a police officer against a citizen; in other encounters a shooting will be averted. We will describe a sequential process of decision making observed in armed confrontations and will suggest that early decisions in such confrontations may either raise or reduce considerably the probability of deadly force being used.

NOTES

1. "In the Matter of Steven Conger," Los Angeles County District Attorney's Final Report, 13 March 1979, pp. 3, 4.

2. J. J. Fyfe, "Shots Fired: An Examination of New York City Police Firearms Discharges," Ph.D. dissertation, State University of New York at Albany, 1978.

3. C. H. Milton, J. W. Halleck, J. Lardner, and G. L. Abrecht, *Police Use of Deadly Force* (Washington, D.C.: Police Foundation, 1977).

4. G. D. Robin, "Justifiable Homicide by Police Officers," *Journal of Criminal Law, Criminology and Police Science* 54, no. 2 (June 1963): 225-31.

5. M. W. Myer, "Police Shootings at Minorities: The Case of Los Angeles," *Annals of the American Academy of Political and Social Science* 452 (November 1980): 98-110.

6. Fyfe, "Shots Fired."

7. Milton et al., *Police Use of Deadly Force.*

8. R. W. Harding and R. P. Fahey, "Killings by Chicago Police, 1969-70: An Empirical Study," *Southern California Law Review* 42, no. 2 (March 1973): 284-315.

9. Myer, "Police Shooting at Minorities."

10. P. Tagaki, "LEAA's Research Solicitation: Police Use of Deadly Force," *Crime and Social Justice*, no. 11 (Spring-Summer 1979): 51-59.

11. R. Knoohuizen, R. Fahey, and D. J. Palmer, *The Police and Their Use of Fatal Force in Chicago* (Chicago: Chicago Law Enforcement Study Group, 1972).

12. A. L. Kobler, "Police Homicide in a Democracy," *Journal of Social Issues* 31, no. 1 (Winter 1975): 163-84.

13. Fyfe, "Shots Fired."

14. Harding and Fahey, "Killings by Chicago Police."

15. A. Binder and P. Scharf, "Deadly Force in Law Enforcement," *Crime and Delinquency* 28, no. 1 (January 1982): 1-23.

16. Harding and Fahey, "Killings by Chicago Police."

17. "Summary of Investigation and Findings of the Ronald Keith Burkholder Investigation," Los Angeles County District Attorney's Office, 6 April 1978, pp. 3-5.

18. Fyfe, "Shots Fired."

19. Milton et al., *Police Use of Deadly Force.*

20. Fyfe, "Shots Fired."

21. Milton et al., *Police Use of Deadly Force.*

22. Los Angeles County, District Attorney's Office.

23. Ibid.

24. Ibid.

25. A. J. Reiss, Jr., *The Police and the Public* (New Haven, Conn.: Yale University Press, 1971).

5 We Pay Them to Make Decisions

PROLOGUE: AN AVERTED ARMED CONFRONTATION

It is obvious that not all armed confrontations result in shots being fired by the police officer; in most cases the encounter is terminated without police shots being fired. A description of averted use of deadly force by a Santa Monica police officer and writer, Barney Melekian, offers insight into the difficulty that officers involved in armed confrontations face, even in which deadly force is eventually avoided:

> *Attention units, stand by to copy information on a 211/187 [robbery/homicide] suspect and vehicle from Venice Division. Suspect is a male, black, 20, wearing a maroon short-sleeve shirt and having a thick mustache. The vehicle is a late-model Cadillac, four-door, dark in color, no further information. Weapon was a .45 caliber chrome automatic. Suspect should be considered armed and dangerous.*
>
> The dispatcher announced this information in a clear monotone tinged with a hint of boredom—just a routine teletype reporting another violent death suffered by one human being at the hands of another. I dutifully copied down the information and continued on patrol.
>
> An hour later, I had already picked up a drunk lying in his own vomit, wrestled with a 15-year-old boy who had taken just enough PCP to convince him that he was living in a horror film, and written a ticket to a 60-year-old woman who was astonishingly familiar with barroom obscenities. That's when I saw a late-model Cadillac sail through a red

light at a major intersection. As I pulled in behind and ran a computer check on the license plate, I saw that the car was a 1975 model registered to someone in Venice. I could see that the driver was young and black and was wearing a white shirt. He sat very still.

Two highway patrolmen were killed while making a routine traffic stop near Sacramento today....

I got out of the police car and walked toward the Cadillac. My backup unit was coming from across town so for the next few minutes I would be on my own. I approached the car, using the flashlight in my left hand to light the interior. I kept my right hand on my gun. The driver kept both of his hands on the steering wheel and stared straight ahead. He was probably just a man in too big a hurry. Or he could be a murder suspect. His basic physical description was the same and his car was close. If he was (he was) the man wanted in Venice.

The lag-time factor always gives the advantage to the suspect. He knows what he wants to do and when he wants to do it. He will always be a little faster than you are. If you forget that you will die....

As I approached to within two feet of the door, the driver turned suddenly toward me. His left hand came off the steering wheel and dropped from my view. I couldn't see what he was doing with it. I didn't want to die, but I didn't want to over-react either. (Once I had to shoot a man who was trying to kill another police officer. There was no pleasure in it, just a numb kind of deadness coupled with gratitude that my partner and I were still alive.) I took my gun out of its holster and held it behind my leg. The driver never saw it.

Before all you hotshots start thinking you're real street cops, ask yourself how many people you've stopped that could have killed you, but chose not to....

No more than 10 or 15 seconds had elapsed since I got out of my car, but already I had made a dozen decisions and there would be more. I walked up to the driver's side window and pressed my leg against the door.

"My I see your license and registration?"

"What the f____ for, man, I ain't done nothin."

"You ran the red light back there."

"It was yellow, man, this is bull____."

"May I see your license, please?"

The man stared at me for what seemed like a long time. What was he thinking? Was he merely annoyed at being stopped, or was he waiting for an opportunity to reach for a gun? His clothing and car differed somewhat from what the broadcast had described, but witnesses make mistakes, and more than an hour had passed since the crime occurred.

The decision and responsibility to display and/or fire your weapon rest ultimately with the individual officer.

Suddenly, too suddenly, the driver turned his head away from me and reached under the seat. My gun came up, paused at my hip, leveled with his head. My finger tightened on the trigger. I leaned forward slightly to get a better angle with my flashlight. Everything moved in super-slow motion. The focus of my whole world was in the driver's compartment of that Cadillac. The man pulled his wallet out from under the seat. Before he could turn back to look at me, my gun was behind my leg. He never knew how close he came, but I do.

No one knows about the hundreds of instances when a policeman decides not to shoot. Perhaps no one cares. After all, people say, we're trained to handle such things, as if training somehow removes or dilutes our humanity.

. . . 117 police officers were killed in the line of duty in 1978. . . .

A decision to shoot when I should not would cost me my career and my livelihood and would burden me forever with the awful knowledge that I had killed or injured another human being in error. A decision to shoot when I should not might also cost me years in prison, for a growing segment of our society would try to imprison me for that decision. But a decision not to shoot when I should might cost me my life.[1]

AVERTED ARMED CONFRONTATIONS

As Melekian suggests, his decision not to shoot the driver of the suspicious car, really might be better described as a series of related decisions. Critical in understanding his decision process (according to the author) and the outcome of the incident were such factors as his previous day's encounters, the fact that police officers had been recently killed while making a routine traffic stop, his assessment of the driver of the car, and the known costs to him if he should make a wrong decision.

As Melekian further notes, only the officer himself knows how close he comes in a given incident to shooting the citizen. Often such averted shootings are not observed by other citizens or officers and are not recorded in official police records. As a result, we necessarily lack systematic knowledge about armed confrontations in which deadly force is not used. Although many police departments keep excellent records on shots fired by police officers, the keeping of systematic records for any but the most spectacular situations in which deadly force could have been used but was avoided is very difficult or, perhaps, impossible. Our research on police use of deadly force has identified more than 100 cases of averted shootings in armed confrontations in four different cities.

We do not know, however, how many averted shootings such as Officer Melekian describes (or encounters where deadly force is displayed by an opponent) an officer faces in a month, a year, or a career. We must rely on estimates of the number of times that officers felt they could have shot but did not shoot in an armed confrontation. In Newark, New Jersey, a survey was conducted with some surprising results. In this very violent city—however, with a very low rate of police deadly force—officers estimated that over a ten-year average career they could have fired but did not in an average of more than a dozen situations (where shooting the opponent would have been legally and tactically justified). Logs of incidents of high-crime-area units, moreover, indicate numerous encounters where circumstances seemed to justify a use of deadly force, but, in fact, officers did not shoot. There is other evidence that police officers shoot in only a small percentage of confrontations in which they could legitimately employ deadly force. One six-officer tactical unit with the Newark department (Target Red), for example, over a one-year period made more than 1,200 arrests, took away 88 guns and 64 knives, had seven shots fired in its presence, and fired but a single warning shot.

Several of the encounters faced by the Target Red team not only involved the perception of danger but its actuality. Consider the incident described in the report below in which officers in this unit (among the most active in the United States in terms of felony contact) disarmed a man with a loaded pistol who seemed intent on escaping at any cost. It is interesting to hypothesize why the officers held fire even as the opponent was apparently contemplating escape or firing upon the officers.

> While on patrol, in an unmarked radio car, in official police uniform, officers were heading north on Camden Street approaching South Orange Avenue. Upon stopping at the corner, officers were approached by an unknown black male. This male stated that another black male, in a black Oldsmobile with New York plates had just threatened him with a small automatic pistol. He further stated that the vehicle was parked on Camden Street with the man in same.
>
> At this point, the man stated that the car was leaving. Officers at this point turned and looked back up the street. A black Oldsmobile with NY plates was observed coming in our direction. Officers at this time blocked the street, blocking the passage of said vehicle. Officers at this point exited the radio car and approached the vehicle which was

occupied by listed suspect. As officers got to the car, the man reached back into the rear of the car and placed something into the rear seat area in the top of a purse. Noted at this time, sticking from the top of the purse was what appeared to be the handle of a pistol. At this point, officers drew weapons and ordered the man to open the doors of the car. The man looked about as if he was going to make an attempt to drive away. Officers again ordered the man to shut the car off and to open the doors. The man complied and was taken from the car. When the man was placed into the radio car, the undersigned went to vehicle and entered the rear seat area. Recovered from the purse which was a Burger King bag was a .25 Cal automatic pistol, loaded with seven .25 cal bullets.[2]

On several occasions the team disarmed men who were at once armed, dangerous, and psychotic. In the following incident, one of the officers grabbed a crazed man's hand as he reached toward his pocket for a loaded .38. Luckily for the officers, speed, timing, and teamwork averted what, given other circumstances, could have been an almost certain shooting. Consider the report below, as well as a follow-up report indicating that the opponent in the encounter was so psychotic that he had to be removed from the holding cell to a psychiatric hospital in a body bag after his arrest:

Due to the amount of robberies, thefts, muggings and drug activity in the area, Target Red Units are assigned to the area as a lookout.

At the above time, Units were in the area, approaching the corner of Ninth Street at Central Avenue. At this time, there were approximately seven men on the corner. The listed prisoner was among them. Both units stopped and watched the group. The listed prisoner looked at Officers put his hand to his right rear pocket, then turned and started walking south on Ninth Street. Officers exited the radio cars, PO [N.] remained and went down the street passed the suspect. The man was looking around and still had his hand on his right rear pocket. At this point, PO [N.] approached from the south, PO [L.] from the east and the undersigned from the north. The man was looking about at the different Officers still with his hand on the pocket. Mentioned Officers continued closer and the man started to take something from his rear pocket. PO [L.] grabbed the man by the belt, PO [N.] grabbed the man's pocket and the undersigned grabbed his hand. At this point, it was established that there was a weapon in the man's pocket. The man was handcuffed and the weapon was recovered. PO [B.] remained with the other radio car as a back up.

The weapon was found to be a loaded .38 cal revolver ... loaded with five .38 cal bullets. Same was confiscated and later submitted as evidence with the proper report by PO [N.].

Officers of unit 310 were dispatched to the North District on a Violent Mental. Upon our arrival officers called for EMB to respond. Officers after a violent struggle put suspect in body bag and transported to MMC to the crisis unit.[3]

In many of their averted shootings, the Target Red officers were able to disarm men who were in the process of firing their weapons. In the incident described below the team confronted a man who was in the process of shooting another man over a drug dispute. The officers were so close that they could actually see the flame leave the gun barrel. The arrested man turned out to be wanted for murder. In a later interview, one of the officers sardonically remarked that when he saw the muzzle go off he "figured he would find out if his vest (bullet-proof) worked."

Officers are assigned to the above area due to the numerous complaints of robberies, larcenies and drug activity.

Unit 131 was in the area and had just stopped a suspicious vehicle with three occupants. As officers were checking the papers to the auto, loud screaming was heard to our left rear. As officers turned, listed prisoner was observed running up the walk. As he reached the sidewalk area, he turned and pointed a small shiny silver object back in the direction of the building. A loud report was heard and flame was observed to come from the shiny object. The officers at this time drew our weapons and called to the man stating that we were Police. The man turned and pointed the item at Officers and as he did so, Officers ordered the man to drop the item. The man complied and he was placed under arrest. The item was recovered and found to be a .22 cal revolver, derringer type, North American Brand, .22 long rifle, loaded with five live rounds and one spent round. Search for shots proved negative.[4]

Other averted shootings faced by the unit involved extremely dangerous persons, although the incidents themselves were not as dramatic as the preceding. The report below describes an arrest of a man wanted for armed robbery and other serious offenses. The officers were able to time their approach so that the opponent had almost no chance of drawing the loaded .38 caliber gun in his pocket. The man was considered to be a known shooter, a man who would certainly try to kill a police officer rather than surrender:

Officers of the Target Red Unit were assigned to the upper number streets of the West and South District due to the amount of robberies of Oil Truck Drivers.

A prime suspect in the robberies was one [D.], B/M 22. . . . This person fit the description of one of the suspects and was alleged to be armed. A check also revealed that the man was wanted for other armed robberies. Warrants at this time had not been issued for the man's arrest.

At approximately 1300 hrs, this date, a general was broadcast over Frequency 5 reference the above suspect. He had been positively identified as a suspect in a robbery this date. Further details are not available at the time of this arrest.

Officers at this time began to look for the mentioned suspect. His known hangouts were checked at various times during the day. One of his known hangouts was the CHIP FROM THE ROCK TAVERN located at S. 16th Street and 14th Avenue. At approximately 1830 hrs, Unit 105 and Unit 131 responded to this location to check for the suspect. He was not on the premises. As Officers exited the premises, the suspect was observed as he walked passed the location. At this time he was in the company of two other men.

Officers entered the radio cars and approached the suspects. As they reached 473 S. 16th Street, Unit 105 pulled in front of the men and exited. Unit 131 pulled to the men's rear. Officers exited and identified ourselves and ordered the men to halt. At this time, [D.] turned and attempted to run north on 16th Street. A brief chase began and the man was apprehended by Officers 105 at approximately 471 S. 16th Street. A brief struggle resulted and the man was subdued. A check of his person revealed a loaded .38 cal, Smith and Wesson, mod. 36 revolver, loaded with three .38 cal bullets.[5]

Other averted shootings evolve from armed confrontations involving irrational opponents. The case described below narrates how the Target Red team successfully disarmed a deranged man who was armed with an M–1 semiautomatic rifle that he had earlier fired at his girlfriend:

I hereby report that at 1941 hours April 12, 1980, Unit 105 P.O. Peter L and I, and Unit 131 P.O. GL and P.O. EN, were dispatched to 15 [R.] Place on a hostage situation where rifle shots had been fired. The [F.] family who resides in a single family house at that location had fled after a grandson, identified as [G.] age 28, had gone berserk. Shots had been fired from a 30 cal. carbine. The suspect was holding his girlfriend, [J.], hostage and was threatening to shoot her. The family alleged that he had fired shots in the house in the past and they considered him extremely dangerous.

Chief V and P. O. S questioned neighbors before any action was taken. It was learned that at least one shot had been heard. Sgt. C and P.O. W went to the rear of the house. The rear door was found to be protected with an attack dog. The front porch was found to be protected with a second attack dog. This left only the side entrance to gain access to the house.

Sgt. C and P.O. W covered the front and rear entrances. Chief V and P. O. S took positions next to an adjacent house where they could observe the side entrance. P.O. N and P.O. L took positions near a parked auto and covered P.O. L and I.

P.O. L called up to the second floor bedroom. He identified us as police officers. He asked the suspect to come to the side door. He said that he would from the bedroom window, but he would not throw out his weapon. P.O. L and I took positions on either side of the side door. The door opened slowly and P.O. L and P.O. N could observe that the suspect had the weapon in his hands. He was lowering it to a possible firing position. They signaled P.O. L and I. P.O. L reached inside and grabbed the rifle, pushing the suspect further inside onto the floor. The rifle was wrestled from the suspect. He was subdued and handcuffed. Sgt. C, P.O. W, P.O. L and P.O. N immediately entered the house and ascended to the 2nd floor bedroom. They found the hostage. She was nervous and scared, but not injured. They recovered a spent 30 cal. cartridge in the bedroom and some live rounds.

Chief V unloaded the weapon. It was found to be a Universal 30 cal. semi-automatic carbine with a full loaded clip and one live round chambered. The safety switch was in the off position. A total of 25 live rounds were recovered.

P.O. L and P.O. N conducted a further search of the house. In the basement numerous 30 cal. bullet holes were found in the wood support beams. The family was notified and they were able to return to their house. The suspect was transported to the West District by Sgt. C and P.O. W.[6]

Why, it might be asked, was deadly force avoided in these encounters, where in other cases the apparently almost identical circumstances resulted in a shooting (and perhaps a fatality)? Specifically one might ask:

1. What critical officer or opponent behaviors make an armed confrontation more likely to result in an averted, as opposed to an actual, use of deadly force?
2. How does the sequential decision process that results in an averted shooting differ from that in incidents in which shots are actually fired?
3. What are the critical social influences upon the officer that determine whether a use of deadly force is averted or actually used in a particular armed confrontation?

One way conceptually to address these questions is to find two cases that are similar or closely similar in circumstances, but differ in terms of their outcomes. We will offer descriptions of two armed confrontations with apparently insane women armed with large knives. One case, which resulted in a fatality, is the celebrated case of the shooting of Eulia Love in Los Angeles in January 1979. This incident is still an object of political controversy, being the subject of four publicized Los Angeles Commission Reports, several hundred news articles, and the congressional subcommittee hearing. The second encounter involved the disarming of a woman with a knife who had just killed a man (who had "stolen" half her liquor bottle). While recognized within the department as worthy of commendation, the second encounter received but a brief mention in the local newspapers soon after it occurred in 1976. It, however, offers a useful contrast to the Los Angeles police officer's shooting of the "Woman with a Knife."[7]

"A WOMAN WITH A KNIFE"

A Use of Deadly Force

The shooting of Eulia Mae Love began as a "routine business dispute" between the gas company and Mrs. Love. On January 3, 1979, at approximately 11:15 A.M., a Mr. John Ramirez, an employee of the gas company, arrived at the home of Mrs. Eulia Love. Mrs. Love, a black 39-year-old mother of four, was told she owed $80 to the gas company. Mr. Ramirez approached the residence and went to shut off the gas meter at the side of the house. Mrs. Love angrily approached Mr. Ramirez, screaming that she would not allow him to disconnect her gas service. She then struck him with a shovel, bruising him on the arm. Mr. Ramirez later said that she was "frothing at the mouth" when he retreated from the Love house. He returned to his office and filed a report. The gas company reported the incident to the Los Angeles Police Department.

Just before noon, Mrs. Love went to a local grocery market to pay her gas bill. When she was told that she could not pay her gas bill there, she purchased a money order for just over $22 to continue her gas service. Later that afternoon, Mr. Jones (also a gas company employee) called the police dispatcher and requested a patrol car to join him at the residence. Mrs. Love came out of her house and spoke to the man, emphatically indicating that she would not pay the full $80 owed. Mrs. Love went back into her house and two or three minutes later emerged with a knife, which she used to hack the branches of a tree on her front lawn. At 4:15 P.M. the Los Angeles Police Department dispatcher placed a call for a patrol car to join the gas company employees ("415 business dispute. Meet the gas man at 11926 South Orchard. Code 2").[8] A few seconds later, Officers E. M. Hopson and L. W. O'Callaghan acknowledged the call.

As the officers approached the house, Mrs. Love yelled at them "You're not coming up on my lawn, motherfuckers, you're not going to turn off my gas!"[9] The officers responded with demands to drop the knife. Mrs. Love continued to yell obscenities, calling Hopson a "cocksucker" and telling O'Callaghan he "could lick her ass." She also yelled, "Use it, if you're going to use it!" (apparently referring to O'Callaghan's and Hopson's drawn pistols). At this point the two officers (who had immediately drawn their weapons) appeared to witnesses agitated and defensive and possibly a bit bewildered. As Mrs. Love backed away from the armed officers eastward along the walkway, O'Callaghan approached the walkway and followed her. He placed his gun in his right hand and pointed it downward. He also removed his baton from his belt and held it in his left hand. Officer O'Callaghan followed approximately six feet behind. Officer Hopson walked to the front lawn of 11932 South Orchard, one house south about 15 feet from Mrs. Love. He carried his revolver in his right hand, pointed downward.

Soon the obvious hatred of Mrs. Love for the officers began to intensify. According to the district attorney's investigators, "Mrs. Love made several right hand knife thrusts at Officer O'Callaghan's midsection."[10] Both officers repeated their attempts to convince Mrs. Love that they would not harm her and ordered her to drop the knife. Alternatively the officers cajoled, threatened, and pleaded with the crazed black woman to drop her knife. However, Eulia Love refused to drop her knife: "Fuck you, ain't no mother-fucker going to shut off my gas!"[11]

One witness saw Mrs. Love's actions as overtly threatening the two officers: "While at the sidewalk, Mrs. Love was waving the knife like a threat . . . Mrs. Love . . . would turn around and yell at them still waving the knife."[12] A different witness emphasized the irrationality of her behavior: "She was very upset or hysterical. . . . He was unable to understand precisely what she was saying. As she was talking, Mrs. Love was gesturing with the knife, moving it up and down in front of her."[13] At approximately 4:20, Mrs. Love suddenly began to retreat backward toward her house. Officer O'Callaghan followed closely. As she retreated, Mrs. Love still thrusted and jabbed at the officers with her knife. O'Callaghan stayed approximately five feet away and tightly held his gun and baton. Several witnesses said that at this point Officer Hopson signaled the gas company employees, as if to mean, "come on," as Eulia Love backed cautiously toward her house. Mrs. Love then suddenly halted at the walkway leading from the sidewalk and faced the policemen with the knife in her right hand. O'Callaghan was now less than five feet from her. Hopson had his gun outstretched and followed approximately ten feet away from the "woman with the knife."

Later, several witnesses concurred that at this point Mrs. Love seemed to relax. She began to lower her arm with the knife and seemed to be edging slowly but certainly toward the house. Instead of her returning to the house, perhaps unharmed, the following seconds would see a series of decisions that altered the careers of the two officers, killed Mrs. Love, and threw the city of Los Angeles into a year-long political turmoil. One witness, Ronald Lewis, described the following seconds as follows: "The white officer knocked the knife from Mrs. Love's hand. The knife fell to the ground at Mrs. Love's feet. When Mrs. Love bent over and retrieved the knife, the white officer hit her again on the shoulder. Mrs. Love began to straighten up, knife in hand. The white officer jumped back about five feet. Mrs. Love had the knife by the handle. While she was straightening up, she threw the knife...."[14] Another witness, William Jones, said: "[O'Callaghan] knocked the knife out of Mrs. Love's hand. He swung at her again. He then tried to step on the knife but Mrs. Love regained possession. She held the knife by the handle in her right hand and moved her right hand and arm back and forth as if she were about to throw it overhand."[15]

It is important to be aware that there was considerable disagreement as to whether Mrs. Love actually intended to throw the knife or merely was threatening the officers with a gesture. Anthony Wolf, for example, commented "The white officer (Officer O'Callaghan) knocked the knife from Mrs. Love's hand. She retrieved it. The white officer jumped back one to two times as Mrs. Love threw the knife."[16] Joseph Harris similarly said, "Mrs. Love picked the knife up and held it by the handle. She stood up, holding the knife in her right hand with the elbow bent and the knife pointing upwards and in line with her head."[17] Sheila Love, Mrs. Love's daughter in contrast, offered that, "The white officer hit Mrs. Love on her shoulder, causing her to fall to the ground. The knife also fell to the ground, a few inches from Mrs. Love's feet. Mrs. Love did not pick up the knife nor did she make any attempt."[18]

There was considerable controversy on other issues as well. Was Mrs. Love's arm moving forward as she was shot? How far did the thrown knife travel in the air (it was found 68 feet from Mrs. Love's body)? What were the final relative positions of Mrs. Love and the two officers? The official police report states, "After the knife was knocked from her hand, she picked it up, holding it by the tip of the blade. . . . She then abruptly stood, raised her right hand over her head, and slowly drew this hand and arm rearward as if preparatory to throwing."[19] O'Callaghan then dropped his baton and shifted simultaneously into a two-handed gun position, less than eight feet from Mrs. Love. Hopson froze in his two-handed, semicrouched position. Mrs. Love then took a step backward and raised the knife with her right hand above her head. No one will ever know for certain what her intentions were in raising her right hand in this manner. Almost instantaneously, both officers fired six rounds each in a rapid-fire sequence; eight of the twelve bullets entered the body. Eulia Love was dead.

During the many reviews regarding the Eulia Love shooting, the question was again and again raised as to how the shooting might have been averted. How might the officers have avoided the circumstances that made the final frame decision perhaps necessary or at least psychologically comprehensible. In explaining what went wrong in the incident later, critics and supporters of the Love shooting focused upon decisions made well before the final decision to use deadly force by the two officers. The "majority report" filed by two LAPD commanders (D. R. Sullivan and M. R. Lanzarone) focused on the officers' efforts to engage Mrs. Love in dialogue and their concern for the children's welfare in Mrs. Love's house, reflected in their concern that Mrs. Love didn't enter the house to threaten the children.[20]

Police critics of the officers' actions focused similarly on early decisions that in effect made the final decision almost inevitable. For example, a minority position written by Deputy Chief M. L. Anderson observed that in large part the threat to O'Callaghan's life was precipitated by the officers' choice of tactics.[21] He suggested that if the officers were ". . . in fear of their lives, they could have stayed behind the car using it as protection when talking to Mrs. Love."[22] He also noted "That their fears were minimal is indicated by the fact that both officers fully exposed themselves and neither attempted to take defensive action. When Eulia Love began backing, the officers advanced approaching even closer."[23] Anderson further questions the officers' choice of tactics, pointing out, "The tactic of handling a firearm in one hand and a baton in the other is poor. This is indicated by the officer's inability to recover his balance after knocking the knife from Eulia Love's hand and then having to drop his baton when using his firearm."[24]

Other observers similarly suggested that the type of information given to the officers, the positioning of the officers (the white officer was consistently closer to the woman than was the black officer), their failure to call for a backup prior to encountering the woman, their inability to elicit community aid in dealing with the woman, the decision to unholster upon confronting the woman, O'Callaghan's positioning of his gun in his strong hand, and even the officers' failure to work out a prior tactical plan may have all contributed to the final, tragic outcome of the incident.

An Averted Use of Deadly Force

The second incident, which occurred in February 1976, involved a young detective confronting an apparently insane woman who had just fatally stabbed a young man who, she claimed, had stolen her liquor bottle, which they had promised to share. It provides a dramatic contrast with the Eulia Love incident. An investigative report described the incident as follows:

At 4:35 P.M., Feb. 12, 1976, Detective Phillips, Badge #46, was traveling west on 16th Avenue, when he observed a black female chasing a black male north to south across 16th Avenue. He observed her stab the black male several times in the back.

The victim ran into the Mr. Hair Barber Shop at 201 16th Avenue and the owner closed the door and prevented the black female from entering.

Detective Phillips got out of his auto and approached the female who was still holding the 8½ inch carving knife and was trying to force open the door. Detective Phillips ordered the female to drop the knife. She turned toward him in a threatening manner. Detective Phillips again ordered the female to drop the knife several times and she finally complied.

She was then placed under arrest by Detective Phillips and taken into the barber shop until Tac Unit #1 arrived and removed her from the scene.

The victim was leaning against the wall with a stab wound in the middle of his chest. He was taken to Martland Medical Center via ambulance and pronounced dead at 5:10 P.M. by Dr. [R.] of stab wounds of the chest and back.[25]

In a statement made to homicide detectives, Detective Phillips described his actions as follows:

> At 4:30 P.M. 2-12-76 I was travelling west on 16th Ave. at 13th St. I observed a black male being chased across 16th Ave. by a black female. While the female was chasing the male I observed her stab him several times in the back, with a long butcher knife.
>
> I stopped my auto in front of 201–16th Ave. just as the male ran into Mr Hair Barber Shop, 201–16th Ave. After the victim entered the shop the owner slammed the door in the suspect's face. When I came within five feet of the suspect she still had the knife in her hand and was trying to force her way into the shop. I stated that I was a police officer and when she turned towards me I identified myself by showing her my badge. She stated "fuck you" and held the knife in a combat position. I commanded her to drop the knife, but she refused. After commanding her several times and talking to her for several minutes I convinced her it was in her best interest to drop the knife. She dropped the knife to the sidewalk and was placed under arrest. She was taken inside the barber shop to await the unit that had been called by a citizen on my request.
>
> Inside the shop I observed the victim leaning against a wall with a stab wound in his chest. When I tried to interview him, he was unable to talk to me. A unit from Martland Medical Center responded and removed the victim to the hospital where he was pronounced dead by Dr. [R.] at 5:10 P.M.[26]

Later we were able to interview the detective regarding his actions in coping with the insane woman with the knife. We were especially interested in the types of actions he took well prior to the woman's dropping the knife that might have had an effect on the final outcome. Just as actions by O'Callaghan and Hopson might have affected the fate of Eulia Love, so too it is clear that the early actions of Detective Phillips significantly affected the outcome of this confrontation.

The context faced by Detective Phillips, as well as his judgment, of course, differed from those evident in the Love shooting. Detective Phillips was off duty when he observed the woman repeatedly stab the younger man in front of the barber shop. The neighborhood in which the stabbing occurred was, as Phillips put it, "known for its numerous stabbings, muggings, and killings." He immediately assessed the antagonists in the incident as "being two winos," given his knowledge about the types of people who "hung out in the area." Upon confronting the young woman, Phillips reported that she muttered something about how "that motherfucker drank my whole bottle up." Interestingly, while Detective Phillips perceived the woman as being both insane and probably drunk, he did not (in spite of his seeing her stab her drinking partner) believe she was an immediate danger to himself. After the woman saw Phillips, she tried to run into the barber shop, but the door was slammed in front of her by the barber. The barber then came out of the shop to assist the officer. Detective Phillips identified himself and kept his pistol unholstered and pointed toward the ground. At this point, he asked the barber to help him, as the barber "knew the woman he kept calling her name, Cindy," and asking her to "act sensible and drop the knife." While verbally abusing the officer ("Fuck you, cop," "fuck you, cop," she kept repeating), she began slowly walking toward Detective Phillips with her knife. ("No one steals my liquor that I pay for.") At this point Detective Phillips kept talking to her, slowly, less than five feet from the eight-inch knife. Phillips kept explaining to her that:

> Since you got a knife and I got a pistol one of us is in trouble. I kept telling her to drop the knife. Calling her name, telling her I would have to shoot if she got any closer. I must have backed up 50 feet. The barber was talking to her all the time. Finally, she just dropped the knife on the sidewalk. We went into the barbershop, handcuffed her and took her in. She's in a mental hospital now.

This incident is revealing in that it is similar to the Eulia Love incident in several respects. Although there are obvious differences in the two confrontations, it might be argued that Detective Phillips faced an even graver initial situation than did the Los Angeles officers; his opponent, for example, had already killed a person with her knife while it was not clear if Mrs. Love had done more than chop at her rose bushes with hers. What, it might be asked, are some of the critical differences in the two incidents? How might one develop some preliminary hypotheses as to their opposite outcomes?

One difference lies in the officers themselves. Officers Hopson and O'Callaghan were typical patrol officers in a rather troubled precinct. Hopson had had two deadly force incidents in the two years prior to the Love shooting. Also black-white pairs in ghetto precincts are at best unusual and possibly invite more stress (both real and perceived) than do all-white and all-black teams.

Detective Phillips was a black detective with an exemplary record in the Newark Police Department. He achieved the highest score on the lieutenant's examination and had an exceptional police record in all respects, having won half a dozen valor medals and other distinctions.

Also, working as a detective in one of the highest crime areas in the United States perhaps gave him a greater reservoir of experience in coping with violence than the California officers.

There are differences as well in the opponents. The encounter of Officers Lloyd O'Callaghan and Edward Hopson and Eulia Love seems almost a chance event. Mrs. Love was born in Vernado, Louisiana, a rural community of 400.[27] She left in 1953 with her family. In 1963, she married William Love, a cook. Together they had four children. The couple seemed relatively prosperous with William earning almost $15,000 per year as a cook. In June 1978, Mr. Love died of sickle-cell anemia. Even before her husband's death, Eulia Love had become obviously depressed. She resigned from her job as a school crossing guard. She also had "fallings-out" with several of her closest friends. Routine confrontations with officials apparently caused her great pain and anguish. The three months it took to have her social security benefits approved from the Social Security Administration were especially painful.

C. P., the other woman, was what Paul Muir[28] would call one of the "dispossessed." An alcoholic resident of the streets, C. P. had little to lose seemingly, either by taking another person's life even for the price of a liquor bottle or by risking her own. After the murder she was found "too crazy to stand trial" and was incarcerated in a mental hospital for the criminally insane, presumably for life.

There are differences, as well, in the setting and scene of the encounters. Eulia Love's home was in a stable working-class area in southeastern Los Angeles. The Los Angeles Police Department and especially the Southwest Precinct were known for the "iron fist" legalistic (J. Q. Wilson's [29] term) approach to law enforcement. The Newark Police Department, although known as tough and occasionally physical, was controlled by a black mayor (Kenneth Gibson) and a black police director (Hubert Williams). At times overwhelmed by seemingly uncontrollable crime on the street, nevertheless the Newark department's reviews and sanctions for abuse of deadly force are among the toughest in the United States. The neighborhood in which the incident took place is at once heavily patrolled and somewhat of a "combat zone" area known primarily for its alcoholism, drug traffic, and violent crimes.

Finally, there were differences in the decisions made by the officers in the two incidents well before the final resolution of each incident. It is these differences in officer decision making (even well before the final frame decision) that we suggest are critical in understanding the final outcome of the incidents. The decision, for example, by Officer O'Callaghan to place his gun in his "strong" right and his baton in his weak left hand probably increased considerably the likelihood that deadly force would be used in the confrontation with Mrs. Love. Officer Phillips' decision to elicit the aid of the barber to help convince C. P. to drop her knife similarly conceivably reduced the probability that deadly force would be used in the encounter.

PHASES IN POLICE OFFICER DECISION MAKING IN ARMED CONFRONTATIONS

To explore the consequences of "early" decisions in armed confrontations, we will propose a descriptive five-phase model of police decision making applicable to both police use of deadly force as well as averted shootings: phase 1: anticipation; phase 2: entry and initial confrontation; phase 3: dialogue and information exchange; phase 4: final frame decision to shoot/not shoot; and phase 5: aftermath.

In addition to increasing or decreasing the probability that deadly force will eventually be used, certain early decisions might either restrict or expand the choices later available to the officer. The dilemma posed in the confrontation's final frame is in many ways a function of choices made earlier in the episode. Thus, for example, an officer who receives a dispatch indicating that an opponent is more dangerous than he really is faces a different emotional and factual situation than an officer (in a comparable situation) who receives accurate information. Similarly, positioning upon physically confronting the opponent and communicating with him might either avert a final-frame decision to shoot or alter the context so substantially that the officer never faces the decision. An officer who similarly discovers, during a prolonged confrontation with an opponent, that he is dealing with an acutely psychotic individual (rather than a more instrumental criminal one) will interpret the man's actions quite differently than would an officer (confronted with the same individual) who had not made those observations. Finally, it should be noted that early decisions by officers may either prolong or curtail the decision process. By seeking cover early in a confrontation, for example, an officer can afford to engage in a more prolonged communication with an opponent than can an officer without similar protection.

A brief word should be said about our uses of phases in this model. First, some shootings that occur very rapidly may not have identifiable stages in the sense we use them. Second, the concept of phases may have different technical and commonsense meanings. Lofland, for example, posits a phase to signify an analyzable component within a social event.[30] Goffman defines repetitive phases within social rituals.[31] In commonsense usage, phases signify regularly occurring periods in types of social events; they also signify choice points at which an activity may continue or be terminated. Viewed in this context, almost any human transaction may be said to have phases. A date between a man and a woman may be said to move in phases toward an erotic encounter. A business meeting may proceed in phases toward either a deal or a disruption of business relationships. A party may move from a getting-acquainted phase to one in which inhibitions become less constrained.

It is in this commonsense context that these phases within an armed confrontation are used. To exemplify further these phases of officer decision making, it might be useful to illustrate briefly each phase in terms of the Love and C. P. confrontations described earlier.

Phase 1: Anticipation

A critical phase in armed confrontations encompasses those minutes from notification, call, report, or dispatch to arrival on the scene where the actual encounter occurs with the opponent. During this period the officers may receive information about the suspect from a dispatcher, fellow officer, or citizen. The words used by others to describe the opponent may greatly affect the set the officer takes toward the incident:

Shooting of Eulia Love

Time
4:10   Dispatcher puts out call "415"—business dispute—"Meet the gas man. . . ." [It has been pointed out that this call may have influenced the final outcome of the final episode.]
4:15   Officers arrive at gas company truck and spend only 30 seconds speaking to gas man. [The decision by the officers not to gather more information from other sources might be seen as an important influence upon the outcome of the episode.][32]

In the case of the C. P. incident, there was no prolonged phase of anticipation because Detective Phillips directly observed her stab the young male.

Phase 2: Entry and Initial Contact

The decisions made by officers on physically entering the scene or first approaching the citizen may have a critical impact on the final outcome of the episode. Here the officer receives direct impressions that may confirm or refute information received earlier about the opponent. An officer who seeks cover immediately in a confrontation with an armed robber, for example, extends this phase and gains greater latitude in reacting to movements by the robber than would an officer who is exposed. Similarly, the officer who gains immediate eye contact with a psychotic citizen possibly reduces the chance that he might use deadly force.

Shooting of Eulia Love

Time

4:18   Officer O'Callaghan unholsters revolver prior to approaching Mrs. Love [as did officer Hopson] and places his baton in his weak hand. [This decision might be seen as a crucial turning point as it obviously limited nonlethal alternatives.]

4:18   From several witnesses' testimony, it seems that the white officer [O'Callaghan] was physically closer to Mrs. Love than was the black officer [Hopson]; the respective distances were six and twelve feet. [Did this affect the final outcome?][33]

Arrest of C. P.

Time

4:37   Detective Phillips approaches C. P. with gun down and badge in hands. [He assumes a firm but unthreatening posture.]

4:38   Phillips positions himself five feet from C. P. and next to barber. [He actively uses the barber in confronting C. P.][34]

Phase 3: Information Exchange

Many, but by no means all, shooting episodes have a phase (possibly verbal, possibly nonverbal) in which there is some communication between the police officer(s) and the citizen. An officer might tell a citizen to "drop his gun" or order him to stop. The officer, similarly, might say something to distract or intimidate the citizen. Some information exchanges with opponents, as with opponents holding hostages, might proceed for hours or even days. Often, this phase in armed confrontations ends with only short epithets. A citizen may threaten the police officer or indicate his contempt for "cops." Sometimes information exchanges may continue for many minutes; frequently they are much briefer. In the Eulia Love case there were more than two minutes of face-to-face dialogue between Mrs. Love and the two officers. The C. P. episode may have lasted five minutes.

Shooting of Eulia Love

Time

4:19a Officers approach Mrs. Love in a threatening manner with gun and clubs drawn. [Would another police approach style have avoided the tragedy?]

4:19b Eulia Love shouts obscenities at officers. Officers react by increasing demands for her to drop weapon. [Was the response by the officers appropriate/avoidable?]

4:20 Mrs. Love began to walk toward her house. Officer O'Callaghan decided not to allow her to continue toward the house and to knock the knife out of her hand. [The report on the incident also notes that Hopson apparently elected not to encircle her, so as to prevent retreat.]

4:21 After Mrs. Love retrieves knife, officers elect not to back away to safety but to try to control Mrs. Love through threats of deadly force and verbal comments. [Backing away to safety was perhaps the only way to avoid deadly force at this point.][35]

Arrest of C. P.

Time

4:38 C. P. utters obscenities at detective.

4:39 Barber and detective demand that C. P. drop knife. [Did presence of known community (nonpolice) person, supporting Phillips affect the episode's outcome?]

4:40 Phillips and barber back into street while certainly and firmly demanding that she drop knife or someone was going to get hurt. [Why did Detective Phillips' verbal tone apparently prove effective?][36]

Phase 4: The Final Decision

At some point in the confrontation, the officer decides either to shoot or that shooting will not be necessary. Occasionally, as in a sniper operation, the final frame might be a deliberate, planned action, given certain contingencies such as the appearance of an armed kidnapper in an open space. In other cases the final frame might simply be the reflexive squeezing of the trigger. A decision that shooting is not necessary may follow disarming the opponent or the display of evidence indicating the opponent is harmless. A decision that shooting is not acceptable may follow bystanders' moving into a region of danger or the realization that the opponent is a youngster.

Shooting of Eulia Love

Time
4:21   Officer O'Callaghan shoots/Officer Hopson shoots Eulia Love [the final frame].[37]

Arrest of C. P.

Time
4:40   C. P. drops knife on sidewalk, is arrested and taken to barbershop awaiting transport to the police precinct.[38]

Phase 5: Aftermath

A confrontation with the opponent often continues whether or not the shooting results in a fatality. In this, the aftermath phase, citizens may berate the police officer or even attack him physically or verbally. In most jurisdictions, following a shooting, the officer is separated from his partner; in some, the officer's gun is, in a symbolic gesture, stripped from him. The rest of the day is spent filing reports, perhaps being questioned by homicide and internal affairs officers, and certainly answering to superiors. For many officers, the next days are disturbing if there has been a fatality or serious injury. Sleepless nights, nonstop talking, and persistent nervousness are common aftermaths—a far cry from the officer portrayed in the film *Bullitt*, who nonchalantly returns home to his lover after a bloody shooting in an airport.

Contact with the opponent whether alive or dead sometimes continues after the shooting. One officer, for example, kept yelling at an opponent he had just shot to "wake the fuck up." Another officer was punched by a wounded opponent while he was placing the opponent on the stretcher. Other officers have reported receiving calls of thanks from opponents for not killing them. Other officers have been threatened, harassed, or even chided by their opponents in deadly force encounters.

Shooting of Eulia Love

4:22–4:25   Officers Hopson and O'Callaghan cover the body and call for an ambulance.[39]

Arrest of C. P.

4:25–5:00   Phillips and barber attempt to calm C. P. down in barbershop awaiting transportation to the precinct jail.[40]

SOCIAL INFLUENCES UPON POLICE OFFICER DECISION MAKING IN ARMED CONFRONTATIONS

We will now turn to some of the social forces that influence police decision making at each phase of the armed confrontation. How do these forces alter the likelihood of various decisions at each phase of the armed confrontation? And how, in the process, are the probabilities of an eventual use of deadly force increased or decreased? Table 5.1 suggests some of the social influences relevant to each of our five phases.

As indicated in the table, specific social influence might be hypothetically related to the outcome of each phase of an armed confrontation.

Anticipation: Prior Definition of the Situation

We have hypothesized that the mode, quality, and credibility of information made available to the police officer regarding the opponent influences the eventual outcome of the incident. One critical source of police information is the dispatcher. Rubinstein well describes the importance of a dispatcher to the urban police officer assigned to a particular job:

> What the dispatcher tells a man when he gives him an assignment is all the policeman knows about what he will find until he actually arrives. The dispatcher must tell him everything relevant to a job in the most economical way, to avoid wasting airtime. . . . The patrolman must have faith in the skill and experience of the dispatcher because what this

TABLE 5.1 Social Influences Upon Officer Behavior in Armed Encounters

Phase	Thoughts and Behavior of Officer	Possible Social Influences
1. Anticipation	Assessment of situation prior to encounter (How dangerous/what type of danger does the opponent represent?)	• Mode of information (dispatch; citizen; other police officer; direct observation • Believed accuracy of information • Prior set of officer toward information
2. Entry and initial contact	Initial positioning and direct information gathering (Confirmation or revision of earlier information; attempts to maximize options/minimize the opponent's options?)	• Physical appearance of opponent • Distance between self and opponent • Safety and cover • Timing
3. Dialogue and information exchange	Information dispensed to opponent and received (Intentions of both police officer/opponent are clarified/elaborated.)	• Information given by opponent (others) • Body language of officer/opponent • Type of communication made by officer • Changes in the degree to which officer controls situation
4. Final decision	Shoot or decide against shooting	• Movements by opponent • Immediate threat by opponent • Dangers to others implied by decision to shoot
5. Aftermath	Coping with the decision (How does officer effectively deal with the actions taken?)	• Certainty of officer in reasonableness of decision • Presence of supportive citizens/officers • Presence of psychological support for officer

unseen person relates to him establishes his initial expectations and the manner of his response to the assignment.[41]

In many cities, a numbered dispatch code is used to provide the officer with information as to the type of incident he might encounter. For example, in California an officer might get a call involving an armed robbery as follows: 211 [armed robbery] in progress. Black male, age 20–25, with gun at 20745 Figuero, at the liquor store. In New Jersey an officer might receive a call such as: 5–60. [B and E— breaking and entering in progress] back of factory. Neighbors saw suspects on roof.

Although, in theory, such systems of communication should provide standardized and accurate information to the officers, in fact, the information may be highly misleading. One officer, for example, received a dispatch indicating that two men were having a fight with guns outside a tavern. When he arrived (with shotgun drawn), he found two friends "fooling around" with billiard cues, "playing like the three musketeers." Another dispatcher indicated that a suspected armed robber was walking with a stiff leg, as if he were carrying "a sawed-off shotgun in his pants leg." A man with a legitimately broken leg, who vaguely fitted the description was nearly shot. Another officer in a state that allows the shooting of fleeing felons received a dispatch that a store of an old man (he knew) was robbed. He fired a warning shot at three tall blacks fleeing the premises through an alley. It later turned out that the robbery was a "petty theft" involving some Halloween candy being stolen by three juveniles (who were narrowly missed by the police officer's bullets). In this same regard, note that the Eulia Love shooting began with the rather innocuous dispatch: "415 business dispute. Meet the gas man. . . ."

There are many reasons for the distortion or inaccuracy of information given police officers relevant to calls for service. One factor is that most reports are initiated by unsophisticated civilians. A citizen, upon seeing a candy bar being stolen, for example, may grab a telephone and say, "There's a robbery taking place at . . .," when, in reality, a petty theft has taken place. This distortion is exacerbated by the fact that in many high-crime areas, police communications are jammed during many periods of the day (especially on a Saturday night). Police dispatchers are guided by coded priorities in dispatching jobs; many citizens know that if they want a police car to come to their assistance, they must convince the dispatcher that a high-priority incident is taking place. Citizens faced with a prowler may report that a "man with a gun" is in their backyard. Similarly, others will report that a "burglar" is an "armed robber" and occasionally that a man has fired a gun.

This escalation of priority may have several consequences for the officer. Some officers may overanticipate the seriousness of the call, believing the information given by the dispatcher. Others may "downplay" the calls because of past experiences "that all calls are exaggerated." ("It's just another black kid in her backyard.") A surprising number of officers may virtually ignore details of the dispatch altogether, preferring to assess the situation by their own observation after their arrival on the scene.

Another consequence of the dispatch "logjam" in a high-crime area is that officers arrive late to almost all dispatched jobs. One officer complained, "Almost all the jobs are more than an hour late. You are more likely to run into someone else's job or something fresh than you are to hit the job that comes over the radio." In the observation of a tactical team by one of us, a unit received an urgent job that indicated a Greyhound bus was being robbed. The officers raced to the scene and found no bus at the location. Further inquiry indicated that the robbery had occurred no fewer than six hours before.

Obviously, not all shootings result from dispatched assignments. In many instances, the information may come directly from citizen to officer, as in this case:

> I was in a bar drinking with a friend when this guy comes in a bit watered down saying, "There's this motherfucker with a shotgun who says he's gonna kill everyone in this bar." I look outside and see "a bar regular" with a cane doing a Fred Astaire act, sure enough shouting soused, but not really hurting anyone. I looked at the guy who had told me about the man and I saw him laughing with his friends, having a big laugh about me rushing to the door. I almost killed him—not the other guy!

Such direct citizen to officer information may, of course, provide critical information to the officer. The officer described earlier who disarmed an irate man with a rifle found out from a neighbor the following information about a suspect who was later disarmed without incident:

> I talked to the lady next door and find out the guy's Ukrainian (I'm Ukrainian too); that he was mad at his old lady; that he had fired his .303 into the ceiling; and that he loved model trains, and also that his name was George. After we got him barricaded, Gary and I moved up the

stairs, and I yell up, "Hey, George, you want to meet another guy named George?" He comes to the door to see who's there. I grab the gun and it's over. After we got him cuffed we sat in the kitchen, drinking beer, talking about Russia and trains. He was a real nice guy, really, just got upset.

Many police officers who are able to use direct citizen information effectively in anticipating an encounter have developed techniques to question citizens critically. One officer, faced with a robber in a back room of a store, asked a witness the following questions:

I said what do you mean a "robber"? What did he take? Did he threaten you? Did he say "give it up" when he took stuff? How old was he? What do you mean you don't know? . . . All this is in less than a minute, but it's important because the answers change whether you can shoot or not if he decides to run, or comes at you.

In some armed confrontations, officers receive relatively detailed knowledge of an opponent from more experienced officers, including specification of modus operandi. One sergeant gave his tactical squad the following information about an opponent:

Watch out for Dinky. He's definitely a shooter. If he goes for his crotch shoot him. A snitch told us he hides a piece down there, a .25. He also may be carrying a sawed-off shotgun in some old newspapers. He supposedly likes to kneel down when he shoots. Our information says he might be a Nam Vet. We also hear that he uses the name Richie, like a nickname; but watch it, he is definitely a shooter. Take no chances with this guy.

Other information is associated with earlier direct personal contact. One officer who purposely aimed for the legs of a fleeing but armed opponent said: "Like I kinda knew Petey and he knew me—not well, but around the neighborhood before and then after I became a cop. I arrested him a few times and I didn't bear him no grudge. I didn't think he'd try and kill me, so I worked extra hard not to have to shoot him. It was like we was almost friends."

Entry and Initial Contact: Definition of Options

Other social influences may influence officers in behavior during the initial encounter of an armed confrontation. For example, upon entering the actual setting of the confrontation, the police officer will, through his actions, seek at once to expand his own options and curtail those of the opponent. One officer described his strategy in an incident described earlier where an armed (and obviously) dangerous murderer was captured by the officer and his partner:

Well we were looking for D. and finally we saw him walking on Avon and Nineteenth. Here, all of the police department was looking for him, paying snitches and stuff and we just see him walking there. Pete and I talk as we ride. I get out of the car and go around the corner waiting. Irvin gets out and cuts over lot to edge of building which he is approaching. Just as he reaches the corner where I am, Pete rides up in the car with the shotgun out. Presto, we got him on three sides. A perfect approach.

A similarly well-executed approach was described by another officer; it resulted in the apprehension of a dangerous felon:

I was in my favorite lunch spot and I hear my waitress tell her sister (they're Italian) that "this guy has a gun." I see this black man standing nervously by the register. I tell her in a loud voice that I'll see her Monday, and pretend to leave but really wait by the post. When he walks by, I put gun to his ear and very softly tell him what will happen if he moves. He just freezes and gives up. He never had a chance. It was all defined by the position I had.

Good position requires an appropriate choice of distance for the circumstances. In the averted shooting described earlier in this chapter, in which the officer successfully reached for the opponent's hand as he reached for a gun in his pocket, there was the obvious requirement of a close initial approach. Other shootings have been averted because the officer was able to "stay away" from an opponent with a sharp object. It might be offered in retrospect that officer O'Callaghan was too far away from Mrs. Love's manipulative action, yet too near to reduce her anxiety about him.

Finding protective, "hard" cover is obviously an effective approach to dangerous situations. One experienced training officer suggested, for example, that although most departments train their officers "in reflexive response to fire," he thought that "the first reflex should be to look for cover, then decide whether you are going to shoot or not. Too many cops think that you can stop someone from killing them with a revolver. I would much prefer a brick wall." Another officer similarly described how he was able to wait out a robber with a pointed rifle because of his adequate cover. "Well, he had this rifle at us, but we had an alley wall between him and me. I just figured I could wait that extra second, knowing that I had that protection."

Conversely, many shootings occur when an officer is "out of position" on entering the scene. One officer, who has only fired one shot in fifteen years (with numerous averted shootings and literally thousands of arrests), described the circumstances of his sole shooting:

> I was stupid. I got in the middle of this crowd with a bunch of Puerto Rican pukes behind me. I got hit from behind by this guy with a bottle. As I was waking up this guy came at me, while I was on the ground, aiming for my head with a tire iron. I'm not sorry I shot him, except I was sorry he didn't die, but it still only happened because of the way I came into the crowd. I won't do it that way again.

Another example of how positioning early in the encounter affects an officer's options may be illustrated by an incident where a California officer, unexpectedly confronting two armed robbers, found himself extremely vulnerable to the expected fire from the opponents. It might be hypothesized that his action in firing a shotgun blast (in a crowded street) was dictated at least in part by the position he found himself in as the men left the massage parlor they had just robbed:

> On February 15, 1980, at 9:33 P.M., Officer ... M, in response to a robbery in progress alarm, drove to 2512 Wilshire Boulevard, Santa Monica. That location is the Ginza Massage Parlor. He arrived there at 9:37 P.M. Officer M observed the building to be lit and there was an "open" sign in the window. He took cover behind a large potted plant approximately 10 feet west of the front door of the massage parlor. He was armed with a shotgun. As he waited, Officer M had the police station telephone the massage parlor to determine if anyone was in the location. He could hear a telephone ringing in the massage parlor, but no one answered it. Officer M was just about to change positions when two men walked rapidly out of the massage parlor. The first one out was holding a gun in one hand and a box in the other. M could not observe the hands of the second man.
>
> At that point, Officer M stood up and yelled, "Police! Freeze." The man with the gun turned toward him and M, fearing for his safety, fired one round in the direction of the two men. [Officer M was in an extremely vulnerable position and approximately 15 feet from the robbery suspect.] Both men turned and ran. The gunman went east, away from M, the other went back into the massage parlor. M then fired another round at the gunman to prevent him from running into an open movie theater on the southwest corner of 26th Street and Wilshire. That

shot struck the window of a lamp store on the east side of the massage parlor. The gunman stopped running and took cover in an alcove entrance to the lamp store. M observed a box thrown to the sidewalk from the alcove, currency spilling from the box. He also heard a metallic click as if a gun striking the pavement. The gunman was ordered out and placed on the ground. He was handcuffed and arrested without further incident. That gunman was subsequently identified as Steven R.

The man that had run back into the massage parlor was found hiding in a rear bathroom of the parlor. It was only then that it was learned he had been wounded. He was taken to Santa Monica Emergency Hospital where he died at 11:04 P.M. He had sustained eight wounds from the first shotgun blast, five pellets lodging in the chest. The entry wounds were in the area of the left shoulder.[42]

The manner of entry into the confrontation context may limit later positioning, as in the following case:

We saw this cab driver with a ragged looking passenger so we followed him from a distance. The car kept driving around, like it was going nowhere. Suddenly at a dark corner the cab turns off its lights. We turn the red light on and the driver jumps out; hey, this guy is robbing me. A second later the robber jumps out with a gun and I go after him and go behind him for about a block and a half. I'm running with a gun in my hand. He's got one in his hand. All of a sudden I turn the corner and see him standing there pointing the gun at me. I tried to shoot but the gun jammed. It turned out that his gun was a replica, of all things. I almost shot him though because of my momentum. I was all off balance.

Clearly, direct observations may drastically revise earlier beliefs about the opponent. One patrol officer, faced with a drunk old man waving a gun on the street, said:

I got a call about a man with a gun—attempted murder. I got to the location and see this old man yelling at his son-in-law and pointing a .22. I looked at his eyes. He was so drunk I didn't think he could hit me with that gun. He was just an old man upset with his son-in-law but not what I expected from the dispatch.

Alternatively, another officer described an encounter in which his initial contact revealed a far greater degree of danger than had been anticipated earlier:

We go to this "boy leaves girl; girl leaves boy thing." She wants him out of the house and all he wants is his clothes and things. Well she decides that the radio was hers not his and he didn't agree and went berserk. I mean berserk. When we got there we were expecting a nothing thing, but now this guy gets totally crazy, throwing light bulbs and stuff. He went from calm to attacking three of us with a broken bottle and a kitchen knife in nothing flat. It took all three of us to get him down and we almost had to kill him.

Many officers report that during the initial encounter they develop "cues" as to how to cope with the opponent. An example of such perception during this phase of initial contact is as follows:

Well I was closing the building [a store] and all of a sudden this guy walks up real slow to the door and sticks a gun in my belly. Now I've been trained in this type of situation to give him what he wants, but he is so nervous that I think, "Hey, this guy is going to kill me out of fear," so when he looks at one of the girl clerks I take a chance and grab his gun, so luckily I'm here. It's all different when you actually see the guy.

Officers tend to believe that the ability quickly, accurately, and objectively to sense an opponent's capacities is critical for survival—both professionally and physically. One officer noted: "It's the ability to judge how dangerous a man is in a few seconds that tells whether you can make it out here; it's a certain look, also, what they do with their hands." Another officer commented, "I usually pretty much discount what I hear from the radio, my partner, a citizen or anyone else; what's more important is to observe anything unusual; anything that will tell me something about the guy; anything to give me a handle on how to deal with the situation."

In summary, two factors seem to be most important at entry in determining the outcome of the incident: the degree to which the officer positions himself to control the situation—that is, expand his options and limit those of the opponent—and his ability to weigh effectively his direct impressions against what he has learned earlier about the opponent. This definition of the circumstances of the confrontation and the new information received will, of course, influence the terms of any dialogue or information exchange between police officer and opponent.

Information Exchange: Mutual Self-Definition
Between Police Officer and Citizen

As stated before, in most, but not all, armed confrontations, there is a meaningful exchange of words or gestures between police officer and citizen. And it is certainly the case that some shootings are avertable by means of information exchange. One officer was faced with a crazed man with a knife in a bathroom. Roughly a year later the officer recalled his dialogue with the man:

> I said in a very calm voice, "Would you please drop the knife." He said, "You're gonna have to take it from me!" We stood there about twenty minutes. I finally kept talking, saying things like, "Do you have a problem we can get settled?" I kept coaxing him and finally he gives up.

Some information exchange involves explanation of his behavior by the opponent, as, for example:

> Well, we go to this bar and hear from a patron that a guy has been stabbed. We go in and see this guy run past us. As he's running, he's turning back, saying, "This guy robbed me before and now he's robbing me again. That's why I stabbed him." Soon I fired a warning shot, but I did think a bit about the circumstances that brought this about.

Many officers report that the most effective communications are those that are least ambiguous as to the intentions of the officer. Among those most commonly used communications are orders, nonambiguous and assertive:

- "Freeze, Police. Don't move."
- "Get out of that car!"
- "Hands on the windshield. Do not move!"
- "Freeze or I'll shoot!"
- "Drop it, asshole!"

Such communications share a well-known, clear meaning and a familiarity through media, fiction, or life to most citizens. It should be added that the tone of voice (its certainty and command presence) may be a more essential element in the dialogue than the communication's content.

Some shooting episodes are characterized by rather ineffective efforts at dialogue with the opponent, where officers communicate very ambiguous messages to the opponent. In some situations, for example, police officers are unable to convince the citizen that they are, in fact, police officers. Language may be a problem. In one confrontation in Los Angeles, two Russian defectors were chasing a thief with a .22 rifle. Soon they were confronted by a group of police officers who ordered them to "freeze," to drop their weapons, and so forth. Only later was it discovered that the men, one now dead, spoke only Russian.

Body language of both citizen and police officer may be important in determining mutual perceptions of the episode. Because, for the most part, the encounter represents the first time the citizen and police officer have met one another, they make important inferences regarding the intention of the other from their body positions, language tones, and movements.

The body language of the citizen may be critically important in determining the outcome of some confrontations. One officer astutely observed: "When he comes you have to interpret quickly. Is he just a drunk wanting to shake hands? Is he going for my gun? Is there a gun in his hand? It's all judgment." Another officer observed that "there is an invisible line; if he crosses it with his toe he's dead." Some body language may signify an end to the confrontation. One officer described an encounter, "Where after I fired this one shot, the guy just ran to a porch and sat down waiting for us to handcuff him." Another officer similarly recalled an incident, "Where suddenly he [the opponent] jumped back into his car and hid there curled up like an infant."

Police body language may be equally important. It is often forgotten that citizens may be irrationally afraid of the police (and, interestingly the police officer may be irrationally afraid of the citizen). A citizen may interpret the actions of a police officer as unreasonably violent and fight (or even shoot) to defend himself. He also may fire, not sure if the policeman is in fact a policeman at all as in the following tragic confrontation described by one eastern city police officer who was one of eight officers involved in the fatal shooting of a tavern owner who fired his gun in apparent fear that he was being attacked:

> We rolled up to this bar to respond to a report of robbery. There were two guys in an old car. One guy has a rifle, the other is asleep. What happened was (we didn't figure this till later) that we arrest the younger guy with the gun without much problem, then the older guy hears the rumpus, wakes up and sees eight white guys (we were all plainclothes) pulling at him. He pulls a .25 and shoots Nick in the neck. We fired and killed him. As he's dying on the way to the hospital, he yells that he thought we were the buglars coming back to rob him. It turns out he owns the tavern. It was a mess.

At times, a combination of cooling words—and, paradoxically, strong, nonlethal force such as a punch or kick—can disarm a suspect without deadly force being used. In the following case, officers lulled an insane, and also armed, man and then "coldcocked" him to get a loaded gun out of his hands:

> Unit #518, Officers E and H also responded to assist at request of Sgt. B. Mr. D. E. answered the door and was apprised by Sgt. B of the eviction notice. At this time, D. E. had his right hand on gun which was half way out of pocket and refused to give up his weapon, threatening, "I'll shoot the police or anybody who comes near me." All four officers were forced to draw their service revolvers in self-defense as Mr. E. continued in his adamant refusal to give up the gun, still ranting wildly that he would shoot anyone who came near him. The officers tried to calm Mr. E. with words and at the same time moved in closer to momentarily distract him. D. E. then started to swing wildly at officers with his left fist, while at the same time holding gun with right hand at officers. After a violent struggle over furniture and floor of room, D. E. was finally subdued and a fully loaded .22 cal. pistol was taken from his person. During the struggle for weapon whereby necessary force had to be used, Mr. E. sustained a slight laceration over left eye. This was treated with a "Butterfly" band-aid by Dr. [C.] at the College of Medicine and Dentistry Hospital.[43]

Another issue involves the officer's ability to establish his identity and authority as a police officer to the citizen. In one confrontation, a black officer accosted a group of Hispanic citizens who were beating an older black man who had bumped into his car. The officer described his dialogue as follows:

> Well I see this old man getting beaten. I'm off duty and come up and say I'm a police officer. I tell them, "You don't have to beat that old man." The man just ignores me, like I'm not there, like I don't exist and keeps beating the man. Finally another guy comes up and hits me with a hammer. As he's coming back I shoot him in the leg. At the trial they all swear they didn't know I was a cop.

Gestures are important communications in some armed confrontations. During one chase, for example, a perpetrator, who was later wounded, "gave the finger" to a police officer as he tried to escape. Grimaces, verbal insults, short epithets, and so on, similarly mark the information exchange of many confrontations. Often, a police officer gains a sense of the personality of his opponent in this type of exchange. One officer, for example, noted that the man he shot was "a real surly guy. Real rude; you could tell by his face." Another officer described a man at whom he later fired a warning shot as follows: "He was just afraid, a typical addict. You know, afraid he'd miss his fix. You could tell by his face. Just a certain type of person who would kill you for a hit of dope."

The phase of information exchange provides an opportunity for the officer to deter nonlethally (possibly verbally) the opponent from creating conditions that threaten his life (that is, pointing a gun at him) or authority (fleeing under certain circumstances). It also provides an opportunity for the officer to gain further information as to the actions of the opponent in response to his commands. For example, an officer commented regarding an incident in which he shot a man in the leg, "When I saw that he wasn't responding to my telling him to freeze, but kept coming, that's when I said, 'Hey I got a problem here.'" When such dialogue fails, the next stop is violence, perhaps deadly.

The Final Decision

The culmination of many armed confrontation is, of course, the use of deadly force by the officer. The opponent has failed to respond to orders to drop his weapon; the officer fears that a certain object is a gun and has no time for dialogue or further dialogue, or the opponent has actually shot at the officer.

Needless to say, the social psychology of final frames is extremely complex, involving the unique characteristics of circumstances, citizens, and officers. In some final-frame situations, one might assume that only the most aggressive would shoot or the most foolhardy or stoic individuals would refrain from shooting. In other situations, individual variation is more understandable.

Many reflexive shootings begin with a shot being fired at the officer. One officer, for example, described the following incident:

> We had heard on the radio that there were these guys shooting people in the bars—it was a Saturday night—and we got a license plate and start rolling down this hill. Soon we spot the car that fit the description of the guys with almost the right plates and we follow them. Soon he starts speeding ahead and we follow him. The guy suddenly slams on the brakes and jumps out of the car and shoots at us with a .45. I was lucky. As I jump out I see him aiming. I shoot and hit him. It was automatic.

Another officer described a situation again involving a shot fired at him, precipitating an automatic response:

Well we started running after this guy, and I, to be honest, thought he would just give up like that, but he runs to a car and fires. Both my partner and I fired through the front windshield and luckily (I guess) hit and killed him. It couldn't have taken more than five seconds.

Other confrontations and final frames may be of even shorter duration. The final frame of the almost instantaneous shooting described earlier was recalled by one of the two officers involved in the incident: "We went into this kitchen after the guy and he just fires at us, just like that. We fired back as soon as we could—just like that. It was like my hand did it without my brain telling me much."

The speed at which such reflexive confrontations occur may be startling. An officer recalled how "the car came towards me, and I though, 'Oh, my God, this is it, I'm going to die,' and I let go a round just as the car was on top of me." Another officer recalled, "My partner yells, 'Watch out he's got a gun.' His arm turns towards me, that's as simple as it was." In some confrontations, the decision to use or not use deadly force emerges out of a hand-to-hand struggle (that may be highly emotional). For example:

> ... Mr. R., who came to within one to two feet of the officer, raised his gun and shot him, striking him in the left side. Both men fell to the ground as Officer B. grabbed R.'s hand and the gun. "I knew he was trying to shoot me again because I could feel the cylinder of the gun turn. Finally I was able to unholster the gun and shoot him."

Other reflexive shootings occur among large groups of officers. In such shootings, the decision to shoot may be a response to the group of officers, rather than to specific actions by the opponent. For example:

> We were in roll call when a "211" [armed robbery] comes over the radio right in front of the station. We all pour out and see this VW with a guy shooting at us. I fired mostly cause everyone else was. I'm not sure if I hit anything.

Other final frames tend to involve far more deliberate actions. One officer describes what he called a premeditated warning shot:

> Well, I arrest this guy and leave him in the back of the car. All of a sudden he starts running while I'm talking to another guy with his cuffs on and all. I don't want to kill him but I'm not gonna let him get away so I take dead aim at his head. I'm a pretty good shot—all 99's at the

range [out of 100], then I move my target about six inches to the left and fire. That stopped him, sure enough.

Some officers indicate that they either attempt to wing or to miss narrowly their opponents. One officer indicated "that I was aiming at the guy's legs. I had to stop him, but I didn't want to kill him." Another similarly replied "that I know they don't like you to do this, but ever since I killed that guy in '69, I have aimed at people's legs whenever possible." Another officer described aiming a shot "between the legs" of a man waving a machete, explaining that he "had to pretend to miss because the department don't like warning shots."

In many incidents, an officer will define a "bottom line" that will determine for him whether or not he will shoot. One officer described an incident where he almost shot a "black Mr. Clean" who had assaulted his partner:

Well, he is on J. and I am behind. I start tugging at him and J. says, "C. he's going for my gun, he's going for my gun." I really feel helpless because this guy has obviously been lifting weights for dozens of years. I pull again and can't move him. I say to myself one more tug and if I can't get him, then I plug the motherfucker right in the fucking ear. Luckily he comes off and we cuff him.

Another officer described an encounter with an older man with a pistol who had already fired at his nephew. Here he indicates how his assessment of the capacities of the opponent determined for him the point at which he would have to use deadly force:

Well he's standing there, yelling and cussing and all kinds of shit. But I see he's an old man and I feel (I may have been wrong) that he couldn't hit anyone with that rifle. Even though he pointed at me or near me I felt I could have waited and come home alive.

An officer with several shootings in roughly ten years described his analysis of final frame decisions this way: "It's like you have to calibrate the situation. If a guy turns toward me with a weapon, he's gone. I've been in Vietnam and I've seen what a bullet can do." Other officers have quite different decision points. For another:

It comes down to this. I will only shoot if I can be almost certain that if I didn't, my life or someone else's would be in jeopardy. When you are going to die, that's it. . . . You are going to die. To be honest, I will put myself in risk with this type of philosophy, but this is the way I am.

At times, final-frame decisions seem as much determined by other factors as the threat posed by the opponent. A common factor in incidents where a decision is made not to shoot is the risk to other officers. One officer described how, during a running gun battle, he was about to shoot when: "This guy is coming right by me maybe 60 feet away, I yell out, 'Halt or I'll shoot.' Level my gun and then see a head appear. It's a police officer. I put my gun down."

Risk to citizens is also critically important; one officer described the following incident: "There was this Puerto Rican guy who shot at Paul and me. We couldn't shoot back because there was this three-year-old kid in the room." Another officer involved in a drug raid says, "We were in this guy's apartment, and he goes for a drawer, but his mother and girlfriend are in the room, so I hold up."

Other decisions to shoot or not shoot seem more a function of momentum than a conscious decision. "I'm chasing this guy and we go around a corner and he's standing looking confused with the gun out. To be honest, I just ran into him. I never even thought of shooting." Another officer described a situation where he fired his gun more to uncock the weapon than anything else:

> Well, I was in this bar and this drunk comes over, grabs me, and says, "Who you calling boy?" I grab my gun and by mistake cock it (as it turns out). I get control of the guy and realize that my big problem will be killing the guy or me by mistake. Finally, I got the gun free and let a shot go into the ground, just so I wouldn't kill either him or me.

It is important to note that even in the officer's mind, some final-frame decisions defy comprehension. Moreover, an officer who either shoots or refrains from shooting will have limited recall of the precise circumstances that existed at the instant in which he fired. Similarly, officers will often fail to recall in the adrenaline-charged moment of the confrontation the precise number of shots fired, at whom they were aimed, or even the number of opponents he confronted.

In some confrontations, one finds decisions against shooting are reconsidered when additional information comes forth. Such confrontations are sufficiently complex to allow several points when the officer must decide whether or not to shoot.

Finally, contrary to widespread public opinion, the decision to shoot is not an easy or light one for officers. As one officer said, "It's a human life held in the balance by slight pressure placed on the trigger of a .38." Another man said, "No one can tell you when to take a human life, not the sergeant, not the I.A., not the law." It is important in this respect to be aware that some officers have "inner guidelines" that are quite different from the department's or their superiors. One officer, for example, commented: "Around here, they say you can shoot at a fleeing felon. But I'm not gonna kill some kid with a TV set." Another man similarly and powerfully observed: "When it comes down to that last moment, it's only between you and God that tells you when to shoot."

The Aftermath: A Strangely Continuing Relationship

One of the interesting—and unrecognized—aspects of police use of deadly force is the aftermath of a police shooting episode. As stated above, often in both fatal and nonfatal shootings, there is an odd continuation of the "relationship" established during the episode. One officer involved in a fatal shooting described how he tried to get his fallen opponent to "wake up":

We went into an alley and I let go a few. I didn't even know if I hit him. Soon I see him sitting there. He looks at me and falls over. I see blood under his jacket. I start doing mouth to mouth resuscitation, yelling at him to get up, to talk. He was dead.

Other postshooting relationships are considerably less cordial. One officer who became involved in a physical fight with a group of Hispanic males, ending in the shooting of one opponent in the leg, described the aftermath of his encounter as follows: "Well, he is lying there moaning and I call for an ambulance. I go over to cover him and tourniquet him and he grabs me and starts punching me. When we get to the hospital the bastard keeps trying to get up and says he's gonna kill me."

A narcotics detective described the aftermath of a shooting during a raid as follows:

Well, this guy goes down with four shots in him. We think he is dead. As soon as he hears the ambulance roll up he starts moaning. He thought we would kill him if we were alone. Anyway even though he takes a shot at us, he has a good lawyer and gets 18 months' county time. Three of them he does and gets the rest suspended. He's out of the hospital, walking around, eating Gino's pizza six weeks later. Now he rides by in his LTD and waves. It's like a joke to him.

After an averted shooting, the officer and opponent may discuss what might have happened. Following the arrest of a young boy with a loaded .32 in a dice game, the young man says to the officers: "I was thinking of going for it, but there was three of you and that's too many. Two of you and I think I might have tried it. A year in jail for a weapon is a long time."

In a few aftermaths there develops a strange bond between the police officer and his former opponent (and at times the opponent's family). A young black patrolman recalled that "this guy I shot in the groin (but didn't kill) would stop my "black and white" and tell his friends, 'that's the man who could have killed me but didn't.'" One officer involved in an encounter in which a store owner was killed by a group of tactical team officers (one of whom was shot also in error by the dead man who thought he was being robbed and fired) made this comment about the scene at the hospital:

> It was very strange. There was G. lying in one bed shot in the throat and there was T. [the store owner] in the other bed. The families just mingled together. G.'s wife went to T.'s bed and held his wife. You would have all thought they were in the same family.

The aftermath of the shooting may see powerful emotions exhibited among partners. One officer remarked that after he and his partner killed a shotgun-wielding escaped murderer (in an incident described earlier): "We just sat there hugging each other, glad to be alive. I just thought about my wife. It was her birthday and said I was glad to be here and hugged my partner. We looked weird but we didn't care."

Another officer shared a memory of an incident in which he was hit five times by a man who was later killed:

> I'll never forget it. Tony just held my hand in the car driving to the hospital. You're gonna make it; you're gonna make it, just like that. I went into a coma for three weeks. Tony never left the hospital. When I got out we lost touch sort of but it's something we'll always share.

Less positive emotions are also released. One officer commented that his partner, who showed great cowardice in a particular incident, attempted to approach him after the incident saying, "We did a good job." The other officer said: "That's the last time I talked to him. I walked to the sergeant and said I won't work with that SOB. He was transferred the next day." Another officer described a scene where his partner and he were surrounded by an angry mob that had gathered after a fatal shooting and his partner began to "lose control":

The guy went down and just began to bleed through his mouth. We called for backup and handcuffed him. A crowd gathered so we drew our guns. They knew he was a pusher and started going through his pockets (believe it or not). I really thought we were going to get it. The backup went to the wrong address. My partner started to lose it. I started ordering him. Like "Unhandcuff him." "Show your gun!" "Look calm," stuff like that. We made it but I can't say it helped our working relationship.

Severe trauma marks the aftermath of some shooting incidents. One officer said, "I broke out in hives thinking about it, that I almost lost my career, that I might go to jail, that I almost killed a guy. I was sick." Another officer noted that "the morning after it was over I just went walking around and kept going back to the spot where it happened. I couldn't get it out of my mind." One lieutenant in charge of a program to help other officers cope with the stress of a shooting said:

There are lots of surprises: like it may come up weeks or even months after it's over, just when you think the guy is O.K. Also it may hit the backup officer and not the guy who actually shot. Like we had a case where this guy shot a guy who was running at him with two broken Coke bottles. The guy who shot was fine. His sergeant who was in the alley calling for assistance fell apart screaming, "Why did it happen, he was so young. . . ." He felt responsible because he left the younger man alone for a minute when it happened.

The end point of the aftermath phase is difficult to define. Some officers report dreaming of the men they shot years after the incident. Legal proceedings may continue for officer and opponent, again several years after the incident itself is terminated. It also should be noted that in a certain sense the aftermath is not a phase in the same sense as the earlier four phases. But it is convenient to designate it as such so that its importance in the overall process is highlighted.

CONCLUSIONS

In this chapter we have outlined a heuristic scheme for analyzing police decision making in armed confrontations. The model we have described should serve as a useful starting point for generating theory aimed at linking "early" tactical decisions to the outcome of an armed confrontation. Reiss[44] and Binder and Scharf[45] have emphasized that many armed confrontations are avertable only at decision points well before the instant when the officer faces an immediate life or death decision: whether to shoot or not shoot.

The approach we describe here to the analysis of armed confrontations has a number of policy implications. One important implication stems from the assumption of the dual responsibility of police officers and citizens in producing violent encounters. Although continued emphasis should unquestionably be made for the police to reduce the inappropriate use of deadly force, the perspective here raises the potentiality of altering citizen behavior in the effort at such reduction. A community education program informing citizens about police expectations and about typical police responses to citizen threats is an example of an intervention focusing on the way that citizens might communicate with police officers to avoid violent confrontations.

Another policy implication is in the area of police decision making. Most attempts to reduce deadly force have focused upon the final decision to use or not to use deadly force. The model of a sequential process in a transaction suggests that interventions to control deadly force might be effectively aimed at an officer's decision well before the final frame. One example of such an early phase intervention is found in the implementation of an administrative operational rule requiring police officers to call for specialized backup support upon confronting an armed, but not immediately threatening, opponent.

A final policy implication lies in the importance of understanding all components in the confrontation in the process of assessing performance and recommending administrative change. Too often, after-the-fact evaluations and, perhaps, policy decisions are based upon superficial aspects of the encounter or upon data available only after the decision to use physical force has been made. Thus, an officer may shoot and kill a burglar emerging from a house when the burglar reaches into his clothing, removes a shiny object, and turns rapidly toward the officer. It may later be determined that the shiny object was a cigarette lighter. Nonetheless, the decision might have been entirely reasonable at the time and in the context that it was made. It also follows that reconstruction of a decision to use physical force without full realization of the perspective of the officer at decision-making time is also frequently responsible for negative, even violent, community reactions.

In Chapter Six, we will continue our analysis of officer decision making, focusing upon officer characteristics related to the repeated use or restraint in the use of deadly force. We will focus upon the psychological capacities that are most critical in effectively coping with armed confrontations: the ability to control fear, perceive reality objectively, employ interpersonal and physical skills, and make responsible moral judgments regarding the decision to use deadly force in an armed confrontation.

NOTES

1. B. Melekian, "A Split-Second Decision," *Los Angeles Times*, July 29, 1979, Part V, p. 5.

2. Newark Arrest Report.

3. Newark Arrest Report.

4. Newark Arrest Report.

5. Newark Arrest Report.

6. Newark Arrest Report.

7. The details of the Eulia Love case come from the "District Attorney Report on Fatal Shooting of Mrs. Eulia Mae Love," April 16, 1979, Special Investigations Division, Los Angeles County District Attorney, Case No. 100–2070.

8. Ibid., p. 12.

9. Ibid., p. 13.

10. Ibid., p. 14.

11. Ibid.

12. Ibid., p. 15.

13. Ibid., p. 16.

14. Ibid., p. 18.

15. Ibid., p. 17.

16. Ibid.

17. Ibid., p. 18.

18. Ibid., p. 19.

19. Ibid., pp. 16, 17.

20. *Los Angeles Times*, October 4, 1979, p. 126.

21. Minority Opinion, Officer-Involved Shooting, DR 79–403 983, March 15, 1979, Los Angeles Police Department.

22. Ibid., p. 2.

23. Ibid.

24. Ibid.

25. Newark Police Department Commendation Report.

26. Newark Incident Report.

27. *Los Angeles Times*, "Woman with Knife from Bucolic Background," April 12, 1979, Section IV, p. 1.

28. W. K. Muir, Jr., *Police: Streetcorner Politicians* (Chicago: University of Chicago Press, 1977).

29. J. Q. Wilson, *Varieties of Police Behavior: The Management of Law and Order in Eight Communities* (Cambridge, Mass.: Harvard University Press, 1968).

30. J. Lofland, *Analyzing Social Settings* (Belmont, Calif.: Wardsworth, 1971).

31. E. Goffman, *Asylums* (Garden City. N.Y.: Doubleday, 1963).

32. Los Angeles County District Attorney Report, Case No. 100-2070, p. 12.

33. Ibid., p. 13.

34. Newark Commendation Report, April 16, 1975.

35. Los Angeles County District Attorney Report, Case. No. 100-2070, p. 16.

36. Newark Arrest Report, April 16, 1975.

37. Los Angeles County District Attorney Report, Case No. 100-2070, pp. 20-25.

38. Newark Incident Report, April 17, 1975.

39. Los Angeles County District Attorney Report, Case No. 100-2070, p. 25.

40. Ibid.; Newark Arrest Report, April 16, 1975.

41. J. Rubinstein, *City Police* (New York: Farrar, Straus and Giroux, 1973), p. 88.

42. Los Angeles County, District Attorney Report.

43. Newark Arrest Report, April 1979.

44. A. J. Reiss, Jr., "Controlling Police Use of Deadly Force," *Annals of the American Academy of Political and Social Science* 452 (November 1980): 122-34.

45. A. Binder and P. Scharf, "The Violent Police-Citizen Encounter," *Annals of the American Academy of Political and Social Science* 452 (November 1980): 111-21.

6 Police Officers Are Human Like The Rest Of Us

SHOOTERS AND NONSHOOTERS

Portrait of Two Shooters

Officer Jethro Hastings (a pseudonym) has shot 11 people in his 19 years on a northeastern city police force. Five of these people were killed, four seriously wounded, and two crippled for life. Officer Hastings feels he was justified in every one of these shootings. "The criminal provides the provocation. They create the circumstances. They create their own problem, the thing that brings it about." In discussing his shooting incidents he demonstrates almost a photographic memory. "We were on a stakeout detail in the northside, when I saw him. I walked by as if to pass him. He turns around and goes to his pocket. I draw out first. As he is dying in the ambulance, he apologizes for having drawn on me."

Officer Hastings is a much decorated officer. He is respected in the community, and of all the black officers in the department he is perhaps the most liberal in political outlook; he is considered radical by some. Hastings explains: "The police officer is a cog in the capitalist system. Dealing with the casualties of the economic system is our job." Not incidentally, Hastings served as a gunner in an airplane in Vietnam. He described in an animated voice what it felt like to be in combat: "40MM's would come out up through the floor. Once I flew 59 'K's' [kilometers] through a gook jungle. The plane looked like some green swiss cheese when we got back. . . . Sometimes when you'd go through the jungle . . . you'd see black pajamas with holes in them. That meant you did your job."

Since becoming a police officer Hastings has gained a reputation as perhaps the city's most aggressive and courageous cop. He has been on tactical, detective, and narcotics units and other specialized squads and details. Other officers speak of him in almost reverent terms: "You should see Hastings in a street situation. He is as cool as a cucumber. Everyone else is shaking, pissing or shitting. Not Hastings. He's cool, like he was strolling in a shopping mall." During the past ten years, in every year but one, he has shot at a human being. In four years he has shot at two persons, in one year three. Hastings loves his work. He rarely calls in sick and has few disciplinary infractions. He also has never in his 17 years of service "been brought up dirty" on a shooting. Hastings says, "They're all justifiable. All brought on by the circumstances that the person brought on himself."

In another city, Officer Samuel L. Jones (another pseudonym) has, in only five years as a police officer, shot seven times, hitting five people and killing three. Officer Jones is a large, red-haired man and talks incessantly about leaving his job. "I think about leaving lots of times," he says nervously, twitching. "Where can I get $23,000 a year with a high school degree. Get me a $20,000 job, and I'm gone." Jones expresses a certain degree of hatred for the criminals he meets on the street. "You should see them. Fucking nigger assholes. Fucking nigger assholes. You should ship them all out of here, back to Africa. The last guy I had to shoot, he comes at me with a broken 'Miller beer wino' bottle. I wished he had fucking died. The fucking jungle bunny was eating Big Macs three months after I shot the dirty motherfucker."

Jones had had numerous problems with his local internal affairs unit, not only for his shootings but for other matters. Once he talked back at roll call to his sergeant. Twice he was caught in a "country bar," while on duty. Seven other times he was cited for such infractions as slovenly appearance, insulting a superior officer, and failure to follow proper arrest procedure. Specific citations refer to "unnecessary force," insulting a citizen, and accidental weapons discharge. "Frankly," says his sergeant ["This of course won't be repeated"] "Jones is an embarrassment to us. If it weren't for the Police Association making it impossible to fire anyone who isn't an out-and-out criminal, Jones would be long gone."

Jones has never been in the military and worked as a laborer for eight years before he became a police officer at age 30. He resents the "college motherfuckers" who run the department and never faced "down a nigger in an alley." He hopes he gets injured badly soon so that he can retire from the department and go "worm farming." He also expresses few regrets about the people he has shot. "A few less miserable cocksuckers. Just saving the courts a little paper and time."

"You Don't Have to Kill Them": Two Nonshooters

George Sullivan (a pseudonym) is perhaps the most decorated police officer in a large inner city department. He has made approximately 6,000 felony arrests during his 13 years, or 500 per year or 2 per working shift. On some days Sullivan has arrested more than ten people for crimes ranging from dealing narcotics to murder. Sullivan is described by his commander as "having no hobbies, but police work. He eats, sleeps, drinks, thinks about police work." When an article appeared in a national magazine including the ten best police officers in the United States, Sullivan was enraged that his name was not included. "What the fuck," he exclaimed, "some motherfucker starts a boy scout camp. What the fuck has that got to do with real police work?"

Sullivan, by his own count, has stripped more than 500 guns and roughly 1,000 knives, beer bottles, clubs, and the like, from the citizens he encountered in his work. He has shot only once. That shooting was after he was assulted by a drug addict, armed with a "2 by 4," from the rear. He sincerely wishes that the guy had died, spoiling his record like that. Most times Sullivan uses cunning rather than his gun to disarm persons. He describes one incident as follows:

> Well I was in this bar and this guy has a gun. I walk in just like this, real slow, and have my Kelolite [six-cell flashlight] out. I say in a loud voice, "Put that fucking gun down or I'll break your thumbs." He just drops it, just like that.

Other times, speed and cunning work to disarm a dangerous criminal.

> You control them, or they control you. You gotta get them up on the wall before they start thinking about things. Also, in this town you gotta get them in the car before a crowd of their friends show up. That's where a lot of shootings take place. Also, watch their hands and eyes, hands and eyes, that's where a lot of shootings go wrong. When I go into a crowd I just watch their hands and eyes, hands and eyes. Never take your eyes off their hands or their eyes. Also never shoot at a fleeing felon, its dangerous to run with your gun. It might go off.

Sullivan recently was made a detective. In less than a week he had alienated the entire detective division for criticizing their productivity. "Lazy bastards. They would rather go to the dentist than arrest people." He is rather proud that he has accomplished so many arrests with so few resorts to his gun. "I have no qualms killing some street asshole who is threatening my life, but short of that, there are other ways to get them in."

Dan Dorsett (again a pseudonym), in a different police department, has never fired a shot in 31 years. Dorsett has (as had George Sullivan) been on every "crazy detail" that existed for the past "umpteen years"—tactical squad, narco bureau, central city patrol. His precinct captain describes Dorsett as a "cop's cop": tough, honest, courageous. "Dorsett is modest so he just doesn't show his medals, but he's got them." The captain adds that he observed that he shoots straight "99's [out of 100] on the range. If Dan misses the center of the target he feels depressed for a month."

Officer Dorsett feels that his military experience makes him less likely to shoot.

> I saw a lot of that shooting stuff over there. I served in Patton's Third Army going towards Bastogne. If you wanted to see shooting and dead people, you had it then. I don't feel I have to shoot most people I face. If you are confident, you can face them down on the street. There may be a time when I'd have to, but let's just say I never faced it in 31 years on the street. Like one time I saw this guy running from another cop on Main Street; I drive down and all of a sudden I see him point a .25 at me. I jumped out of the car and took him down. Don't ask me why I don't shoot. I just didn't feel it was necessary.

Dorsett would much rather talk about his seven children, five of whom are pursuing advanced degrees, than about police shootings, but he does express a modest opinion about what makes a police officer shoot or not shoot in a split-second decision:

> Part of it is luck. The rest can be explained by two things: the ability to be able to control your fear in a crisis situation when any normal man would be scared out of his mind. Another thing is the skill in handling your weapon, but more important is people.

Thus, Dorsett thinks that beyond luck there are two things that decide what will be the outcome of a particular confrontation: confidence and competence. "That's the two things. If you are competent with your hands and gun, and confident in your ability to use them, you will do okay on the streets. Problem is many guys don't know how to use their gun and get afraid when they think they might have to use it."

CRITICAL COMPETENCIES IN COPING WITH ARMED CONFRONTATIONS

What is that makes an officer become involved in many shootings, as in the cases of Officers Hastings and Jones, and why do others avoid shooting people, like Officers Sullivan and Dorsett? What competencies seem to be critical for an officer to cope effectively with large numbers of armed confrontations without using deadly force? A response to this query will be attempted in this chapter.

Clearly, part of the differences among the officers may be explained by the number of confrontations faced by each officer. An officer's propensity to use deadly force might be evaluated by a ratio analogous to the batting average is baseball. Just as a batter who gets 100 hits in 300 at bats (or hits at a .333 average) is considered to be a better hitter than a player who gets only 75 hits in as many at bats (he hits at only a .250 average), so, too, we must use a baseline to balance for number of opportunities; that is, we must relate the number of times an officer actually fires to the number of armed confrontations he has encountered. Thus, for example, an officer who has experienced many armed confrontations, say 100, and only fires three times may have a lower shooting rate than does an officer who fires only twice but faces far fewer, say ten, confrontations.

To illustrate this concept of shooting ratio, we offer in Table 6.1 three hypothetical officers, each with different shooting ratios: shots fired/armed confrontations. As the reader will observe, officers differ both in terms of the times fired at citizens and in the number

TABLE 6.1   Hypothetical Shooting Ratios of Three Officers

$$\text{Shooting average} = \frac{\text{number of shots fired}}{\text{number of armed confrontations}}$$

Officer A: Shoots 3 times in 100 armed confrontations, or a .03 shooting rate

Officer B: Shoots 2 times in 10 armed confrontations, or a .20 shooting rate

Officer C: Shoots 1 time in 3 armed confrontations, or a .33 shooting rate of armed confrontations faced: The first officer fires at a .03 rate (3/100); a second officer fires at a .20 rate (or 2/10); and a third officer fires at a .33 rate (or 1/3). These examples make clear that judging an officer's propensity to shoot must be done not only in terms of the numerator (shots fired) but in terms of the denominator (number of armed confrontations) as well.

There is a major problem in operationalizing this ratio, however. The denominator for a particular officer is very difficult to determine. There are simply no systematic records of armed confrontations. The number of times an opponent is faced with a weapon or, more meaningfully, the number of times an officer believes an opponent might have a weapon, is, in effect, unknown. But even if the figures for the denominators were available, the obtained ratios would not provide the full answer.

As we observed in Chapter Five, early actions and decisions by the police officer—the way he interprets information, engages the opponent, and communicates information to him—may increase or decrease the number of armed confrontations the officer faces. For example, an officer who frequently stops his car while off duty to check out suspicious persons in his neighborhood will almost inevitably have a higher armed confrontation rate than will an officer who remains oblivious to all but the most blatant criminal activities seen in off-duty circumstances. An important difficulty, then, in the officer shooting ratio construct is that the denominator is a function of the activity level of the officer. It will be large for an aggressive officer and small for an officer who avoids dangerous situations except when there is no other choice.

Incidentally, it should be noted that various indirect procedures have been used to estimate contact or hazard rates. Various investigators have used such indexes as violent crime rates, felony arrests, and murder rates to serve as indicators of hazard or contact.[1] These are, of course, all encompassing statistics that may conceal important differences in actual hazard. A particular officer, for example, might confront more criminals determined to shoot their way to freedom, although his felony arrest rate is identical to that of another officer. And the quality and implications of violent crime rates, felony arrests, and so forth vary considerably among cities and even precincts within a city.

Although it is difficult to ascertain an officer's (or department's) precise armed confrontation rate, it appears, when estimates of armed confrontations are accounted for, that wide differences in officer shooting rates exist. Officer Jones, for example, may have encountered 20 armed confrontations and fired in 7 of them. Both Officers Sullivan and Dorsett apparently have encountered at least several hundred armed confrontations and have only one shot between them. How, we might ask, do we explain these differences in the individual propensity to shoot? What competencies do the nonshooting officers possess that make them able to cope effectively with numerous and possibly extremely difficult and dangerous armed confrontations, and rarely fire.

To explore these issues we will look at four psychological dimensions related to the police officer's use of deadly force: the control of human emotions; the discrimination of real and apparent events in shooting confrontations; interpersonal, physical, and weapons skills; and moral judgments regarding the decision to shoot. We will hypothesize and demonstrate (but certainly not prove) the following relationships:

1. That officers with poor emotional control, inability to perceive events accurately in rapidly occurring encounters, poor skills, and primitive moral judgments will be more likely to shoot than will other officers (of course, controlling for contact rates).
2. That the above capacities may bear upon decision making in both the early phases of the encounter (see Chapter Four) and in the final frame.
3. That these competencies may be said to interact in that a deficiency in one area may make other competencies more difficult to implement—a frightened officer may be unlikely to use his demonstrated interpersonal skills in a terror-inducing encounter.
4. That the ability to cope in an armed confrontation requires a high level of skill in each of these four areas, and that training and experience might increase these competencies, thus making inappropriate uses of deadly force less likely.

Human Emotions and the Decision to Use Deadly Force

Human emotions reflect a central psychological dimension related to police use of deadly force. In a single encounter, an officer may feel terror, fear, sympathy, shame, and horror. Clearly, the ability to monitor appropriately such emotions may bear heavily upon the final outcome of the episode.

Sympathy or abhorrence toward the opponent may be an important factor in determining how long an officer will wait out a particular ambiguous (not immediately or certainly life-threatening) provocation. One officer described an encounter with a knife-wielding insane man as follows:

> When I go to this 5-50 [mentally disturbed person call] I meet this woman who tells me her son is crazy and is from Central State Hospital and begs me not to hurt him. I must have backed off three full city blocks trying not to hurt that lady more than she's been hurt.

Another officer described a situation where he had a report that a man had a loaded shotgun under a beach towel:

> A citizen tells us there's this guy over here with a shotgun. We go to check it out and there's this older Hispanic man with what looks like a gun under this towel. D. and I yell "put it down, put it down," but he's real drunk. He doesn't understand. Finally we take the towel off and see it's a machete he's keeping for self-protection. I think it was his eyes. He didn't look like a bad guy. I kind of liked him; I think if he acted a bit different, who knows?

In other episodes a lack of empathy may influence, if not actually determine, the officer's decision to shoot:

> There was this "B and E" in an old woman's house. This addict took this old lady's sewing machine that she used to make clothes with for the people in the neighborhood. It was like a piece of her was stolen by the guy. I was so mad. When we finally found him, and he died, I was thinking more about that lady and less about him. After it was over the lady didn't want to know about the guy (even though there was an ambulance), but rather just grabbed her sewing machine and hugged it like a child.

Obviously, a particularly important emotion is fear. Officers who have been involved in deadly force situations frequently describe them as "hair-raising," "spooky," "terrorizing," or "insane"; they portray their own reactions as ranging from "sheer terror" to a "calm panic." These emotions obviously make deliberate decision making difficult. One officer noted that he almost went into shock, believing that "this was it, I might really die." Some officers will even show extreme physical reactions to the emotional stress of the shooting situation. A young black officer, for example, described to us his response in a situation where he "came within a hair" of killing a paraplegic man armed with a loaded shotgun:

> It all started when _____ and I had gone Code 7 [stopped for dinner]. A guy came from out of the chicken place and said, "There is a guy in

the back of the parking lot." I went through the restaurant while _____ went around the side. I see this guy in a wheelchair with a shotgun. I pulled my revolver out of my holster, not sure what to think. My heart is pounding, "Can I kill a cripple?" I tell the guy to drop his gun. He doesn't do anything but slowly turns towards me. . . . Finally he dropped his gun. He was a little snockered, but wasn't going to kill nobody. When I sat down to eat I had to put a napkin over my pants to cover the urine. It was fear!

Rubinstein quoted an officer involved in his first shooting as saying, "These two guys [involved in a holdup] come running out and they shot at me. I pulled my gun but, honest, my arm was shaking so bad that I couldn't hold it steady."[2]

Then there is the emotional response of unrealistic detachment. A female officer, who froze when a man pulled a gun at her, said that "it was like time standing still. It wasn't real." This type of response to a shooting episode closely approximates that in military combat or a civilian catastrophe. In this component of what is called a "traumatic reaction," the person's emotions become detached from what is immediately happening to him or her. The person becomes unreasonably objective. Events seem to be observed by another person. One officer, faced with a shotgun-wielding escaped murderer, described his experience: "I thought about my wife who was sick at the time. It was like the seconds were hours." Another officer similarly said: "When I heard a voice behind me say, 'Eat it cop,' and heard the shot it was like I was in the movies. I didn't believe it was real until I somehow jumped through a window and started shooting."

As we pointed out in Chapter Four, early events in the encounter may influence the emotions of both the officer and the citizen. Toch,[3] Westley,[4] and Muir[5] have suggested that some potentially violent police transactions with civilians "escalate" in affective pitch, mutual hostility, and danger. They imply that such violence-inducing transactions are perhaps most common in social situations where the civilian may be psychologically construed as "the enemy"—common, of course, in police-citizen transactions in racially polarized and economically divided communities. Toch argues that at least some armed confrontations begin with either a nonverbal or verbal evocative communication, which gradually leads to open hostility and possibly the death of or injury to the citizen or the police officer.[6] Such transactions, according to this perspective, create in the officer a psychological state wherein he is increasingly angered, frightened, threatened, terrorized, and humiliated. For these cumulatively debilitating emotions, some individuals may find violence a tempting release.

Certain types of confrontation are viewed by police officers as possessing a high risk of emotional escalation. One police office shared with us his reaction to a near shooting at a Hispanic wedding celebration:

> I was called to this Chicago wedding . . . (things always start there). All of a sudden, after we told them to shut up . . . this heavy asshole comes over, pours wine on me and calls me a motherfucking "cuerpo" [pig]. I pull out my gun and say to myself, if these cocksuckers don't back off, I'm taking some of them with me. Luckily the backup team got there just as I'm getting agitated.

Hatred in itself is often a key emotion in armed confrontations. Although few officers will actually kill out of pure anger, often there is a point where the angry, sometimes brutal, side of human nature may be revealed in even the seemingly most mild-mannered police officers. Rubinstein suggests:

> Very few policemen use physical force gratuitously. A man will cajole, joke, advise, threaten, and counsel rather than hit, but once his right to act is questioned, once his autonomy is threatened, he is prepared to respond with whatever force is necessary. . . . The policeman who says, "If some bastard hurts me, I'm not gonna just win, I'm gonna get even, and he's gonna know I hurt," is expressing a thought that violates the law, but one that cannot be eliminated because the law allows policemen to treat alleged criminals differently from people who are not criminals.[7]

Such feelings of hatred are usually directed at criminals who threaten either the officer or his partner. After capturing three teenaged black males who had robbed a 50-year-old woman and then pointed a gun at an officer, an older black officer told them in no uncertain terms: "What I hate most of all is wise-ass niggers who don't respect life and law and property. I want to do you little motherfuckers in." Another officer, just after wounding a man who had shot at him, indignantly told the lieutenant investigating the incident, "What do you expect me to do. The motherfucker shot at me. The motherfucking, cocksucking bastard shot at me!"

The hatred a police officer may feel toward individuals who are perceived as threats to his life is no small consideration in a psychological understanding of police use of deadly force. The charged emotions of any potential shooting confrontation can lead to actions and responses that, while not rational, are readily understandable responses to the provocation. Wambaugh, in *The New Centurions*, describes an episode in which a young Chicago officer, Serge Duran, has his life threatened by a juvenile gang member:

"They're bailing out!" Milton shouted and Serge looked up to see the Chevrolet skidding to a stop in the middle of Soto Street as all four doors were flung open.

"The one in the right rear fired the shot. Get him!" Milton yelled as Serge was running in the street before the radio car finished the jolting sliding stop.

Several passing cars slammed on brakes as Serge chased the *Rojo* in the brown hat and yellow Pendleton shirt down Sota and east on Wabash. Serge was utterly unaware that he had run two blocks at top speed when suddenly the air scorched his lungs and his legs turned weak, but they were still running through the darkness. He had lost his baton and his hat, and the flashlight fluttering in his swinging left hand lighted nothing but empty sidewalk in front of him. Then his man was gone. Serge stopped and scanned the street frantically. The street was quiet and badly lit. He heard nothing but his outraged thudding heart and the sawing breaths that frightened him. He heard a barking dog close to his left, and another, and a crash in the rear yard of a rundown yellow frame house behind him. He turned off the flashlight, picked a yard farther west and crept between two houses. When he reached the rear of the house he stopped, listened, and crouched down. The first dog, two doors away, had stopped barking, but the other in the next yard was snarling and yelping as though he was bumping against a taut chain. The lights were going on and Serge waited. He jerked his gun out as the figure appeared from the yard gracefully with a light leap over the wooden fence. He was there in the driveway silhouetted against the whitewashed background of the two-car garage like the paper man on this pistol range, and Serge was struck with the thought that he was no doubt a juvenile and should not be shot under any circumstances but defense of your life. Yet he decided quite calmly that this *Rojo* was not getting another shot at Serge Duran, and he cocked the gun which did not startle the dark figure who . . . was in the intense beam of the five-cell. Serge had already taken up the slack of the fleshy padding of the right index finger and this *Rojo* would never know that only a microscopic layer of human flesh over unyielding finger bone kept the hammer from falling as Serge exerted perhaps a pound of pull on the trigger of the cocked revolver which was pointed at the stomach of the boy.

"Freeze," Serge breathed, watching the hands of the boy and deciding that if they moved, if they moved at all. . . .

"Don't! Don't," said the boy, who stared at the beam, but stood motionless, one foot turned to the side, as in a clumsy stop-action camera shot. "Oh, don't," he said and Serge realized he was creeping forward in a duck walk, the gun extended in front of him. He also realized how much pressure he was exerting on the trigger and he always wondered why the hammer had not fallen.

"Just move," Serge whispered, as he circled the quivering boy and moved in behind him, the flashlight under his arm as he patted the *Rojo* down for the gun that had made the orange flash.

"I don't got a weapon," said the boy.

"Shut your mouth," said Serge, teeth clenched, and as he found no gun his stomach began to loosen a bit and breathing evened.

Serge handcuffed the boy carefully behind his back, tightening the iron until the boy winced. He uncocked and holstered the gun and his hand shook so badly that for a second he almost considered holstering the gun still cocked because he was afraid the hammer might slip while he uncocked it.

"Let's go," he said, finally, shoving the boy ahead of him.

When they got to the front street, Serge saw several people on the porches, and two police cars were driving slowly from opposite directions, spotlights flashing, undoubtedly looking for him.

Serge shoved the boy into the street and when the beam of the first spotlight hit them the radio car accelerated and jerked to a stop in front of them.

Ruben Gansalvez was the passenger officer, and he ran around the car throwing open the door on the near side.

"This the one who fired at you?" he asked.

"You prove it, *puto*," the boy said, grinning now in the presence of the other officers and the three or four onlookers who were standing on porches, as dogs for three blocks howled and barked at the siren of the help car which had raced code three to their aid.

Serge grasped the boy by the neck, bent his head and shoved him in the back seat, crawling in beside him and forcing him to the right side of the car.

"Tough now that you got your friends, ain't you, *pinchi jura*," said the boy and Serge tightened the iron again until the boy sobbed, "You dirty motherfucking cop."

"Shut your mouth," said Serge.

"*Chingra tu madre*," said the boy.

"I should have killed you."

"*Tu madre*."

And then Serge realized he was squeezing the hard rubber grips of the Smith & Wesson. He was pressing the trigger guard and he remembered the way he felt when he had the boy in his sights, the black shadow who had almost ended him at age twenty-four when his entire life was ahead.[8]

The passage suggests some of the powerful, and ugly, emotions that may be vented at a suspect during a violent encounter. It also indicates how a particular type of suspect might produce an especially powerful response on the part of the police officer. Rubinstein describes a similar incident where an officer was disarmed by a man who shot at him, although he later was able to wrestle the suspect to the ground.

> "We were rolling around, you know, and he still had the gun and I was holding on to his hand so he couldn't shoot me. I was biting him on the face and kicking, my mouth was filling up with his blood and he was screaming. When he gave up, I just stood there holding my gun and I really wanted to kill him. I did, but I just couldn't shoot. I smashed him with the butt."[9]

Such responses by police officers might be exacerbated by events that occurred immediately preceding the armed confrontation. A fight with one's wife, a drunk throwing up on one's shirt, financial problems, or other tensions might create a climate of temporary emotional "risk" for the officer. One California officer, for example, who had recently buried his mother, angrily pummeled a citizen who, during a liquor store dispute, called him a "motherfucker." Also, a long shift of heated confrontations (especially where there is a death of an officer) may find an entire squad, precinct, or even department with badly frayed nerves.

Specific preludes to a potential shooting episode may increase the likelihood of a heated emotional response by the officer. High-speed chases are infamous among police officers in this respect. Often a chase will last for many minutes and miles, posing great risk to the officers as well as citizens; simply following a speeding car for several miles can be unnerving in itself. A sergeant described the aftermath of one chase as follows:

> Well, we was following this guy through at least six towns . . . up into LA County, down again into Orange County. We had three cars from our PD involved, and two from _____. Anyway, finally this kid crashes into a big RV on the street after they had gone more than 20 miles. I get to the scene and I see the officers roughin' him up, you know, smacking him with nightsticks, hitting his ribs. I decided to let them get it out. If I tried to stop them, next time they might kill the guy before I get there.

Calls just prior to an armed confrontation might seriously affect an officer's attitude and emotional state during the confrontation itself. For example, one officer who had witnessed a brutal beating of a family just moments before being dispatched to a "shots-fired" call involving the same suspects, and the call resulted in a fatality. Often a "crazy job" in which an officer must respond to a "man with a gun," "an armed robber," "a DOA," or "shots-fired" call may seriously affect his emotional equilibrium in a subsequent armed confrontation. Supervisors say that the last two hours of a difficult shift may find men in an extremely vulnerable psychological state. One sergeant in a high-crime urban police department commented:

> I don't know how to put it, but by midnight on Saturday night, I've got a bunch of lunatics out there. They tell the dispatchers to go fuck themselves if they don't like the job. They are hungry, are thinking about getting laid in a few hours, and really don't give a fuck about anything. If we don't have enough supervisors out there (and that's usually the case) watch out.

Thus, the role of emotions in a heated armed confrontation is an important factor to consider in some shooting decisions by police officers. This factor is ignored in many discussions of police use of deadly force. Just as it is misleading to pretend that warfare is conducted by soldiers dutifully and stoically facing death (and rationally deciding to kill the enemy), so too is it misleading to fail to understand that the police officer, as a human being, may be terrified in a potential shooting confrontation.

Common responses to this terror might be anger, hatred, and a desire to humiliate the opponent. (Alternatively, as discussed earlier, some officers may show greater compassion or empathy for some opponents as opposed to others.) On occasion, bizarre (and sometimes tragic) outcomes are explained on the basis of the intense emotions. An off-duty officer mistakenly shot and killed his wife who was being fondled by a robber/molester; in another encounter an excited officer shot his own windshield, which he neglected to notice was in the line of fire in a car-to-car shooting exchange. Such errors would be less likely were not the emotional demands of armed confrontations so extreme, or if the officers involved were under better control in the most extreme of human encounters.

Distinguishing Appearance from Reality
in Armed Confrontations

A related psychological factor is the factual ambiguity implicit in armed confrontations and the officer's ability to define objective reality in a heated and rapidly occurring confrontation. In rapidly evolving shooting incidents, what is believed true may not appear later in fact to be true. Many errors in the use of deadly force may be related to the inability to define accurately the facts of the shooting encounter. The majority of shooting situations occur at night under conditions in which it is very difficult to distinguish appearances from reality.[10] One suburban patrolman described to us the following episode:

> A guy and a woman robbed a _____ store in _____. An officer told the guy to stop, and the guy told the gal to get along; so we chased them up the freeway. I followed the pursuit. The pursuit got off the freeway. They went right in front of me! I heard on the radio "245b—_____"— this officer. This means assault with a deadly weapon on an officer. Everyone assumed that meant they shot at him—that they were armed and dangerous. Later I found out that what happened was that he rammed his car, which is also assault. They got in front of me. I got involved in the pursuit. I got along outside, and I rolled down the window. I was about to shoot. I noticed the driver was a woman. I say to myself, if I see a gun coming, I shoot. I also noticed that her fender was busted. She couldn't get over 50 mph. The rubber was tearing at the wheel. . . . Finally we ran 'em off; no one gets hurt, shot. It's funny. I almost shot thinking that they had a gun.

This confusion as to what Thomas calls the "definition of the situation"[11] is compounded by the reality that many officers involved in shooting episodes are in a heightened state of emotional turmoil. Even though an officer may respond appropriately to a confrontation, he may only have the vaguest conception of the actual facts facing him. Postshooting interviews often reveal important differences between the events reported by the shooting officer and the facts that are later established to have occurred. For example, one officer reported five shots being fired in an incident that actually saw more than 30 exchanges of gunfire. A decorated officer who had been involved in a shooting episode described ironically how he had "pulled a Wyatt Earp" (shot the gun out of a suspect's hand): "There were these two 'hypes.' They came towards me about 15 feet apart with what looked like '22's.' I instinctively fired. My heart was going crazy. I got a medal for shooting the gun out. I only told a few people that I was really shooting at the other guy. I really didn't see exactly what happened."

Another officer commented, in retrospect, about how a confused situation, rapid time perspective, and heightened emotions created a situation where he almost shot a fellow plainclothes officer:

> There was a situation where a guy was shot. Officer B says, "Hey, there's a guy been shot," and calls for help. He says, "I don't know if the suspect is still in the house or not." Everyone who was working was there. (Later he found out the guy had shot himself because of his ex-wife.) A lady comes from next door yelling, "There's a man in my backyard. He's wearing a blue shirt and he's got a gun." We've got shotguns cocked and loaded . . . and I almost shot . . . but it turns out it's a plainclothes officer from another P.D. who's answered the call.

Factual confusion in armed confrontation might be related to the fact that police officers, according to several studies,[12] hit only a small percentage of the people they shoot at. Estimates of the shots-fired to person-hit ratio vary from 1:6 to 1:2 of all shots fired at human targets. This is especially interesting in that we find numerous examples of officers missing several shots from distances as close as seven to ten feet. One officer described a shooting after a Molotov cocktail was thrown during a riot in the 1960s at a group of six officers standing on a streetcorner. The officers fired more than 20 shots at the man, *all* of which missed. Another officer fired five shots at a man standing less than six feet from him, missing with every shot!

The confused factual context of an armed confrontation at times will have tragic implications, as was the case with intense emotional response. Officers will in fact make shooting decisions based on what they believe to be true, which, of course, may prove quite different from what in fact is true. The following article from the *New York Times*, dealing with a shooting among out-of-uniform officers, provides an example of the consequences mistaken perceptions play in a shooting situation:

Woman Slain in Gun Fight Between Off-Duty Officers

> A 24-year-old woman was fatally wounded early yesterday in the East New York section of Brooklyn when caught in the crossfire between a Housing Authority officer and a Correction Department officer who were exchanging shots because of a dual case of mistaken identity, the police said. Both off-duty officers were wearing street clothes at the time.

The shooting started when the correction officer saw a housing patrolman standing gun in hand over a man and a woman and apparently mistook him for a robber. The woman had been arguing with the officer about trying to get her car out of a parking space.

The victim of the shooting was Maria Pellot of 749 Franklin D. Roosevelt Drive. She was killed in a parking area at Pitkin Avenue and Crescent Street as she stood near her car. She had been visiting friends in the area.

The two officers involved in the gun battle, in which nine shots were exchanged, were Housing Officer James Gibson, 31 years old, and Correction Officer Robert Johnson, 26. Detective John Britt, who was passing at the time—shortly before 1 A.M.—halted the shooting and disarmed the two men.

As Detective Britt later reported, the other officers were crouching behind cars when approached.

He said that he had drawn his gun, and showing his police shield to Officer Gibson, asked him to stop shooting. But the officer kept firing. Detective Britt said that he then approached Officer Johnson and persuaded him to cease shooting. Then he and Officer Johnson, shouting to Officer Gibson, convinced him that they were officers and got him to desist.

Mrs. Pellot was taken to Brookdale Hospital where she died of a bullet wound in the stomach.

Officers Gibson and Johnson were questioned at the Sutter Avenue police station and released pending further investigation. An autopsy is to be performed on the woman, and a ballistic test will be made to determine whose weapon had fired the fatal shot. A loaded .25-caliber automatic was found at the scene of the shooting.

The incident started when Mrs. Pellot tried to get her car out of parking space and found it was blocked by Officer Gibson's double-parked automobile.

Officer Gibson, who lives nearby, saw her and went to his apartment to get his car keys so that he could move his vehicle. When he returned, he saw Mrs. Pellot hitting his car with a pipe in frustration.

The officer tried to take the pipe from the woman. A passerby saw the struggle, went to Mrs. Pellot's aid and punched Officer Gibson in the face. The officer then drew his service revolver and said he was going to arrest them.

At this juncture, Officer Johnson—on a passing bus—saw Officer Gibson holding his gun over the man and Mrs. Pellot. Officer Johnson got off the bus and fired. The two men, unaware that the other was an officer, then started their gun battle. The pedestrian fled.[13]

An episode described in Chapter Four from Los Angeles similarly involved a tragic and mistaken perception of reality. Two Los Angeles police officers were protecting a murder witness when a 15-year-old boy hurdled the fence into the yard of the witness. The homicide investigator for the department related the shooting to the fact "that the officer was blinded by floodlights from a nearby apartment building," leading the officers to believe that he was attacking the witness. According to the LAPD press release:

> The subject (young Washington) climbed atop the fence ... and was apparently preparing to jump into the yard when he was observed by the Metropolitan Division officers. Officer Holland identified himself as a Los Angeles police officer and ordered the subject to "freeze." He failed to comply, jumped from the fence into the yard and started to turn toward the officers. Based upon the subject's surreptitious entry into the yard, the officers believed that he was armed and would attempt to accost the witness. Officer Holland fired three rounds from his service revolver, fatally wounding the subject in the head.[14]

Another case of mistaken identity occurred in East Los Angeles, involving the slaying by the police of a non–English-speaking Mexican man who had taken a toy plastic gun out of the garbage can and was carrying it home to his children. After he failed to obey an order to stop by two officers, he was killed. Similar confusion might be illustrated by a case where a hostage was shot because a SWAT team officer confused him with one of his captors. Another tragic incident involved a suburban police officer who was called to a "burglary in progress" in the home garage of a carpenter. As he approached the open garage he saw a man with a long "pointed" object. He called to the man "to freeze." The man turned toward the officer. The officer fired three shots, almost fatally wounding the man. The wounded man turned out to be the homeowner, who was carrying a tire iron while chasing a group of teenagers who had burglarized his garage. Fyfe described an incident where a New York police officer killed two armed Puerto Rican males who were seen standing with pistols above a young well-dressed black boy. Subsequent analysis showed that the men he killed were the owners of a "bodega" that had just been robbed by the boy who the officer presumed to be their innocent victim. The boy, who was arrested, was later discovered to have been pointing a small revolver at the two men who were trying to hold him at bay.[15]

Even under the best of circumstances it is difficult for the most experienced officers to distinguish fully facts from images. An officer will commonly believe an opponent is firing at him when other officers behind him are in reality firing at the opponent. In the dark, cigarette lighters may appear to be pistols; a man reaching for his ID may look as though he is reaching for a weapon.

An interesting issue in this respect involves the relationship of cultural differences to mistaken perceptions. Perceptions are influenced by the set with which a situation is approached, and different kinds of people produce different sets in officers. A person of a given minority group may appear more dangerous than a middle-class Caucasian in similar circumstances. Similarly, the time of day or week, culturally defined body language (for example patterns of gesturing), and even dress might have a significant impact upon the officer's subjective assessment of the danger of a particular encounter, and that set could affect perception.

It should be noted, as well, that there are numerous cases of "misreading" social reality that result in jeopardy or death to the misperceiving police officer. One officer we interviewed soon after a shooting described how he spent several seconds in a dangerous situation attempting to decide if a man behind him was a fellow officer just "fooling with him": "I was on patrol in _____ looking in an alley on a reported 459 [burglary]. I didn't see anything and started back to the car. All of a sudden, I heard this guy behind me say, 'Freeze, copper,' from behind this fence. I didn't believe it at all. It wasn't like real. When I heard a cap go off I decided it was for real and dove in some bushes." Another officer refused to shoot a man who shot twice at him because he wasn't sure the "gun was real." The weapon later turned out to be quite real, a .38-caliber revolver that had misfired. Another officer was shot when he walked into a middle-class neighborhood and "missed" a very real gun in the hands of a housewife.

Police communication techniques, as discussed in Chapter Four, may contribute to the often mistaken social perceptions of the officer faced with a decision to use deadly force. Dispatch calls may suggest extremely misleading appraisals of potential suspects. At times a dispatcher will refer to a getaway car brushing a police car as "assault on a police officer with a deadly weapon." Other departments will transmit a "man with a gun" call to an officer without qualifying the source of the information. In some cities, suspect descriptions will be extremely vague, fitting literally hundreds of persons. Also, officers may be lulled by dispatched information, which they might downplay or even dismiss. The following is an illustration:

At about that night we had arrested three people for "false reporting." What they were doing was calling "man with a gun" because they felt that was the only way they were going to get service. One woman, believe it or not, was a schoolteacher who wanted medical help for her son and called in "man with a gun." Anyway, that night we get our fifth, I said fifth "man with a gun" call. We are ho-humming it up the Colonnade Apartments elevator, just jiving, us and a team from East. Anyway the door opens and we nearly shit seeing this guy with a gun. That taught me something.

It would seem reasonable to hypothesize that there exist psychological differences among individual officers' ability to perceive and interpret information and effectively act on it. They themselves believe that some officers have almost an uncanny ability to recognize and accurately assess dangerous situations (as was illustrated by the case of a nonshooting officer earlier). One officer described another as possessing "antennae that other guys didn't even know were there." Another officer was described as "being able to see things you or I never would. Like we are passing a bus station and he sees something that looked like a bulge in this old guy's pants. We pass the guy, walk up on him and whammo, a loaded .45. I never saw nothing." Other officers are similarly noted for "having tunnel vision," or, as one commanding officer suggested, "seeing only what they want to see." One officer, he said, "became so fixated on a pistol held by a man he confronted in a tavern that he failed to observe the detective shield the man held in his other hand." Luckily his partner disarmed him before he shot the detective, who was holding an armed robber at bay.

The role of officer perceptions in coping with armed confrontations seems to be an important area for future research. What percentage of shootings, we might ask, result from erroneous (even if reasonable) interpretations of situations? It also seems important to determine if some officers more quickly and accurately identify ambiguous perceptions than do others. Does, for example, heavy contact with armed confrontations increase an officer's ability to recognize important cues in subsequent violent encounters? It also seems important to investigate new training models that would effectively train officers in rapid and accurate assessments of the ambiguous "facts" encountered in armed confrontations.

Clearly, the factual ambiguity of many shooting situations may increase the emotional anxiety of the officer, just as the fact that the officer might be afraid or even terrorized, and this state may reduce the probability that he will be able accurately to distinguish fact from image in a rapidly occurring armed confrontation.

Interpersonal, Physical, and Weapons Skills and the Police Decision to Use Deadly Force

Negotiating skills are essential for avoiding deadly force in confrontations that include prolonged social interaction between the citizen and police officers. And such confrontations are far from rare. Milton et al. found that 32 percent of shooting deaths occurred in response to domestic disturbance incidents, which typically involve extended discussions.[16]

In addition, officers, through clear, nonambiguous commands are often able to avoid the types of encounters that escalate into armed confrontations. It is quickly established that the officer is "for real" so that limits are not tested by the citizen. One officer with no shooting incidents in 11 years claims that he has been successful in potential dangerous encounters because he has a calm, clear voice that "tells the other guy I would just as soon kill him as not" (see our earlier illustration of the forcefulness of George Sullivan).

There is some evidence that it is possible to improve by training the negotiating skills and command presence of officers. Bard's analysis of a New York City police crisis intervention team indicates that the range of behavior repertoires available to officers might be increased.[17] The police were encouraged to develop their own style of coping, guided by their perceptions of the citizen. Research evidence indicated that the response repertoires of the officers expanded along with the officers' sense of mastery in coping with disputes. A similar project in Connecticut documented an increased rate of officers' successfully coping with family disputes.[18] In this study, 18 trained officers encountered 1,388 disturbances without a shooting incident or officer injury. Studies reported by Driscoll[19] and Helb[20] found greatly lowered violence rates among officers trained in crisis intervention techniques and strategies.

Some officers seem to develop a successful style of dispute management without formal training. Muir, in his *Police: Streetcorner Politicians*, describes an officer who was noted for his ability to resolve family disturbances and similar conflicts peacefully. This officer rarely found it necessary to use physical force in even the most violent disputes:

Joe Wilkes realized that any chance for long-run pacification of a family squabble depended upon the family members' reattaching themselves to those friendships, traditions, and concerns which they felt were important.

So in a family beef, Joe Wilkes talked. "My own personality is to talk," he said. He articulated a perspective of hope for the husband and wife: "We talk about his possibilities—about everything he had possibilities for." . . . He tried to expand their self-interest, what he called their "ego" and what others referred to as pride or dignity.[21]

A young California officer described to us how he disarmed a psychotic and suicidal woman:

> It was a slow night. We got a "925"—suicide in progress—call in a seedy motel. We go to the door. There's this filthy woman sitting on the bed with a gun. She is obviously a "total looney tune." She says she is going to shoot. The sergeant says, "Let's go get her." I say, "Come on, she's crazy." I go in and start talking. I look right at her eyes, talking slow. Then it dawns on me. She's lonely and needs someone to take care of. I say, "I'm really nervous, could you give me a cigarette?" She does. A minute later she lets me sit on the bed. Soon I ask for her gun, "for safekeeping." She gives it to me.

Numerous instances occur where imagination, humor, guile, and poise averted the use of deadly force. For example, another officer subdued an armed and large (and obviously extremely paranoid) man by opening the door of his police car and telling the man, "Hey, look, you can hide from them in here. Duck down, they won't see you here." The man huddled in the car until backup officers arrived. A Honolulu staff sergeant said that the extremely low shooting rate in his city was in part attributable to the fact that in Polynesian culture it is considered unmanly to resolve conflicts by deadly force when guile, physical (but nonlethal) force, or cunning could do the job as well. "It is more macho here," he said, "to knock him physically on his ass or to bullshit him out of it." An officer in Southern California was observed by one of the authors when he and a younger officer were told to respond to a call that 11 Samoans with knives were going after their landlord. There had been a dispute with the landlord over the rent. The younger officer drew his weapon as he left the car to approach the young men. "Put it away," the older officer said. "How many bullets you got?" he asked his younger partner. "Six," was the reply. "Well, we won't be needing those then!" As he left the car the older man yelled to the Samoans using a few key Samoan phrases, "What's going on here?" The men told him of their complaint and offered to "put away their knives." They disbanded without incident.

The techniques used by officers to avoid violent citizen encounters are almost as varied as the personalities of officers. One officer, known for escaping "hairy" incidents without violence, said he had "joked" more guns out of people's hands than he could remember. An eastern city police officer described a situation in which he approached a juvenile with a gun, taking it out of his hand by saying, "You ain't old enough for the draft yet, wait a year." Another officer disarmed a "huge, insane gorilla-type guy" with a knife by convincing him that he "would hold his knife for him so the cops wouldn't find it." An officer in another eastern city marched up to the door of a gun-wielding insane suspect who had barricaded himself with a hostage, and demanded a "cold beer." When he was led to the refrigerator he disarmed the suspect.

Often, physical skills are important. An officer who can physically control an opponent may, in some circumstances, avoid a level of threat that would warrant the use of deadly force. Speed in apprehending a suspect, in cuffing him, and in getting him into the police car may thus avoid some escalated armed confrontations. In Honolulu, all police officers receive substantial training in effective (and difficult to learn) martial arts techniques. Sometimes even a "fatherly" vigorous arm can control a potentially dangerous citizen.

Conversely, in many departments some officers are known for their ability to unnecessarily escalate minor disputes into major altercations. One officer was described by another officer as "pissing people off regardless of race, nationality, religion, or political creed." Dispatchers in this city were under standing orders to route this officer away from any "major problems." At rollcall the captain told this officer, "X, you must love getting your shirt ripped off. You do it all of the time." In one month, Officer X managed to beat up a child molester, wrestle with a drunk in a parking lot, and provoke a hopeless fight with six sailors on leave. Later, X's sergeant explained that "X was an expert" in magically turning parking tickets into riots.

Wambaugh offers a marvelous example of this type of officer in his description of Roscoe Rules, one of the characters in *The Choir Boys*. In one incident the hapless Rules and his partner Whaddayamean Dean, whose favorite sport was to get "scrotes" (virtually any citizen) to "do the chicken" by choking them with various and sundry chokeholds, managed to create a major battle with two hod carriers. The two policemen confronted the hod carriers, one black, one Chicano, while they were involved in a relatively minor disagreement:

"I think we can quiet them down," Whaddayamean Dean said as Roscoe stood on one foot like a blue flamingo, rubbing his toe hopelessly on the calf of his left leg.

"Can I talk to you?" Whaddayamean Dean asked the Mexican, walking him to the other end of the hall while Roscoe Rules hustled the silent black thirty feet down the stairway.

"I don't want no more trouble outta you," Roscoe whispered when he got the hod carrier to a private place. "I ain't gonna give you no trouble, officer," the black man said looking up at the mirthless blue eyes of Roscoe Rules which were difficult to see because, like most hotdogs, he wore his cap tipped forward until the brim almost touched his nose.

"Don't argue with me, man!" Roscoe said. His nostrils splayed as he sensed the fear on the man who stood hangdog before him. . . .

"What's your name?" Roscoe then demanded. "Charles ar-uh Henderson," the hod carrier answered, and then added impatiently, "Look, I wanna go back inside with my family, I'm tired of all this and I just wanna go to bed. I worked hard. . . ."

But Roscoe became enraged at the latent impudence and snarled, "Look here, Charles ar-uh Henderson, don't you be telling me what you're gonna do. I'll tell you when you can go back inside and maybe you won't be going back inside at all. Maybe you're gonna be going to the slam tonight!"

"What for? I ain't done nothin'. What right you got . . . ."

"Right? Right?" Roscoe snarled, spraying the hod carrier with saliva. "Man, one more word and I'm gonna book your ass! I'll personally lock you in the slammer! I'll set your hair on fire."

Whaddayamean Dean called down to Roscoe and suggested that they switch hod carriers. As soon as they had, he tried in vain to calm the outraged black man.

A few minutes later he heard Roscoe offer some advice to the Mexican hod carrier: "If that loudmouth bitch was my old lady I'd kick her in the cunt."

Twenty years ago the Mexican had broken a full bottle of beer over the head of a man for merely smiling at his woman. Twenty years ago, when she was a lithe young girl with a smooth sensuous belly, he would have shot to death any man, cop or not, who would dare to refer to her as a bitch.

Roscoe Rules knew nothing of *machismo* and did not even sense the slight, almost imperceptible flickering of the left eyelid of the Mexican. Nor did he notice that those burning black eyes were no longer pointed somewhere between the shield and necktie of Roscoe Rules, but were fixed on his face, at the browless blue eyes of the tall police-man.

"Now you two act like men and shake hands so we can leave," Roscoe ordered.

"Huh?" the Mexican said incredulously, and even the black hod carrier looked up in disbelief.

"I said shake hands. Let's be men about this. The fight's over and you'll feel better if you shake hands."

"I'm forty-two years old," the Mexican said softly, the eyelid flick-ering more noticeably. "Almost old enough to be your father. I ain't shaking hands like no kid on a playground."

"You'll do what I say or sleep in the slammer," Roscoe said, remembering how in school everyone felt better and even drank beer after a good fight.

"What charge?" demanded the Mexican, his breathing erratic now. "What fuckin' charge?"

"You both been drinking," Roscoe said, losing confidence in his constituted authority, but infuriated by the insolence which was quickly undermining what he thought was a controlled situation.

Roscoe, like most black-glove cops, believed implicitly that if you ever backed down even for a moment in dealing with assholes and scrotes the entire structure of American law enforcement would crash to the ground in a mushroom cloud of dust. . . .

"You honky motherfucker!" the black hod carrier yelled when he finally exploded. He tossed a straight right at Whaddayamean Dean which caught him on the left temple and knocked him free of the Mex-ican and over the kneeling body of Roscoe Rules who was hoping des-perately he wouldn't puke from the kick in the balls.

Roscoe aimed a spunky blow at the black hod carrier's leg with his unauthorized, thirty-four ounce sap which pulled his pants down when he wasn't careful to keep his Sam Browne buckled tightly.

Hit 'em in the shins. They can't take that, thought Roscoe, swing-ing the sap weakly, relying on folklore to save him now that he could not stand up.

But the hod carrier did not seem to feel the sap bounding off his legs as he and the Mexican took turns punching Whaddayamean Dean silly.

The redhead had lost his baton and gun and was bouncing back and forth between the two men. "Partner! Partnerrrr!" Whaddayamean Dean yelled, but Roscoe Rules could only kneel there, look up in hatred and wish he could shoot the nigger, the spick and his puny partner.

Then Roscoe fell over on his back, nursing his rapidly swelling testicles, spitting foam like a mad dog.

It ended abruptly. There had been men, women, and children screaming, encouraging, cursing gleefully. There had been bodies thudding off the walls, doors slamming. Then silence.

Roscoe Rules and Whaddayamean Dean Pratt were alone in the hallway. Both on the floor, uniforms half torn off, batons, hats, flashlights, guns and notebooks scattered. Whaddayamean Dean lay moaning, draped across an overturned trash can. Roscoe Rules felt his strength returning as he struggled to his feet, keeping his balls in both hands for fear if he dropped them they'd burst like ripe tomatoes.[22]

Although the portrayal of Roscoe Rules is, of course, more caricature than reality, there is truth in Wambaugh's portrayal in that at least some conflicts involving police deadly force are precipitated by heavy-handed and unskilled police interpersonal communications.

Roscoe Rules's "black glove" law enforcement style is by no means the only type of police behavior that may lead to an inordinate number of unnecessary confrontations. One officer, for example, with a very weak self-image (his description) and poor voice control (his supervisor's description) shot three times in situations where citizens failed to recognize his identity as a police officer. Another officer insisted on giving a sidewalk lecture to a man he had just arrested on a narcotics charge (instead of placing his prisoner in the car and driving off). Before he had finished his lecture, a crowd developed to "seize his prisoner." A warning shot was finally fired to disperse the crowd, almost precipitating a full-blown riot. In other instances, failure to cuff a prisoner properly has resulted in shots being used either to fend him off or to recapture him.

It should be noted that officers may be more or less skilled in particular situations. One officer, who had survived several hundred armed arrests while in a tactical unit without firing a shot, became involved in a series of off-duty squabbles that resulted in shots being fired. Conversely, officers who seem to possess unusually effective crisis intervention skills may not have the positioning, shooting, and teamwork skills required to effectively handle such armed confrontations as those encountered in planned narcotics raids.

It might also be noted that the focus upon verbal skills by Bard[23] and others in avoiding the escalation of encounters is perhaps most appropriate to confrontations with unarmed, drunk, insane, or angry persons. These encounters are but a small proportion of armed confrontations faced by police officers and an even smaller proportion of police shootings. Many encounters require sheer physical strength. In the situation described below, an imaginative, and strong, officer was able first to fool the opponent by feigning paralysis and then physically overcome him, thus avoiding an almost certain shooting encounter:

> There was knowledge that a young black male was holding up subway passengers at Norfolk and Orange streets. We decided to stake the place out (two members of the tactical squad, myself and my two partners). It was very cold. We waited and waited. The tactical squad left. We waited some more. Finally, my partners left their positions, came over to me and asked what we were going to do. It was extremely cold and it appeared the suspect was not going to show up. As we stood there talking together, the suspect came bounding down the steps. He was armed and began waving the gun about, covering all of us simultaneously. He asked us to raise our hands. I responded that I was paralyzed and could only raise one arm. (Actually, my hand was on my gun inside my pocket.) As another subway approached the platform, the suspect glanced in its direction. This afforded me the opportunity to draw my weapon, yet I did not shoot for fear that the bullet might ricochet off the steel beam and strike one of my partners. Instead, I wrestled the suspect to the platform (luckily, I was lifting weights and stronger than him), confiscated the gun which, incidentally, he had stolen from another officer earlier. With the aid of my partners, we got the handcuffs on the suspect.

Skills that only tangentially belong in this section are those related to the use of "nonlethal" weapons. Skill with a nightstick, sap, flashlight, chemical shield, or mace can avoid some uses of deadly force. And various new nonlethal weapons show promise of ending a confrontation without a shooting. Several departments have been exploring the use of a "Taser gun," which fires disarming darts into the citizen. The darts penetrate the skin and a stunning electric charge is sent via wires connected to the darts. Los Angeles police personnel recently patented a "leg grabber," useful in certain types of armed confrontations; the device grabs the legs of a person in a viselike manner. Some officers who were involved in the emotionally charged shooting of a psychotic citizen in Los Angeles worked to invent a nonlethal "beanbag stun gun" to control such persons. The technology of these supplementary weapons makes them useful only in certain incidents, usually those involving a citizen not armed with a gun where there is enough time for deliberate police actions.[24]

Paradoxically, perhaps, proficiency and familiarity with lethal weapons might deter some shooting decisions. One very experienced LAPD commander commented: "One of the strange things in this area is that the SWAT team is trained to hit you in the eye from 100 yards, after they have run 100 yards in full equipment, yet they almost never kill anyone." This paradox is documented in many cities where the most proficient SWAT trained officers will confront dozens of violent persons each year and kill no one.

A related paradox may be found in the area of ammunition. The type and effectiveness of ammunition used by a police department may affect the decision to use deadly force by increasing or decreasing the officers' faith that the weapon, if fired, will in fact "stop" an opponent. Some officers commented, for example, that few of them had confidence in the .38 hard point bullet used by several departments, including the Los Angeles Police Department. These officers suggested the possibility that the reason O'Callaghan and Hopson fired their weapons as many times as they did at Eulia Love is because they were not sure that the bullets issued to the department could stop a strong and crazed individual. One officer thought that, had a more potent hollow point bullet been issued, fewer shots would have been fired. He also speculated that the officers might have waited an instant longer if they believed a single shot would have stopped Mrs. Love.

Sheer marksmanship may also paradoxically help an officer avoid certain uses of deadly force. An officer who is a dead-eye shot can (if permitted) fire a warning or "limb" shot, whereas a less skilled man must shoot to kill. One extremely skilled marksman (an officer who has shot "100s" [perfect score] for several consecutive years) described a warning shot as follows: "As he ran I aimed at the center of his head and then moved the target over six inches creasing his scalp. He stopped as soon as he felt that old .38 whistle by." And, it might be recalled, Dan Dorsett, a nonshooter, is an expert marksman.

The level of social, physical, and technical skills of the officer thus may affect the use of deadly force. In some situations, knowledge of and ability in alternative strategies may allow the officer to avoid the use of deadly force. This dimension of skill seems most relevant to an armed confrontation where there is sustained dialogue between citizen and police officer. In other situations, the ability to gain tactical superiority through positioning seems uppermost. Obviously, heightened emotions and the clarity with which the intentions of a perpetrator are defined might greatly affect the level of skill an officer can bring to bear in a given armed confrontation. In this sense, there can be an interactional effect between an officer's level of emotional control, his ability to recognize and act upon objective facts, and his level of interpersonal and physical skill.

Officer Moral Judgment and Police Use of Deadly Force

Another psychological dimension related to police use of deadly force is the moral judgment involved in the decision to shoot. Many officers recognize that the decision to use deadly force represents an explicit moral judgment on their part. One officer commented, "It's like playing God." Another man suggested, "It weighs on you all the time, that you can take someone's life and it would be wrong." The officer described earlier who shot and killed a driver of the fleeing stolen recreational vehicle offered:

> Well, I don't think that anybody else is going to shoot him, and it looks to me that there is only one thing that is going to happen. What are we going to do? Drive off the exit.... He is going to keep killing people ... He's going to hit people ... this thing has got to stop.... I told [other officer], we got to shoot him.... If it was unfair to any-body, it was unfair to us being there.

After a shooting confrontation, some officers often go through long periods of moral deliberation and despair regarding their actions. One older officer described a shooting incident he was involved in more than ten years earlier: "In 1963 I shot a boy who was running away from a Safeway [store]. It was a legal shooting. I even got a medal. Everyone said 'nice shooting, nice shooting,' but it stunk. If I had known what I know now, that young man would be alive today. I didn't see it was wrong, then, but now I do."

Some officers assert their moral responsibility and seem to defend actively the moral rightness of their actions. One officer who shot a fleeing juvenile insisted on viewing the body of the man he had just shot:

> I guess I should. I shot the guy. I just don't want to walk away from it. ... I looked at him and I said that guy is dead.... People were con-cerned about how I felt. "How you feel; how you feel?" I didn't feel bad. Pretty soon I began to wonder—how am I supposed to feel.... I didn't feel bad because I had done my job. Some of the decisions were made because we were the only people there to do it. We couldn't shirk the responsibility. That was to me the reason we were doing them. It was the potential risk to the rest of the people on this freeway, not

because we felt that we just wanted to kill someone, not because if we didn't kill him he was going to kill us. . . . There was that possibility, but that wasn't it. It was the fact that we were put in the position that we had already seen many people being hurt, the potential of death to somebody. All of them who were innocent! That is what we are ready to do. That is what we are called upon to do. That's what we are ready to do. If we backed off again we didn't know how far this thing is going.

Other officers seem far less willing to express their actions in terms of moral responsibility. One officer blamed his actions on "instinct"; another said, "You couldn't hardly see who you were shooting at in that dark"; an officer who killed a fleeing felon commented with seeming black humor, "Well, it saved the county a trial."

Beyond the acceptance of moral responsibility is the issue of when and under what conditions individual officers believe it is morally right to use deadly force. Statistically, as stated above repeatedly, officers shoot in only a small proportion of the situations where they might legally or even dutifully shoot, according to departmental guidelines.

Assuming that moral considerations become more pressing in decision making as one moves closer to the operational context, the set of forces operating on an officer may be conceptualized as in Figure 6.1. The outermost circle represents the broadest set of forces—statute and case law. The next circle represents administrative or departmental policy, which is necessarily no less stringent than law. The third circle, moving inwardly, reflects police informal culture: the practice informally encouraged and allowed. Although this force may, in theory, be no less stringent than law or policy, it is clear that this is not always the case in practice. But where there is that type of discrepancy, there will eventually and necessarily be corrective action by the chief, city officials, the courts, the community, or a combination of the preceding. Finally, the innermost circle represents the conscience, the inner controls of the deciding officer himself. We have given several examples of officers who feel and express a good deal less restraint than police culture, policy, or even law would require; however, we have also pointed out that more generally the greatest restraint comes from the officer himself. That brings to mind a conversation one of us had with an officer regarding the newly implemented, highly restrictive shooting policy for the department in Birmingham, Alabama. To the question, "Are you upset by the new policy?" came the response, "Hell, it doesn't make any difference to me, I'm not going to shoot anyone anyway."

FIGURE 6.1 Circles of Moral Decision Making

Our position is summarized below in the comment of a commander in a police department with a very high citizen-to-citizen murder rate:

> Look, let's face it. If people shot to the limit of when they could shoot there would be bodies all over the place. The department is tougher than the state statutes, and informally, we discourage some aspects of our guidelines in other than the most extreme situations. For example, our guidelines say you can shoot a felon in certain circumstances; but unless it's a murderer or something, you don't do it. But still even under these conditions there are guys who have their own rules. Even if their life is on the line, they are willing to take chances where other guys won't.

Another officer, who had faced several armed confrontations, similarly commented: "I'm willing to go that extra step, that extra mile for a person. That's the way I am. It's not like it's the law; it's a life, that's what it's all about."

Both organizational and individual factors determine the bounds of the inner circle defining the specific circumstances that, for a given officer, justifies the use of deadly force. Uelman and others have suggested that the chief of a particular department may convey to officers a particular moral atmosphere through his pronouncements, guidelines, review decisions, and operating rules governing police officer deadly force.[25] A department, for example, may communicate much about its concern for a citizen's life by the care it takes to review shootings and to train its officers. A commander with a "hard-charger" mentality may communicate to officers his expectations that violence will be condoned or protected in certain cases. A department's policy guidelines may also implicitly indicate either a concern or a disregard for human life by the types of restrictions it places on the taking of human life.

Differences over officers in moral judgment regarding the use of deadly force was investigated by Scharf.[26] He used Kohlberg's conceptualization of moral reasoning[27] to interpret the moral position of officers regarding the use of deadly force. This psychological approach analyzes the structure of moral reasoning as opposed to the content of particular moral judgments. According to Kohlberg, each moral stage represents a unique mode of processing moral information. Each successive stage possesses an increasingly adequate and reasonable framework for resolving moral conflict and for interpreting moral probabilities. The theory asserts that some moral perspectives are *truer* or *righter* than others as measured by their legal logical consistency. Moral reasoning has been found to be positively correlated with legal reasoning by Tapp[28] and others.

Stage 1 in Kohlberg's system is the punishment and obedience stage, or a naive rational hedonism. Stage 3, or "good boy/girl" orientation, becomes associated with collective opinion. At stage 4, there is a shift toward fixed definitions of law and society; the law is justified in terms of its order-maintaining function. Stage 5 is a legalistic-contract orientation in which law becomes the agreed-upon contract among social equals, with duties of stage and individual clearly defined and regulated. At stage 6, Kohlberg argues that there is a universal basis for ethical decision making. The law here is a repository for broader social principles and is subordinate where law and justice conflict. Each stage suggests quite different concepts to define what might constitute justifiable homicide. At stage 5, for example, homicide is justifiable given a clear utilitarian mandate that only by taking a life can other lives be saved. At lower stages, the concept of justifiable homicide may be understood in terms of particular societal standards, interpersonal feelings, or self-interest. Table 6.2 contains full descriptions of Kohlberg's six moral stages.

According to Kohlberg's theory, officers at lower moral stages have a quite different conception of a legal statute than do officers at higher ones. Complex legal ideas as "necessary force and reasonable force" are difficult concepts for individuals below stage 4. The approach assumes that police officers will in fact make a conscious moral evaluation that is critical in deciding whether or not to use deadly force in a particular situation.

TABLE 6.2   Stages of Development

Preconventional

Stage 1:	Obedience and punishment orientation. Egocentric deference to superior power or prestige, or a trouble-avoiding set. Objective responsibility.
Stage 2:	Naively egoistic orientation. Right action is that which instrumentally satisfies the self's needs and occasionally others'. Naive egalitarianism and orientation to exchange and reciprocity.

Conventional

Stage 3:	Good-boy orientation. Orientation to approval and to pleasing and helping others. Conformity to stereotypical images of majority or natural role behavior, and judgment by intentions.
Stage 4:	Authority and social-order-maintaining orientation. Orientation to "doing duty" and showing respect for authority and maintaining the given social order for its own sake. Regard for earned expectations of others.

Postconventional

Stage 5:	Contractual legalistic orientation. Recognition of an arbitrary element or starting point in rules or expectations for the sake of agreement. Duty defined in terms of contract, general avoidance of violation of the will or rights of others, and majority will and welfare.
Stage 6:	Conscience or principle orientation. Orientation not only to actually ordained social rules but to principles of choice involving appeal to logical universality and consistency. Orientation to conscience as a directing agent and to mutual respect and trust.

Source: Peter Scharf, *Readings in Moral Education* (Minneapolis, Minn.: Winston Press, 1978), p. 336.

TABLE 6.3   Moral Stage and Shooting Decision

| | Decision on Shooting Dilemma | |
Moral Stage	Shoot	Don't Shoot
1. Preconventional (stages 2 and 3)	4	1
2. Conventional (stages 3 and 4)	5	9
3. Postconventional (stages 4 and 5)	0	5
Total	9	15

In Scharf's study, 24 officers were randomly selected from two western state police departments.[29] The sample included 18 patrolmen, 4 sergeants, and 2 lieutenants. The officers ranged in experience from 6 months to 27 years. Exactly half this group possessed college degrees; the mean age was 30 years. An interview schedule, including moral dilemmas faced by police and citizens, generally was used. The general dilemmas were based on those developed by Kohlberg, carefully standardized in terms of rating procedures. A shooting dilemma asked officers to decide if it was right to shoot a suspect who was holding a hostage in a convenience store. It was assumed that it was 50 percent probable that he could kill the perpetrator without harm to the hostage and 30 percent probable that if he did not shoot, the perpetrator would shoot the hostage. Descriptive analysis revealed an apparent association between moral stage and decision on the "shooting dilemma." The results are summarized in Table 6.3.

The preconventional (stage 2; none was scored at stage 1) officers in our sample tended to view the hostage dilemma as a problem of personal authority and control. For example, the five police officers scored at stage 2 showed a concern with power and domination. One officer remarked:

> I go into a situation and attempt to show control. I am kind of like a rooster. I am going to show everyone who is boss. I first get control, then I decide what to do. . . . I try to get them to respect my uniform— to know that I am the law!

In responding to the dilemma involving the hostage, typically there was more concern with the officer's own life than that of the hostage: Question: What would you consider in deciding to shoot?

"It would depend on whether or not he fired at me. That's the first thing. . . . If he shoots at me and misses—he's a dead man."

The stage 2 officer's conception of utility in determining whether to shoot seems simplistic. Often in these interviews, the opponent is stereotyped as a "bad guy" and dealt with accordingly. For example, one officer said: "The bad guys can hit innocent people as well as me. They are probably not as good a shot as I am; they are more likely to hit someone than me. . . . They are the bad guys . . . they are potential dangers when they walk out on the street."

There was often a tone of cynicism in these interviews. One officer suggested that "blowing away a bad guy was doing society a favor." Another officer referred to the courts as "the asshole of the criminal justice system, blowing out what we put in." Another patrolman noted that "most guys don't shoot because that can get you sued."

The 14 conventional (stages 3 and 4) officers showed quite different moral reasoning than did the preconventional subjects. Although the stage 2 police officers were concerned with concrete consequences to themselves or others, the conventionally reasoning subjects showed a far greater concern with the procedural legality of particular actions. For example, one officer with a rather religious stage 4 moral philosophy responded as follows to the "Heinz" dilemma (asking whether it would be right for a man to steal a drug if his wife were dying of cancer and there was no other alternative):

It's God's law. "Thou shalt not steal." No if's, and's, or but's about it.
I might do it, but it would be wrong. When they were transporting the
Ten Commandments, God said, "Don't touch them." They started to
fall, and a guy grabbed them and he dropped dead. It's the same thing.

In the hostage situation, the officer used a similar law and order philosophy:

The law says that I have probable cause if he goes toward the woman.
Thirty percent is enough for probable cause in the eyes of the law. I
would say, "You kill her and you are going to die." The law would say
that if I shot, it was justified. He was threatening her life. I would be
within my rights.

Similarly, another officer, who also scored at stage 4, suggested that the penal code pretty much defined his obligations in the situation. Moral obligation is defined by what is legally permissible rather than by what actually is for the greatest good:

> I'd be more inclined to shoot than not shoot. Like, there was a guy who had 56 arrests. Given that kind of background, I think the law would back me up in shooting. . . . He's threatening another person. You would be justified in that circumstance. If you tried other means and there was no other way, then that's the way it has to be.

The conventionally reasoning subjects showed a great concern with others' evaluations of their actions. One officer suggested that his sergeant "would go along with shooting in this situation." Another officer told about several instances where he was "reamed out" for making a mistake. A patrolman who scored at stage 4 similarly offered: "Look, we got a supervisor looking over our shoulder making sure we enforce the 80,000 laws on the books." Generally, the conventionally reasoning subjects perceived few ambiguities in the law: "There aren't that many tough decisions to make. The only decision you make is how to handle the people while you are carrying out the decision. But the decision is right here [in the penal statute book]."

The most postconventional or principled (stage 5; there were no clearly stage 6 officers in our study) officers demonstrated quite different perspectives from those seen in either preconventional or conventionally reasoning officers. These officers suggested that, although taking a life would be justified under certain circumstances, it must be regarded as a last "in extremis" strategy. One officer suggested:

> Taking a life must be the ultimate thing. It's like playing God. I would never shoot unless a life were in imminent danger. Shooting for property makes no sense at all. We don't have capital punishment for theft. The important thing is saving the life. I would even be further tempted to take chances with my own life than that of an unarmed civilian. It would take less of an overt action to shoot with a civilian than myself, but it's still an extreme step.

Whereas many of the preconventional and conventional officers made little distinction between shooting to save a life and shooting to stop a fleeing felon, the postconventional stage 5 officers saw these two justifications quite differently. One officer said:

> I have a principle—my own philosophy. I won't shoot unless my life or someone else's is absolutely in danger. If it's my life, and I can still flee, I won't shoot. . . . A thief, it's different. There's no life. As long as he does nothing to threaten me, I won't do anything. If he runs from the car I will pursue; but I will not shoot.

This same officer similarly made a clear distinction between what is legally right and what his conscience defines as morally acceptable:

> If it's 20 percent that he would shoot the hostage, this seems different than 50 percent. At 50 percent (though I know the probabilities can change quickly), then I might shoot if I was sure I could save the hostage. At 20 percent there is a substantial chance that through sealing off the area, of just talking the guy down, I can get out of this with no harm to anyone.

Characteristic of the stage 5 interviews was the perceived sanctity of human life. Most of the officers indicated that any solution not violating a human life was preferable to a solution in which a death occurred. These officers also shared a common moral respect for the perpetrator's life, which was not articulated by the preconventional and conventional officers. Whereas these lower stage officers often assumed that the perpetrator was either a "hype" or a "bad guy," the postconventional officers tended at least to cite mitigating factors: "Perhaps the guy was panicky," had gotten "into a bad position," and so forth. This concern for the life of the perpetrator as well as that of the hostage or potential bystander was unique among the morally postconventional subjects.

The moral values of the individual officer are probably most important in explaining differences in officer shooting behavior in those situations where the threat to the officer is ambiguous, or in cities with very open-ended guidelines, as, for example, those allowing the use of deadly force against fleeing felons. Thus, when one officer risked his life by hitting a low caliber rifle out of the hand of a young boy with a tennis racquet, other officers (commenting on the incident) suggested that the risk taken by this officer was inappropriate for them. Conversely, some "quick-firing" officers seem to believe that almost any threat to them justifies the use of deadly force to protect themselves.

In regard to fleeing felons, many highly principled officers simply do not believe that the capture of a fleeing felon justifies the taking of human life, whereas most lower stage officers find this practice consistent with their moral values.

While we do not have the corresponding moral levels for the officers cited below, the variety of moral reactions to shootings is well depicted. One officer commented, in regard to a shooting: "Look, I didn't like it, but I don't think about it. It was unfortunate, but I'm a professional, and dealing with this type of situation is part of my job." Another officer similarly involved in a near fatal shooting said bluntly, "I only felt bad the motherfucker didn't die. A few weeks later he was in his LTD selling dope and waving at me as he went by." Others placed the moral burden upon the (deceased) opponent. "He puts the situation on himself. It is the opponent who created the circumstances that got him killed. I'm just reacting." For other police officers, the shooting creates immense moral turmoil. One officer said, "I break out in hives just thinking about it." Another man described seeing "the face of the man I killed in crowds, on the faces of players in a basketball game, just anywhere." Still another officer simply and articulately said: "It [the fatal shooting] made me realize the implications of the job, of what I am doing. That I am hired to decide when to kill."

Finally, it would seem that fear, the perceptive clarity of the situation, and the officer's collection of abilities determine the degree to which moral concepts are operationalized in a given incident. The officer who is afraid and cannot control the fear may not be able to assess the shooting situation rationally. Similarly, the officer who erroneously perceives the threat posed by the citizen or lacks nonlethal alternatives faces a different moral dilemma from that faced by a more perceptive and socially skilled officer.

CONCLUSIONS

In this chapter we have described some of the competencies required of police officers forced to cope effectively with armed confrontations, emphasizing various psychological capacities affecting the propensity to use deadly force. We have considered not only the individual capacities an officer needs to cope with an armed confrontation but how such capacities might interact. An officer, for example, who is extremely fearful in a particular encounter may not be able to define reality objectively, or be able to bring to the situation effective interpersonal skills. We have further suggested that these capacities may affect decision making well before the final frame in which the officer must choose whether or not to shoot. Thus the ability to

assess information critically may affect an officer's preparatory behavior as he anticipates a particular confrontation, how he assesses
the scene upon arrival, and how he interprets a citizen's response to
his commands or orders.

There is, too, an interactive effect between situational characteristics and abilities. That would account for an interesting phenomenon that may exist: Our informal, undocumented observations
make it appear that officers who shoot several times over a period of
time shoot in very similar situations. One officer, for example, fired
four times, all in off-duty situations in bar fights involving women. A
tactical team officer fired no fewer than six times in duel-type confrontations with armed felons. Another officer fired three times in
situations preceded by physical altercations with a citizen. An officer
fired three times in situations where citizens failed to recognize him
as a police officer, due to his slight demeanor and apparently nonasser-
tive communication skills. Another man, apparently in panic, has
fired three times at cars he felt were about to assault him.

The evidence is far from conclusive, but consistency does seem to
indicate that the personal characteristics of the officer interact with
circumstances. That, of course, may amount to little more than the
observation that there is at least some consistency of personal characteristics across situations. In any event, it does seem clear that certain
officers in particular encounters are far more likely to use deadly
force than are other officers in similar encounters, and that officers
who are at risk in one type of confrontation may not be at any
special risk in another. The officer who had been in four off-duty bar
confrontations in which shots were fired had been involved in more
than 200 prepared on-duty confrontations with armed persons,
without a single shot fired in any of these incidents.

Some people object to the focus on psychological abilities in
analyses of the use of deadly force on the grounds that it stresses the
"bad apple" in the police barrel rather than the badness of society
and its "repressive" forces, the police.[30] Our emphasis has been on
the diversity of abilities over officers, and not on the concentration
of negative ones in a few ("bad") officers. Although we are not willing to deny that there are officers who are so ill-equipped psychologically for police duties that society would be better off if they were
in different occupations (indeed we have provided examples of such
officers throughout this treatment), our feeling is that this category
is quite small. Vastly more important, in our opinion, are the array
of differing capacities, their mutual interaction, and their interaction
with situational characteristics.

Empirical research in this area is extremely difficult. As Inn has observed, officers involved in shooting episodes tend to have an unusually high attrition rate.[31] In addition, there are the major difficulties associated with the assessment of differential capacities.

It is our feeling that many shooting policy statements (like the cockpits of many airplanes) are not designed for human beings. Humans differ in relative capacities, strengths, weaknesses, and so forth, and the best of us are limited in which we can do under stress in a rapid time frame. In short, these policies may be asking the human beings who became police officers to perform at unrealistic levels.

Our analysis also suggests a framework in which to analyze training related to police deadly force. Few training programs have attempted to conceptualize the varied and complex competencies necessary to implement a responsible deadly force policy. Most training, as we will observe in Chapter Seven, focuses upon one or possibly two isolated competencies. Shooting simulators attempt to train police officers quickly to identify threats against them. Some crisis intervention training approaches focus almost exclusively upon the verbal skills useful in dealing with a limited range of disputes. If training is to be effective in reducing the aggregate number of police shootings, it must focus on multiple psychological dimensions, emphasizing those capacities that might influence police behavior in a wide range of armed confrontations. Also, such training should be conducted in environments simulating the complex, and often bewildering, conditions in which deadly force episodes usually take place. From our observations, this approach to shooting training is rare in police departments. The New York Police Department's "outdoor" training is exceptional in that there has been an effort to base training on the competencies required to cope with the most common types of shooting incidents.

The approach we have taken here may also be useful to develop hypotheses relevant to both personnel selection and management. In selecting police officers who would be at minimal risk in terms of inappropriate police shootings, it might be useful for selection boards, test developers, and others to review their conception of the types of competencies required in street confrontations. As we have taken pains to argue in this chapter, the capacities required for such a task may be far more extensive and complex than has previously been recognized. It also may well be that as important as are the specific capacities of the officer is also his ability to implement these capacities in the heat of an armed confrontation. This would suggest the development of assessment centers designed to measure officer abilities under conditions similar to those found in street conditions.

In terms of the management of police personnel, it would seem important to put more emphasis on the tracking of officer behavior in various circumstances than is currently done by effective supervisors. It would seem possible to recognize an officer who is prone to react excessively to particular types of situation and, through reassignment, reduce the risk of a particular officer confronting a particularly risky type of opponent or situation, thus reducing the likelihood of deadly force. To illustrate, one officer, who had experienced a series of shootings in armed raids, was transferred (in spite of his unusually effective arrest record) to a detail in the department's emergency services division. Since this transfer, more than three years ago, he has been in numerous confrontations with insane persons and others, but none involving a use of deadly force.

In Chapter Seven we will shift our focus toward the impact of law and departmental policy and procedure upon police use of deadly force. We will describe differences in departmental deadly force rates and relate these differences to administrative policy and procedure designed to reduce the use of deadly force—for example, shooting guidelines, training, operational rules, and shooting review policies. In this analysis of administrative policies to control police deadly force, we will emphasize the political forces constraining effective policies to monitor and prevent killings by and of police officers.

NOTES

1. For example, J. J. Fyfe, "Shots Fired: An Examination of New York City Police Firearms Discharges," Ph.D. dissertation, State University of New York at Albany, 1978; R. W. Harding and R. P. Fahey, "Killings by Chicago Police, 1969–70: An Empirical Study," *Southern California Law Review* 46, no. 2 (March 1973): 284–315; and M. W. Meyer, "Police Shootings at Minorities: The Case of Los Angeles," *Annals of the American Academy of Political and Social Science* 452 (November 1980): 98–110.

2. J. Rubinstein, *City Police* (New York: Farrar, Straus and Giroux, 1973), p. 330.

3. H. Toch, *Peacekeeping* (Lexington, Mass.: Lexington Books, 1976).

4. W. A. Westley, *Violence and the Police: A Sociological Study of Law, Custom, and Morality* (Cambridge, Mass.: MIT Press, 1970.

5. W. K. Muir, Jr., *Police: Streetcorner Politicians* (Chicago: University of Chicago Press, 1977).

6. Toch, *Peacekeeping.*

7. Rubinstein, *City Police,* p. 327.

8. J. Wambaugh, *The New Centurions* (New York: Dell Publishing, 1978), pp. 112-14.

9. Rubinstein, *City Police*, p. 330.

10. As mentioned in, for example, Fyfe, "Shots Fired"; and C. H. Milton, J. W. Halleck, J. Lardner, and G. L. Abrecht, *Police Use of Deadly Force* (Washington, D.C.: Police Foundation 1977).

11. I. A. Thomas, "The Definition of the Situation," in *Theory and Society*, ed. T. Parsons (Cambridge, Mass.: Harvard University Press, 1967).

12. For example, Fyfe, "Shots Fired."

13. *New York Times*, April 3, 1976, p. 4.

14. Los Angeles Police Department Press Release, May 1979.

15. Fyfe, "Shots Fired."

16. Milton et al., *Police Use of Deadly Force*.

17. M. Bard, "Family Intervention," *Journal of Criminal Law, Criminology and Political Science* 60 (1969): 247-50.

18. As cited in Toch, *Peacekeeping*.

19. L. Driscoll, "Crisis Intervention Among Police Officers" (Lexington, Ky., 1976, unpublished).

20. Donald Helb, "A Review of Crisis Intervention Training in Connecticut," 1974, unpublished.

21. Muir, *Police*, p. 98.

22. J. Wambaugh, *The Choirboys* (New York: Delacorte Press, 1975), pp. 40-43.

23. Bard, "Family Intervention."

24. For a discussion of the use of nonlethal weapons, see D. Johnson, "Hardware/Software: 'Stop or I'll Throw My Net at You," *Police Magazine* 4, no. 2 (March 1981): 23-28.

25. G. F. Uelman, "Varieties of Police Policy: A Study of Police Policy Regarding the Use of Deadly Force in Los Angeles County," *Loyola of Los Angeles Law Review* 6 (January 1973): 1-65.

26. P. Scharf, "Deadly Force: Moral Reasoning on Police Hypothetical Dilemmas," in *Criminology Yearbook* (Santa Monica, Calif.: Sage Publications, 1980).

27. L. Kohlberg, "Moral Reasoning and Moral Education," in *Readings in Moral Education*, ed. P. Scharf (Minneapolis, Minn.: Winston Press, 1978).

28. J. Tapp, "Child's Garden of Law and Order," *Psychology Today*, April 1971.

29. Scharf, "Deadly Force."

30. For example, P. Takagi, "A Garrison State in 'Democratic' Society," *Crime and Social Justice*, no. 1 (Spring-Summer 1974): 27-32.

31. A. Inn, Concept paper presented to the National Institute of Justice, Washington, D.C., 1979.

7 Administrative Control

INTRODUCTION

The Paradoxes of the Administrative Control
of Deadly Force

A police chief in a mid-Atlantic area city glanced nervously at the report on his desk. An officer with seven years' experience had shot a man armed with a .22 pistol. On casual glance the shooting would seem noncontroversial, almost routine. The report tersely indicated that the officer was faced with an apparent threat to his life and fired only after he had been shot in the thigh. This shooting was in reality, however, anything but routine. The officer had been disciplined twice in the two previous years for excessive use of force against black gang members. Three years before he had shot a kneecap off a 16-year-old boy who had broken a bottle when he was cornered in a schoolyard by the officer (and three others). Also, the current shooting involved a politically active black man in the "hardest" core ghetto area in the city.

As the chief was just finishing the report, a black reporter from a local newspaper called to ask him if he had a comment about a reported witness to the shooting who claimed that the victim was shot more than two minutes after the officer was shot. The chief responded that he was unaware of any such witness. "Well, you'll be reading about it in the evening paper," the reporter said. He abruptly hung up. The next call came from the Police Protective Association. The president of the association was at the other end of the telephone line to urge the chief "to express support for all the city's officers in this report. . . ." Anything else, he said, "might demoralize the troops." He added that he could take no responsibility for how they might respond if the officer was disciplined.

In the afternoon, the chief visited the wounded officer in the hospital. The man was not seriously hurt but seemed disoriented and defensive. His eyes twitched and he smiled blankly. Later that afternoon, the chief received a petition from a group calling itself the Citizens' Coalition Against Police Abuse, demanding that the chief immediately fire the offending officer. The petition also called for a "citizen's audit" of the department's shooting policies, training, and review processes. The chief later met with the captain in charge of the shooting review team; the grave captain handed him a detailed report containing the following:

> Officer X encountered a black male, age 23, who pulled a pistol from his jacket while on his porch at 22 Joseph Avenue, after Officer X questioned him about the whereabouts on an acquaintance. The officer told the man to drop his weapon. The man fired two shots from a .22 pistol at Officer X, wounding him in the left thigh. The officer returned fire, killing . . . .

"I.A., good as you can get," the captain grimly offered. "The broad who said that he waited to blow him away was full of shit. Two cops saw it differently. Those people will always stand up for their own."

The chief asked for the service, personnel, and psychiatric records of the two backup officers, both veterans with long service in the precinct with Officer X. Their service records indicated a series of unusual incidents; one officer was accused of covering up a beating; the other man was accused of participating in a "late nite cop party" at a local brothel. Neither, however, was sufficiently substantiated to warrant a shift in assignment or suspension.

At 5 P.M. the mayor called: What was the chief going to do about his shooting? Did the chief know that a rally was planned that night in the Baptist church? The chief spoke to the district attorney's office before leaving for home. The D.A. wanted the paperwork on the shooting by the next morning. He said he'd had more than a dozen calls about it already. "What," he wanted to know, "was the chief going to do about *his* shooting problem?"

Similar pressures have been faced over shooting incidents by police chiefs in Los Angeles, Birmingham, Miami, Oakland, Philadelphia, Chicago, and many other cities during the past several years. In this chapter, we will consider several of the techniques, procedures, and policies available to the chief to minimize occurrence of the phenomenon and to make handling easier if it does occur. We will outline the usefulness of formal administrative policy, training procedures, operational rules, and shooting review procedures in reducing the rate of deadly force by police officers. We will also address some of the forces that counteract the effective implementation of a forceful organizational approach to control the use of deadly force; we will consider, for example, the conflicts faced by the chief, who desires at once to protect the lives of innocent citizens from police force abuse and to maintain sufficient political support (both within and without the police department) to continue to administer his department effectively. The police association, for example, is likely to oppose virtually any imposition of a firmer, more restrictive rule or approach.

In our discussion of the administrative control of deadly force, we will build on the arguments developed earlier. In previous chapters, we have described the sequential (and complex) nature of decisions to use deadly force; we have argued that the bewildering array of personal and situational forces that interact in armed confrontations makes the administrative control of police deadly force extremely difficult. In emphasizing the psychological complexity of the police decision to use or not use deadly force, we hope to have conveyed the exceedingly difficult judgment demanded of an officer required to implement almost any deadly force policy. This emphasis is illustrated by the comment of one police chief who stated, "You can attempt to control your department but you never can keep your officers from thinking and making judgments."

The difficulties of the administrative control of police deadly force are compounded by the reality that its use within the context of a democratic society by necessity poses powerful dilemmas. As a West German police officer interviewed by Berkeley[1] observed, "Democracy is awfully hard on the police." The officer continued, stating that during the Nazi period Hermann Goring said, "When a policeman shoots, I shoot." In a democratic society, in contrast, there are forces to reduce shooting to the minimum level consistent with public order. Moreover, reviews of shooting may be open to public scrutiny, and there is always the threat of investigation by the press. This normally places a very demanding burden upon both the police officer and the police department.

These difficulties are intensified by the occupational realities of policing. Street police work demands great organizational autonomy for its operatives (from patrol officers to commanders to detectives). Police departments are also, by necessity, highly cohesive social units governed more by informal norms than by formal procedures. The specific tasks of police work demand that its officers make rapid decisions (often irreversible ones), mostly with little direct supervision.

The task of controlling police deadly force is further compounded by both the actual danger faced by police officers and the officers' general perceptions of such danger. Since 1968, about 100 police officers have been killed in the line of duty each year. In addition, the media, police unions, and various political forces have heightened public awareness regarding the risks to police officers of violent criminals. No police chief can afford to control police use of deadly force at the expense of either police safety or, as important, the appearance of police safety. The nature of the beast is such that it is possible for a chief to feel deep moral concern about the use of deadly force in his department but can do little to change matters.

Variation in Departmental Rates of Deadly Force

It will come as a surprise to no one that there are pronounced differences in departments in the rate of use of deadly force. A recent report by the International Association of Chiefs of Police (IACP) contains comparisons of justifiable homicide rates of police departments in more than 50 major U.S. cities, covering the period 1975–79. Homicide rates by police are expressed in terms of such factors as citizen homicide rate, violent crime rate, and numbers of police officers and citizens in the various cities.[2] To illustrate, Table 7.1 shows justifiable homicide by the police in these cities per 1,000 violent crimes; and Table 7.2 shows justifiable homicide by the police per 100,000 population. The entries are yearly averages. The cities of Sacramento and Portland, for example, have low rates of justifiable homicide by police on both bases; New Orleans and Birmingham are high in both. But, although St. Louis is second highest on the population basis, it is, because of a very high crime rate, further toward the center of the distribution on a violent crime basis.

Using the data in Table 7.2, one can note that the police in Sacramento killed .08 people per year per 100,000 population, whereas New Orleans police killed 2.3 per year per 100,000 population. This indicates a rate of police homicide in New Orleans that was almost 30 times higher than the rate in Sacramento. (It should be mentioned that population is resident population; there could very well be a difference in transient population between these cities and between other cities.)

Assuming that there are not vast differences in shooting accuracy over the represented police departments, the differences reflected in the two tables show, more or less, differences in rates of deadly force. Obviously a complex array of social, political, and administrative factors influences the rate of use of deadly force in a particular police department. Two cities with identical resident populations may confront very different numbers of dangerous and armed offenders; and transients, not reflected in resident counts, may have a high proportion of criminals. Crime rates, arrest patterns, and local gun sale policies contribute to the hazard in a particular city or department and have an effect on deadly force rate. Administrative policy and shooting review procedures may similarly affect rates. Although it is difficult to develop an agreeable standard by which to judge a police department's rate of shooting, it seems clear from existing studies that cities show broad variation in the rates of deadly force irrespective of how the number of shooting incidents are compared, by population, number of officers, or any other criterion.

Administrative Intervention and Changes in the Rate of Police Deadly Force

An indication of the importance of administrative policy in determining the rate of use of police deadly force may be found in examining changes in the shooting rate within cities that have experienced major administrative changes related to shooting practices. Atlanta, New York, and Newark were all, by means of administrative changes, able to effect drops in rates of police use of deadly force. Lee Brown, public safety commissioner of Atlanta, for example, commented that following major policy reforms in 1975, the rate of deadly force sharply declined:

> In Atlanta in 1971 there were 12 citizens killed by police; in 1972 there were eight; in 1973, 17; in 1974 there were 12; in 1975, seven; in 1976, five; in 1977, six; and this year to date there have been three.
>
> For the number of people shot but not killed by the police during the same eight-year period, there are no data available prior to 1973. In

TABLE 7.1 Rate of Justifiable Homicide by the Police to 1,000 Violent Crimes, 1975–79

Standard Format Listing		Rank Order Listing	
Akron	.44	Sacramento	.07
Albuquerque	.41	Boston	.13
Austin	.30	Newark	.17
Baltimore	.57	Portland	.19
Birmingham	1.63	St. Paul	.20
Boston	.13	San Francisco	.26
Buffalo	.29	New York	.27
Charlotte	.28	Charlotte	.28
Chicago	.75	Buffalo	.29
Cincinnati	.57	Miami	.30
Cleveland	.67	Austin	.30
Columbus	.56	Toledo	.36
Dallas	.77	Albuquerque	.41
Denver	.46	Minneapolis	.43
Detroit	.84	Honolulu	.43
El Paso	.94	Akron	.44
Fort Worth	.47	Denver	.46
Honolulu	.43	Fort Worth	.47
Houston	1.60	Seattle	.50
Indianapolis	1.02	Tampa	.53
Jacksonville	1.38	Columbus	.56
Kansas City	.74	Cincinnati	.57
Long Beach	1.16	Baltimore	.57
Los Angeles	.70	Rochester	.58
Louisville	.83	Norfolk	.60
Memphis	.75	Cleveland	.67
Miami	.30	Washington	.68

City	Rate		City	Rate
Minneapolis	.43		San Jose	.68
Nashville	.97		Omaha	.68
Newark	.17		Los Angeles	.70
New Orleans	1.81		Kansas City	.74
New York	.27		Phoenix	.75
Norfolk	.60		Memphis	.75
Oakland	.77		Chicago	.75
Oklahoma City	1.05		Oakland	.77
Omaha	.68		Dallas	.77
Philadelphia	1.24		Louisville	.83
Phoenix	.75		Detroit	.84
Portland	.19		San Diego	.85
Rochester	.58		St. Louis	.91
Sacramento	.07		El Paso	.94
St. Louis	.91		Nashville	.97
St. Paul	.20		Tulsa	1.01
San Antonio	1.07		Indianapolis	1.01
San Diego	.85		Oklahoma City	1.05
San Francisco	.26		San Antonio	1.07
San Jose	.68		Wichita	1.11
Seattle	.50		Long Beach	1.16
Tampa	.53		Philadelphia	1.24
Toledo	.36		Tucson	1.28
Tucson	1.28		Jacksonville	1.38
Tulsa	1.01		Houston	1.60
Washington	.68		Birmingham	1.63
Wichita	1.11		New Orleans	1.81

Rate = yearly average of justifiable homicides by police divided by yearly average of (1,000) violent crimes.

Mean = .70.

Source: K. J. Matulia, A Balance of Force (Gaithersburg, Md.: International Association of Chiefs of Police, 1982), p. 79.

TABLE 7.2 Rate of Justifiable Homicide by the Police to 100,000 Population, 1975-79

Standard Format Listing		Rank Order Listing	
Akron	.24	Sacramento	.08
Albuquerque	.35	Honolulu	.11
Austin	.12	Austin	.12
Baltimore	1.06	St. Paul	.15
Birmingham	1.74	Charlotte	.20
Boston	.23	Portland	.21
Buffalo	.25	Boston	.23
Charlotte	.20	Akron	.24
Chicago	.74	Buffalo	.25
Cincinnati	.49	Toledo	.27
Cleveland	1.04	San Jose	.31
Columbus	.37	Fort Worth	.32
Dallas	.83	Albuquerque	.35
Denver	.46	Newark	.37
Detroit	1.63	Columbus	.37
El Paso	.40	Omaha	.38
Fort Worth	.32	Minneapolis	.38
Honolulu	.11	San Francisco	.39
Houston	1.10	El Paso	.40
Indianapolis	.67	Seattle	.44
Jacksonville	1.16	Rochester	.46
Kansas City	.90	Denver	.46
Long Beach	1.18	San Diego	.48
Los Angeles	.89	New York	.48
Louisville	.60	Cincinnati	.49
Memphis	.60	San Antonio	.50
Miami	.51	Norfolk	.50

City	Rate
Minneapolis	.38
Nashville	.70
Newark	.37
New Orleans	2.13
New York	.48
Norfolk	.50
Oakland	1.32
Oklahoma City	.86
Omaha	.38
Philadelphia	.94
Phoenix	.52
Portland	.21
Rochester	.46
Sacramento	.08
St. Louis	1.77
St. Paul	.15
San Antonio	.50
San Diego	.48
San Francisco	.39
San Jose	.31
Seattle	.44
Tampa	.66
Toledo	.27
Tucson	.72
Tulsa	.59
Washington	1.05
Wichita	.52

City	Rate
Miami	.51
Wichita	.52
Phoenix	.52
Tulsa	.59
Memphis	.60
Louisville	.60
Tampa	.66
Indianapolis	.67
Nashville	.70
Tucson	.72
Chicago	.74
Dallas	.83
Oklahoma City	.86
Los Angeles	.89
Kansas City	.90
Philadelphia	.94
Cleveland	1.04
Washington	1.05
Baltimore	1.06
Houston	1.10
Jacksonville	1.16
Long Beach	1.18
Oakland	1.32
Detroit	1.63
Birmingham	1.74
St. Louis	1.77
New Orleans	2.13

Rate = yearly average of justifiable homicide by police divided by yearly average of population (100,000).

Mean = .66.

Source: K. J. Matulia, A Balance of Forces (Gaithersburg, Md.: International Association of Chiefs of Police, 1982), p. 81.

that year, 51 citizens were shot by the police; in 1974 there were 22; in 1975 there were 19; in 1976, three; in 1977, one; and to date this year there have been four.[3]

The work of Fyfe[4] with the New York Police Department provides another important example of the impact of administrative reform on the rate of police deadly force. The creation of a shots fired review board in 1972 and a change in department shooting policy were followed by a substantial drop in the rate of deadly force. That effect and the subsequent patterning are shown in Table 7.3.

Although there are confounding factors from year to year—changes in crime rate, number of employed police officers, and so forth—the almost steady decrease since 1972 makes an alternate explanation much less reasonable. Kansas City, Missouri, has shown a decrease in police shooting incidents from 40 per year to 17 per year. Los Angeles experienced a decrease in police killings of civilians from 33 in 1977 to 14 in 1979. The fatality rate in Newark has decreased from an average of 8 killings by police officers in 1967–71 to an average of roughly 2 per year under the administration of Hubert Williams in 1974–82. Shots fired at persons were reduced from 72 in 1971 to 43 in 1980. Other cities that have reported similar declines in the rate of deadly force include Detroit, Washington, D.C., and Seattle.

The possibility that these declines in deadly force are related to extraneous factors such as declines in population, number of officers, or crime rate needs to be rigorously examined, but this possibility seems unlikely, given the available data. Although population has

TABLE 7.3 Shots Fired, Wounding of Persons, and Fatalities by New York Police Officers

Year	Shots Fired	Woundings	Fatalities	Percentage of Annual Reduction/ Increase of Shots Fired
1973	556	121	54	−29.5
1974	470	109	56	−15.46
1975	439	97	41	−6.5
1976	374	86	42	−14.80
1977	414	98	49	+10.6
1978	372	80	41	−10.1
1979	364	72	30	−.2

steadily declined in many of these urban areas, crime rates have either remained constant or have risen in each case. In some cities, the total number of officers has slightly decreased due to financial constraints; however, the average workload per officer and the per officer contact rate with violent persons has probably increased.

MANAGEMENT STRATEGIES TO CONTROL POLICE DEADLY FORCE

In thinking about strategies to control use of deadly force by police officers, one must consider the nature of police decisions to use deadly force as well as the array of methods available to regulate these decisions. As we emphasized in earlier chapters, the decision to use deadly force often occurs with extreme suddenness, under unprepared conditions. Such decisions are most often made under emotionally stressful conditions in which it is most difficult to distinguish appearance from reality. Also, police officers vary widely in terms of their moral outlook and the psychological skills they bring to a confrontation. Finally, a use of deadly force is by nature an irreversible decision.

Organizational theory suggests that it is difficult to ensure compliance with policy guidelines aimed at regulating an activity that requires a complex judgment on the part of trained personnel. Although it is relatively easy to attain compliance when activities are routine, as in production-line work, activities that require complex judgment and decision making, as those of a lawyer or surgeon, are far more difficult to control. In these judgment-dependent activities, only actions that are grossly negligent—for example, those actions for which virtually no justification may be found—typically will be subject to direct administrative sanctions. One reason for the difficulty is the organizational necessity to protect the decision maker from unfair after-the-fact evaluations that may not take into account the context in which the judgment was made. That factor was discussed earlier when a distinction was made between reasonable and right decisions.

Etzioni suggests three general models of organizational control: coercive, instrumental, and normative.[5] Coercive control emphasizes intensive scrutiny and draconian punishments for noncompliance. Instrumental control implies product and performance in monitoring and achievement for rewards. Normative control achieves compliance through intensive socialization and indoctrination rather than direct monitoring and sanctioning. Most organizations requiring complex judgments by key personnel will use either instrumental or normative methods of control. A corporate division head, for example, will be evaluated by the profitability of his division, as determined by a rigorous audit of the division's finances. Other professionals, such as physicians, professors, and lawyers (and even SS commanders— Etzioni's example), are typically controlled more through adherence to a common normative ideology. What Etzioni calls semiprofessions, such as social work, policing, and teaching, frequently employ more coercive techniques to ensure compliance, when appropriate behavior is defined and compliance is considered important by the organization. It is important to note in this context that what may be considered important to outside observers is not necessarily important to policymakers in the organization.

Law enforcement officials rarely publicly articulate the strategies they use to ensure officer compliance to departmental rules. It should also be noted that the chief's stated approach to dealing with his own officers may be startlingly different from those he applies to the larger society—both criminals and other citizens. Thus, one very "liberal" chief who demonstrated great public concern for the civil rights of citizens was a notorious martinet in terms of ensuring officer compliance to departmental rules (including adherence to "haircut" standards). A hard-line public law and order chief, on the other hand (in charge of a huge city police department), initiated few disciplinary actions against officers, including those charged with serious abuse or negligence.

In any event, the point is that broad management strategies for controlling deadly force must often be inferred, and the inferential process is fraught with risk. The constructions that follow are, thus, to be understood as approximations, although they do have similarities to a more general typology of organizational control (see, for example, McGregor[6] and Argyris[7]).

Types of Control

Strategy A: Severe and Punitive Sanctions

This strategy assumes that the individual police officer is scarcely more governable than the criminal he is supposed to arrest. One chief summed up his shooting policy by indicating that "any guy who makes a mistake gets his ass." Officers found violating shooting guidelines will often be fined or suspended or even fired. Prosecution may be encouraged where there is a hint of criminal action. A bit of Hobbesian thinking may be found in the defense of this strategy to control police deadly force. One internal affairs lieutenant commented, "These guys, if you let them run wild, you would find dead bodies all over the streets. You have to show them who's in charge." Fear of the internal affairs department is an integral part of this administrative strategy. One seasoned officer described the head of internal affairs in his department "as the scariest thing since Godzilla!" Another internal affairs chief was described "as being so scary even the chief is afraid of him."

Strategy B: The Marginal Utility of Control

This strategy is far more often practiced than preached. It is charitable in its views toward the line police officer, suggesting that if armed officers confront armed citizens often enough, some citizens will inevitably be killed by police officers. Errors from this point of view are seen as regrettable, but largely unpreventable. One assistant chief frankly said: "If I did all the things the liberals wanted me to do, then *maybe* I'd save one life" (of the roughly 20 lives lost due to the police use of lethal force each year in his city). Management control using this approach is achieved by following standard procedures. All shootings are investigated; few result in serious disciplinary actions or legal charges against the officers. Strategy B officers in internal affairs tend to be rather sympathetic with the "street" realities of patrol officers. In a few of the Strategy B cities we reviewed, the head of the shooting review board was also the head of the SWAT unit. Internal affairs officers tend to view many of the shooting cases as either "righteous" or, at worst, "questionable but acceptable." One head of a shooting review board noted that most of his cases involved "bad guys with guns." What do you expect the guy to do, put flowers in the "bastard's teeth"?

Strategy C: They Have to Be Taught

This strategy emphasizes, as one would guess, the role of training and education in the control of police deadly force. This strategy suggests that the officer is faced with a decision that few men can be expected to implement successfully without a great deal of support, supervision, and training. In one city, the chief mandated monthly shooting qualification of officers in both silhouette and standing situation shootings. This department offered officers no fewer than five programs that related at least in part to the use of deadly force:

a complex shoot/don't shoot program, a program in crisis intervention skills, stress-management seminars, a class on legal aspects of
force, and a class on nonlethal force and emotionally disturbed persons. In Strategy C departments, officers involved in ambiguous or
controversial shooting situations are more often assigned to retrain-
ing than they are disciplined. The head of a shooting review board
characteristically observed that his "tactical reviews" were immediately "recycled" into the training program to correct future "tactical,
psychological, or legal mistakes."

Strategy D: Stepping Back

The implicit strategy is far less sanguine about the malleability
and trainability of the police officer than is Strategy C. The way to
control police shootings is to avoid the types of situations that are
likely to produce controversial use of deadly force. Policies are both
defensive and reactive: "Problem officers" are given desk jobs, risky
chases are broken off, field commanders in the field lecture on their
particular "aggressive practices," SWAT teams are called in whenever
possible, pursuits are discouraged, and controversial encounters are
avoided. When shooting incidents do occur they are reviewed somewhat defensively. One internal affairs captain admitted: "We don't
normally do any investigation unless there is a complaint." Another
internal affairs sergeant observed: "We try to keep things as quiet as
possible; that's the message we get from above—don't make waves
unless you have to."

This four-part typology, of course, suffers from all of the limitations of similar efforts to conceptualize types of police administrations or functions (see Wilson,[8] for example). Many departments, in
fact, use multiple strategies in controlling their officers' use of deadly
force. Also, this typology of organizational control strategies ignores
the relationship of the type of strategy used to control police deadly
force to broader departmental style. For example, Strategy D (stepping back) would be expected in a department with what Wilson calls
a "watchman" policing style; similarly, Strategy C, emphasizing
training, is consistent with a department that has a "service" orientation; and Strategies A and B would be expected in departments with
what Wilson might term "legalistic" orientations to policing.

Even a preliminary typology as the one presented here, however,
is useful in emphasizing the diversity in attitude in the control of
police deadly force. Uelman[9] and Williams,[10] among others, have
emphasized that it is the overall tone of a department that deter-

mines the scope of management mechanisms used to control police deadly force—guidelines, training, operational rules, review procedures, and so forth—and possibly (controlling for other factors) the frequency with which officers in the department will use their guns against citizens. One chief argued this position as follows:

> It's not so much training or guidelines or any specific measure. Rather it is the attitude the chief executive takes towards the problem. You will find, for example, many departments with similar sounding paper policies having very different operational policies and also will find very different shooting rates. It's something else! It's the whole approach the top guy takes to the problem. Whether or not he's serious about what they do with those guns.

Specific Management Policies

Recently, attention has been focused upon specific administrative mechanisms to reduce the rate of police deadly force. Chapman[11] has argued that each police department should develop a specific shooting policy that systematically encompasses all relevant components in a unified package. The development of that sort of policy, he believes, should take into account the social, legal, personnel, and demographic realities unique to the particular police department. It should include specific provisions for guidelines, training, operational rules and procedures, and shooting reviews. We will review each of these four provisions, attempting to conceptualize the ways in which each contributes to the end result. We will also explore some recent innovations in each area and focus upon some of the difficulties implicit in each mechanism.

Guidelines

One administrative means of controlling police use of deadly force may be found in shooting guidelines used to restrict police shooting to specific situations. Such guidelines are most often more specific and restrictive than statute law. As recently as 1970, many departments had no guidelines beyond such truisms in personnel manuals as "Leave your gun in your holster until you intend to use it." But that has changed considerably over the last decade. The survey by the IACP mentioned earlier in this chapter found that every department that responded to its questionnaire had a written policy, and many of these policy statements contain moral, ethical, and constitutional discussions, as well as specification of when shooting is appropriate and acceptable.[12]

The 1977 Los Angeles Police use of firearms policy below is a model of a comprehensive, intelligible, yet sufficiently open-ended policy. It replaced a far more ambiguous policy allowing the shooting of any type of fleeing felon.[13] This document was created following a series of shootings with political repercussions. The policy reflects intensive study, dialogue, and compromise among various functions and between the department and its constituency. The availability of such a document makes public the expectations and standards of the department while preserving freedom of interpretation for the officer. This type of document also articulates a general departmental philosophy regarding the use of deadly force.

Policy

I. PREAMBLE TO THE POLICY ON THE USE OF FIREARMS.
The use of a firearm is in all probability the most serious act in which a law enforcement officer will engage. It has the most far-reaching consequences for all of the parties involved. It is, therefore, imperative not only that the officer act within the boundaries of legal guidelines, ethics, good judgment, and accepted practices, but also that the officer be prepared by training, leadership and direction to act wisely whenever using a firearm in the course of duty.

A reverence for the value of human life shall guide officers in considering the use of deadly force. While officers have an affirmative duty to use that degree of force necessary to protect human life, the use of deadly force is not justified merely to protect property interests. It is in the public interest that a police officer of this Department be guided by a policy which people believe to be fair and appropriate and which creates public confidence in the Department and its individual officers.

This policy is not intended to create doubt in the mind of an officer at a moment when action is critical and there is little time for meditation or reflection. It provides basic guidelines governing the use of firearms so that officers can be confident in exercising judgment as to the use of deadly force. Such a policy must be viewed as an administrative guide for decision-making before the fact and as a standard for administrative judgment of the propriety of the action taken. It is not to be considered a standard for external judgment (civil or criminal litigation) of the propriety of an action taken. This is a matter of established law and also a process for courts and juries reviewing specific facts of a given incident.

II. **NECESSITY THAT OFFICERS BE ARMED.** As long as members of the public are victims of violent crimes and officers in the performance of their duties are confronted with deadly force, it will remain necessary for police officers to be properly armed for the protection of society and themselves.

III. **REASON FOR THE USE OF DEADLY FORCE.** An officer is equipped with a firearm to protect himself or others against the immediate threat of death or serious bodily injury or to apprehend a fleeing felon who has committed a violent crime and whose escape presents a substantial risk of death or serious bodily injury to others.

IV. **PROTECTION OF GENERAL PUBLIC.** Regardless of the nature of the crime or the justification for firing at a suspect, officers must remember that their basic responsibility is to protect the public. Officers shall not fire under conditions that would subject bystanders or hostages to death or possible injury, except to preserve life or prevent serious bodily injury. Firing under such conditions is not justified unless the failure to do so at the time would create a substantial immediate threat of death or serious bodily injury.

V. **MINIMIZING THE RISK OF DEATH.** An officer does not shoot with the intent to kill; he shoots when it is necessary to prevent the individual from completing what he is attempting. In the extreme stress of a shooting situation, an officer may not have the opportunity or ability to direct his shot to a nonfatal area. To require him to do so, in every instance, could increase the risk of harm to himself or others. However, in keeping with the philosophy that the minimum force that is necessary should be used, officers should be aware that, even in the rare cases where the use of firearms reasonably appears necessary, the risk of death to any person should be minimized.

VI. **THE USE OF DEADLY FORCE.** An officer is authorized the use of deadly force when it reasonably appears necessary:

    A. To protect himself or others from an immediate threat of death or serious bodily injury, or

B. To prevent a crime where the suspect's actions place persons in jeopardy of death or serious injury, or

C. To apprehend a fleeing felon for a crime involving serious bodily injury or the use of deadly force where there is a substantial risk that the person whose arrest is sought will cause death or serious bodily injury to others if apprehension is delayed.

Officers shall not use deadly force to protect themselves from assaults which are not likely to have serious results.

Firing at or from moving vehicles is generally prohibited. Experience shows such action is rarely effective and is extremely hazardous to innocent persons.

Deadly force shall only be exercised when all reasonable alternatives have been exhausted or appear impracticable.

VII. JUSTIFICATION LIMITED TO FACTS KNOWN TO OFFICER. Justification for the use of deadly force must be limited to what reasonably appear to be the facts known or perceived by an officer at the time he decides to shoot. Facts unknown to an officer, no matter how compelling, cannot be considered at a later date to justify a shooting.

VIII. SUSPECTED FELONY OFFENDERS. An officer shall not fire at a person who is called upon to halt on mere suspicion and who simply runs away to avoid arrest. Nor should an officer fire at a "fleeing felon" if the officer has any doubt whether the person fired at is in fact the person against whom the use of deadly force is permitted under this policy.

IX. YOUTHFUL FELONY SUSPECTS. This Department has always utilized extreme caution with respect to the use of deadly force against youthful offenders. Nothing in this policy is intended to reduce the degree of care required in such cases.

X. SHOOTING AT FLEEING MISDEMEANANTS. Officers shall not use deadly force to effect the arrest or prevent the escape of a person whose only offense is classified solely as a misdemeanor under the Penal Code.

XI. FIRING WARNING SHOTS. Generally, warning shots should not be fired.

XII. DRAWING OR EXHIBITING FIREARMS. Unnecessarily or prematurely drawing or exhibiting a firearm limits an officer's alternatives in controlling a situation, creates unnecessary anxiety on the part of citizens, and may result in an unwarranted or accidental discharge of the firearm. Officers shall not draw or exhibit a firearm unless the circumstances surrounding the incident create a reasonable belief that it may be necessary to use the firearm in conformance with this policy on the use of firearms.

Other departmental policy statements are far less comprehensive, restrictive, and clear than that of the Los Angeles department. But no modern ones are like the one reported by Chapman,[14] which consisted of the not too useful aphorism, "Never take me (i.e., your gun) out in anger, never put me back in disgrace." The city of Charlotte (North Carolina) Police Department's statement below is an example of a rather terse and almost incomprehensibly open-ended departmental shooting guideline:

DEADLY FORCE

1. The officer may use only that amount of deadly force which is reasonably necessary. If a peaceful means is at his disposal and would serve as well, he must use it. If another means exists for dealing with the situation, it must be used.

2. The officer may use deadly force.

3. The officer is justified in using deadly force only when reasonably necessary.

PUBLIC SAFETY

A. WARNING SHOTS: The danger to innocent bystanders must be taken into consideration.

B. CALL FOR ASSISTANCE: The rules pertaining to warning shots apply except if there is no other way to summon assistance.

C. MOVING VEHICLES: . . .

Summary: When discharging a firearm, an officer *must* consider the lives and safety of others.[15]

The effectiveness of restrictive guidelines has been well documented in a series of recent studies. A report by the police commissioners in Los Angeles[16] has shown that the implementation of the restrictive Los Angeles guidelines has had a major impact upon the use of deadly force by police personnel since their adoption. Meyer states:

> Commencing in 1978, there was a substantial decrease in persons shot (hit) and persons shot fatally. The number of persons actually shot— that is, hit—changed little prior to 1978, and the number of persons shot fatally did not decline prior to that year. The number of persons shot increased through 1976; the number shot fatally increased through 1977. About eighty persons per year were shot from 1974 through 1977. This number decreased to 63 in 1978 and 61 in 1979. . . . About thirty people per year were shot fatally from 1974 through 1977, but the number of shooting fatalities dropped to 20 in 1978 and 14 in 1979.[17]

Similar results have been found to follow implementation of more restrictive guidelines in other cities, as noted above. Fyfe demonstrated that the promulgation of a new general order regulating deadly force produced a significant decline of deadly force by New York police officers during the next several years. He concludes:

> Our examination has demonstrated that a considerable reduction in the frequency of police shooting accompanied New York City's direct intervention on the firearms discretion of its police officers. Further, our data indicate that this reduction was greatest among the most controversial shooting incidents: shootings to prevent or terminate crimes, which frequently involve police shots at fleeing felons. To the extent that this New York experience may be generalized to other agencies, therefore, an obvious consequence of the implementation of clear shooting guidelines and their stringent enforcement is a reduction of injuries and deaths sustained by suspects who would face far less severe penalties even if convicted after trial.[18]

The administrative shooting guidelines and shooting incident review [Temporary Operating Procedure (T.O.P.)-237] were promulgated in August 1972. The effect of T.O.P.-237 on police shootings is evident in the following picture of ratios of felony arrests to shootings over the years: 1971–47.6; 1972–41.2; 1973–61.3; 1974–80.6; 1975–86.9. Clearly, officers in New York shot far less frequently after 1972, using felony arrests as a basis for comparison over the years. In terms of actual numbers, Fyfe found that shooting incidents reached the level of 149 during the period May–June 1972, decreased to 141 during July–August 1972, and remained below those levels through 1975 (when his study ended).

In Seattle, a reduction from 20 shooting incidents per year to fewer than ten followed the creation of a more restrictive shooting policy. Changes in shooting guidelines in both Detroit and Washington, D.C., seemingly reduced the rate of deadly force by roughly 40 percent in Detroit and 35 percent in Washington, D.C. It is uncertain whether the reductions stem entirely from the restrictions on the types of situations in which deadly force may be used (for example, not against a felon fleeing from a property crime), or if there is an attitudinal change with impact upon shootings within the self-defense justification category, and similar allowed categories, not directly affected by the change in guidelines.

Rubinstein,[19] along with many police officers and their associations, have pointed out that policy statements that are too encompassing may inhibit police functioning and even endanger the police. And a review of guidelines by Gigliotti[20] suggests that some are even more confusing than the state justification statutes (for example, "Officers should not be allowed to fire at felony suspects when lesser force could be used; when the officer believes that the suspect can be apprehended reasonably soon thereafter . . ."). He ironically observes that "applying the necessary *permitted* force is a feat rivaling the Amazing Kreskin" (supposed mind reader of some repute).[21] Shooting guidelines may reduce the discretion to shoot, but they will not do away with the need to process information, evaluate it, and decide whether or not to shoot on the basis of a multitude of factors.

Even police departments that have specific administrative shooting guidelines frequently allow the officer broad latitude in deciding when to shoot. As mentioned in Chapter Four, police officers shoot in only a small percentage of the instances in which they are legally or administratively justified in doing so. Similarly, Kaplan's report regarding the Los Angeles police suggested that guidelines simply define an outer circumference of what is administratively defensible, and that the circumference is large even when the guidelines are strict.[22] The police officer still has the burden of distinguishing "between a shooting that is *necessary* and one which is legally allowable." The "tightest" of guidelines thus allows the shooting of a relatively large number of persons if officers were to shoot in nearly all situations where they were administratively permitted to shoot.

In addition, restrictive guidelines may create conflicts between statute and administrative definitions of permissible deadly force. In

Peterson v. *City of Long Beach*, the court ruled that the city of Long Beach could be held civilly liable to the standards set in its administrative guidelines.[23] The decision states that a city could be sued if it failed to meet the stringent standards set in its public guidelines. The court ruled that statements in a police department manual are formally "regulations," with all attendant legal requirements. This, as one California chief observed, created a dilemma between a "city's conscience" and its "pocketbook." The chief went on to observe that "the formulation of restrictive guidelines might cost his city 10 or 20 million dollars over the next several years." Other cities (for example, San Jose, New York, and Los Angeles) have been sued by police unions demanding that these departments return to less restrictive state shooting statutes.

In summary, although restrictive guidelines do indeed reduce shootings within their specified domain—as, for example, no shooting at felons fleeing after burglaries—they seem of much more limited use in a broader range of situations—as, for example, when people are, or may be, in danger.

Training

We will consider several aspects of police training that carry implications for the use of deadly force. One of these is actual shooting. It is widely believed that existing training offered in the area of technical shooting is inadequate. Most departments simply offer static target shooting during preservice training, supplemented by periodic (semiannual, quarterly, or monthly) requalifications. Often such technical shooting is conducted totally divorced from any possible street conditions, for example, shot fired at static targets in daylight more than 60 feet away. Typically, officers will fire 20 or more shots at paper targets on command of the training officer. Such training may be supplemented by "double-action" firing (two shots at a time) or a shotgun course.

Critics point out that such range shooting does not prepare officers for real-life armed confrontations. For one thing, realistic levels of stress are certainly absent from such training exercises. Observations of officers who had achieved high scores in static training revealed that accuracy scores tended to plummet dramatically when the men were harassed by range officers or after they ran 100 yards. Furthermore, officers will often practice shooting while firing from an arm rest in a static position. As one officer who had been involved in several shootings sarcastically commented, "It's completely unrealistic, a police Disneyland. You have time to set up; no one is trying to kill you and you aren't completely stressed out from six other insane assignments. Also you're not moving and the target's not moving. Otherwise the training is fantastic here."

It should be noted that in many departments training of all sorts is relegated to the position of a very low priority activity. "Roll-call" training may be terminated when there is almost any sort of competitive need. And officers who fail to "qualify" at their periodic shooting trials are often simply returned to duty. Also, many cities, faced with severe budget cuts, have chosen to curtail or suspend training activities.

Some cities have made intensive efforts to improve training related to deadly force. Several police departments in the past few years have developed new approaches to train officers in rapid shooting judgments. The Riverside (California) Police Department has developed with Motorola a quick perception reaction shooting program called "shoot/don't shoot." The approach was described in a "60 Minutes" television program and has been adapted as a major film training program by Motorola Films that is widely used in both medium-sized and large departments.

The Riverside Police Department's "shoot/don't shoot" program is conducted in an indoor training range. Each officer in the department must qualify monthly in the program. A film is projected on a blank sheet of paper placed roughly ten yards from the officer, presenting the officer with a dramatized shooting encounter. The range master instructs each of a pair of shooters to fire his or her weapon only when necessary, consistent with the laws of the state of California and the guidelines of the Riverside Police Department. The officers are then placed in darkness in their shooting stalls, told to load their weapons, and are presented with a brief film vignette (roughly 1 to 4 minutes) portraying a possible shooting situation, projected on the paper target.

In one such situation, the officer is confronted by a group of three Hispanic men who first hesitate upon an order to halt and then turn and raise a concealed pistol at the officer. A related scenario shows an irate housewife who quickly draws (and fires) a concealed pistol at the police officers viewing the film. Another shows a man hovering over a man who has been shot in the head. This man, who is holding a pistol, turns out to be a neighbor who has found his friend shot and has naively picked up his gun. In another vignette, police officers respond to a "burglary in progress" in a convenience store.

An older man turns quickly toward the officers and slowly and somewhat incoherently explains that he is the manager of the store. Another situation portrays a "robbery in progress" call in a variety store. The officers observe a black soldier in front of the counter and a pretty (and white) female behind the cash register. The black soldier turns out to be the victim of the robbery. The female perpetrator rapidly points her weapon and fires at the officers. In each simulation, the officer must choose when to fire and must fire with sufficient accuracy to hit the appropriate target.

Officers observed participating in this training exercise made several errors repeatedly; several were outgunned by the opponents on the screen, and others shot with little accuracy. Also, several innocent citizens were shot by the trainees. (In one simulation, we saw an innocent victim shot by each of six officers we observed go through the training.) One simulation showed a "reported" armed person near a railroad trestle. The trainee encounters (on the film) a somewhat disoriented young man who ignores all orders to halt. Suddenly the range master fires from the darkness to simulate an unexpected real shot being fired in a tense situation. In each training session we observed, the officers in training began firing almost instantaneously with the range master. The disoriented young man turns out to be a deaf mute who was reaching for a wallet with a card which read "I am deaf and dumb." One lieutenant who shot the man through the head exclaimed as he walked forward in the darkness to observe his score: "Oh, my God, I probably shot a cop," obviously realizing the gravity of reflexive response.

An improvement of the "shoot/don't shoot" approach has been developed by September and Associates, located in Tukwilla, Washington. The company has developed a computer-synchronized slide tape simulator that can be modified by altering or speeding up or down the sequences of slides. The simulator can diagnose an officer's "early" or "late" response to a simulated shooting situation.

The September and Associates training simulation begins with the officer in the dark at the Washington State Criminal Justice Academy training range. The trainer hands a young recruit a .38 "short special" loaded with blanks and tells him "to react as you would on the streets." The trainer seeks to instill enough tension in the trainee to "simulate at least some of the tension of an armed confrontation." Finally, a dispatch like the following is heard in the dark: "Robbery in progress, black male with shotgun—7012 77th street." Suddenly five slide projectors acting sequentially portray a police car slowly approaching a 7–11 store. As it arrives, a young robber runs toward the officer from the 7-11 store with what appears to be a sawed-off shotgun and immediately turns toward him. The officer fired at slide 76 when the robber leveled his gun at him. At frame 78 the "armed robber" shoots. "Good," says the trainer, "you got him." When, in a follow-up scenario, the trainee delayed firing (perhaps distracted by a pretty girl who ran across the 7-11 parking lot) and was "shot" in frame 104 while responding in frame 105, the training officer observed, "Well, next time shoot a bit quicker—but, OK."

The September and Associates program, in its attempt to develop scenarios that closely correspond to actual armed confrontations, has developed computer simulations of videotapes of actual police/citizen armed confrontations. It also attempts to ensure that such factors as lighting, duration of the incident, and distance between police officers and citizen correspond to the realities of actual shooting incidents.

Another program, which seemingly is very responsibly conceived, but uses no unconventional technology, is the New York Police Department's outdoor range program. The attempt is to make shooting simulations correspond to actual street conditions. If reported shootings over a six-month period take place in alleys that are three yards wide, then the New York outdoor range simulations correspond to that type of physical condition. Similarly, shooting distance, race of opponent, time frame, and other dimensions all are made to correspond to observed patterns in recent police-citizen shooting encounters.

The Riverside, Seattle, and New York shooting programs obviously reflect major advances over static range firing. But there is still an element of the "officer survival" orientation in them, particularly in "shoot/don't shoot." In the more blatant cases of "officer survival" focus (as opposed to a balancing of risks over all lives in jeopardy), we have noted a level of suspiciousness that approaches paranoia among exposed officers. The probability of an inappropriate shooting could increase considerably.

Various police departments have developed interesting extensions of training related to the use of deadly force. In Rochester, New York, police officers receive eight hours of training in the "ethics of the use of deadly force." In New York City, trainees receive instruction in "legal training related to police use of deadly force." In these programs, officers discuss "gray" areas in the law, as well as the policy and practice of the use of deadly force. In the New York program, the recruits receive indoctrination in the legal philosophy underlying the city's use of deadly force guidelines, and recruits discuss shooting incidents in which the guidelines are ambiguous, analyzing past cases in which the use of deadly force was appropriate or not. In one New York police training class we observed, the recruits discussed a case in which an officer had been knifed by an insane man. His partner shot the main while he was fleeing from the scene (after the assailant dropped his knife). He justified his decision on a little used "imminent peril" clause in the New York State statute; this allows for the use of deadly force against unarmed persons when they present "imminent peril" to others. The recruits animatedly discussed a variety of cases involving the imminent peril clause and the types of situations where a decision to shoot would be justified or not.

A related training program was developed by one of the authors.[24] Two teams of ten police officers received 36 hours of training discussions about the moral implications of hypothetical shooting situations. Officers in one simulated situation were given an order to report to a building where they met a "neighbor" (actually a plainclothes officer), who was reporting a family disturbance. This "neighbor" told them that a man "inside the house was about to kill his wife." After the trainees resolved the simulated situation (some by shooting the man, others not), a discussion followed on the decision each officer made and the justification for it.

Another very important, but often neglected, type of training involves tactics likely to reduce the risk of armed confrontation. As Rubinstein observes, poor tactics often contribute to an officer shooting in an armed confrontation:

> From a purely technical point of view, the patrolman had initially made an error by failing to close the distance betwen himself and the suspect, allowing himself no alternative but to leave or to use his gun. If he had charged the man immediately upon suspecting him of some misdeed ... the patrolman would have avoided the chance of a much more serious incident.[25]

This type of street savvy is very difficult to teach, but a few departments have attempted sophisticated tactical training programs with varying success. The New York tactical training program uses cases in which the situation is either controversial or leads to increased hazards for the officer. One case (mentioned by the trainers as stimulating productive and apparently useful discussion) illustrated what the trainer called a "mass reflective response" to an armed confrontation:

Two officers on foot patrol were advised by a civilian that a movie theater was being robbed. The officers cautiously approached the theater and the suspect, who was in the manager's office, heard them knock on the door and announced that he was coming out with the manager. The officers then radioed for help as the suspect left the manager's office and entered the theater's ceramic-tiled lobby with the manager at gunpoint. Eighteen foot and motor patrol officers responded to the call for help and confronted the suspect in the lobby which faced directly upon the street. As they took up various positions on the street, the patrol supervisor entered the lobby, holstered his gun and tried to coax the suspect into surrendering. The patrol supervisor suddenly lunged at the suspect, and both fell to the floor. As both began to rise, seven of the officers fired 31 shots at the suspect, who had a gun in hand. The perpetrator fell, instantly killed by multiple gunshot wounds. The patrol supervisor suffered five gunshot wounds in his left arm and both legs. Four of the other officers present were also struck by bullets which had apparently ricocheted off the lobby's tiled walls. One officer was hit in the right arm, the second in the right thigh, the third in the left side and right leg, and the fourth in the left cheek. The suspect's gun was recovered fully loaded.[26]

The trainer offered suggestions as to how tactical errors created "an overresponse to the situation" and entertained ideas from the officers how the situation might have been tactically avoided.

In many cities, special units are given ongoing tactical training regarding barricaded suspects and hostage negotiations. Difficult problems are staged, and officer responses are scrutinized and corrected. Often, when time permits, officers preparing for a particularly dangerous armed raid will rehearse the tactical plan before the raid. Possible contingencies are discussed in advance and plans are made to prevent officer-to-officer cross fire or unnecessary exposure to fire from opponents.

Such tactical training attempts to influence officer decision making well before the actual decision to shoot. This, we argued in Chapter Four, is essential for successful outcomes to many armed confrontations. The efficacy of such training (whether formal or informal) is reflected in the observation by many police officers that "prepared" armed confrontations (in which training and behavioral rehearsal is possible) produce relatively few actual shootings compared with unprepared confrontations (where little preparation or training is possible). The usefulness of such training is further indicated in the relative rarity of shootings compared to the overall rate of armed confrontation among units that are given intensive tactical training, such as LAPD's SWAT Team, NYPD's Street Crime Unit, and Newark's Target Red.

Most tactical training is conducted informally through peer supervision and often through debriefing contacts with armed citizens. It might be hypothesized in this respect that officers in units that have long experience in working together (presumably thus developing tactical plans to meet most situations) and high contact rates with armed persons over time will reduce the risk of shots being fired in any particular armed confrontation. This hypothesis (if confirmed) would indicate that coping with armed confrontations is a trainable skill involving complex tactical strategy techniques that are trainable through experience.

Another type of training teaches officers the interpersonal skills likely to avoid dangerous conflicts with agitated citizens. Such training is, of course, most relevant to armed confrontation with an extensive "information exchange" with the opponent (for example, a family disturbance encounter). In Fresno, California, police officers participate in role-playing exercises (with actors of Hispanic descent) simulating a Mexican wedding. In New York City, officers learn skills useful in dealing with disputes involving a wide range of the city's polyglot population. This type of training focuses upon the interpersonal skills necessary to avoid at least some shooting confrontations. Bard's training experiments sought to teach officers the skills and tactics likely to reduce the possibility of "unnecessary" escalation of conflict that might lead to a police use of force.[27] Crisis intervention skills and nonlethal martial arts are taught in many police departments. The Honolulu Police Department, with a very low shooting rate, offers recruits many hours of training in martial arts. There also has been effective use of simulation, often staged by professional actors (see Schwartz[28]), to train officers in techniques to cope with violent citizens.

New York's social science training program offers an example of a well-thought-out police crisis intervention program. Recruits receive training in the psychology of violent persons and advice on how to deal with emotionally disturbed persons. Specific techniques are taught to "shape down" violent and psychotic or paranoid persons. Transactional analysis is taught as a means of understanding and avoiding violence using communication strategies to defuse violent encounters through assertive commands, distractions, and even humor. The trainees learn this strategy through lectures, role playing, and peer assessment of videotapes illustrating different strategies to defuse violent encounters.

It is obvious that no amount of training, no matter how sophisticated, will reduce unnecessary shootings to zero. There are, for example, many situations encountered by police officers in armed confrontations for which no training presently exists. Thus, while perhaps one-fourth of all shootings are encountered by off-duty officers, virtually no means exist to train officers in the responses appropriate to the unique dynamics of off-duty armed confrontations. And a limitation in even the best training is found in what might be called the questionable "hidden curriculum" (or latent value assumptions) of some training programs. The "hidden curriculum" might suggest to the young officer attitudes regarding use of deadly force quite different from those he might encounter in the department's training manual. For example, we observed one trainer in a department with an uncomfortably high police shooting rate deliver a lecture on the "legal aspects of deadly force" commenting (as an aside) to the recruits: "Now, of course, what we tell you in here is the theory of it; if you are in an alley with some prick with a .38, just make it look like he went for you. I won't ask any embarrassing questions."

Similarly, field supervisors can convey to an officer an attitude toward deadly force that may not be congruent with the department's training manual but may have as important an impact. One young detective was observed leaving a briefing in which he was ordered to transport a dangerous prisoner to a county jail. The captain, we were told, explained the assignment to the officer while he rotated the barrel of his revolver (perhaps for emphasis), concluding his speech by saying, "Now Smith, remember—don't lose the son of a bitch." It would seem reasonable to assume that this "briefing" constituted as important a "training experience" for the young detective as did the 40-odd instruction hours on the "legal and ethical dimensions of deadly force" he received at his local training academy. It might also be added that because of such value conflicts (and also technical limitations in existing training approaches), training in itself will be unlikely (in the absence of other changes) to successfully control fully police deadly force.

Operational Rules and Procedures

Operational rules and procedures constitute another administrative mechanism to control the rate of police use of deadly force. Operational rules in police work seek to regulate police behavior in encountering particular types of citizen behavior. For example, an operational rule may prohibit chases of juvenile joy riders, or forbid the use of mace against insane persons. In many other professions, it should be noted, operational rules are used more effectively than in police work. In the airline industry, for example, pilot behavior is restricted by use of very specific and empirically based operational rules. Such rules are redefined and reverified through ongoing investigations of both actual and averted aircraft disasters (lightning storms, forced landings, near collisions, and the like). A pilot, for example, when faced with an emergency such as a serious downdraft, burning engine, or near collision is instructed to respond in terms of clearly defined procedures. Many of these operating procedures require pilots to forsake intuitive reactions to emergencies and engage in procedures that have been found to cope effectively with specific emergencies. Thus, if an engine catches fire on takeoff, the pilot is instructed to level his aircraft *prior* to attending to the fire. Operational rules are defined for virtually every situation a pilot might plausibly encounter. An airline pilot's rulebook for such emergencies may cover more than 300 pages.

Police operational rules are far less formalized and detailed—and all too frequently neglected. They are, however, potentially very

TABLE 7.4 Fresno Rules for Responding to Potentially Violent Opponents

Levels of Force				
LEVEL 1	*LEVEL 2*	*LEVEL 3*	*HIGH RISK*	*FELONY*
Basic enforcement contact	Passive Circumstances suggest a threat to officer safety	Aggressive Actions, threats, or general circumstances threatening officer safety Ask for backup Notify supervisor Mace and baton level Take cover	Overt act Information Observation Accompanied with present ability to do bodily harm to officer Ask for backup Notify supervisor Firearms display (semiready position) Take cover	Crimes of violence Ask for backup Notify supervisor Firearms display (ready position) Take cover

Source: Fresno Police Department Operations Manual (1979).

important techniques for the administrative control of deadly force, as they define how specific categories of incidents are to be dealt with. Some departments have developed explicit operational rules for guiding officers in coping with possible use of force situations. The Fresno Police Department's rules for responding to potentially violent opponents in its "General Order on Use of Force" may be seen in Table 7.4. The rules are aimed at structuring officer responses to varying types of risk posed by opponents.

Reiss has persuasively argued that the creation of specific operational rules to deal with specific circumstances provides effective measures to control police use of deadly force in that "the earlier one intervenes in a causal sequence that the more likely one can alter its course."[29] Such operational rules, he argues, can effectively "rule out" those situations that are most likely to result in fatal or serious injuries to either citizen or officer.

Often, departmental operational rules are very narrowly focused in ordering officers to deal with a particular type of confrontation in a particular manner. Reiss offers an example of a possibly effective operational rule of that type, an order implemented after five officers fired at a psychotic man armed with a pair of scissors, a total of 24 shots. The new order created an operational rule that required officers to call supervisors or specially trained service officers (skilled in the use of mace and other techniques) rather than attempt to resolve a confrontation with a psychotic person themselves. Other common operational rules order officers to attempt to contain rather than rush barricaded suspects; order them not to engage in certain types of high-risk pursuits; and require police officers to call specialized types of personnel (for example, SWAT teams) to cope with particularly dangerous confrontations.

Clearly, informal police operational norms may be as important in controlling deadly force as are formal regulations. In almost every police department, one observes police cultural norms that define how to deal with particular types of confrontation. One set of such informal norms deals with discretion in terms of confronting particularly dangerous situations. One officer explained a norm of that sort in his department as follows:

> You have to remember. We had one of the worst riots back in the 60's. When we see a situation, let's say a group of blacks standing on the street corner, possibly with guns, virtually every guy here will pass it up, knowing that it's too dangerous to take them on unless you've got three or four cars to spare. It's like an informal code: *Restraint!*

Another department had an informal rule on displaying guns on certain types of calls that contradicted its formal rule. An officer explained this norm as follows:

> It's a set thing in the Pittsford area that if you get a family beef call, or whatever at night, you unholster, no matter what. The department says you can't unholster without seeing the other guy's gun, or something that's a threat, but you come with us any night and I bet you don't see one guy go up a back alley or staircase with his gun still in his holster.

Other informal rules may affect very subtle, though important, aspects of police behavior in armed confrontations. One informal norm deals with the time allowed for an officer or team to "clear" an assignment. In some departments, officers are encouraged to approach a building quickly, thus decreasing the time needed to "clear" a particular assignment. In one department, the sergeant would place a walkie-talkie call to officers who he felt were "fooling around," taking too long on a particular job. Other departments encourage greater caution in approaching "unknown or suspicious" circumstance calls.

Another type of informal norm governs pursuit of certain types of opponents. Some departments instill norms in their officers that encourage back alley chases of fleeing suspects. One supervisor, for example, chastised a young officer for not following an armed youth into the back of a darkened factory. Other departments discourage such chases, fearing the risk of a shooting should the opponent suddenly turn on a lone officer armed with a gun. One officer described his department's policy as follows:

> Here it's an unsaid thing, like "you gotta let them go." Like they seem to feel that most of these chases the guy will get away anyway and it's not worth the risk of you plugging the guy if he turns on you. Once he gets a step or two on you, it's good-bye and if he's bad enough maybe you try to get him later.

Other risk situations may be similarly avoided by informal norms. One department virtually forbade two-man teams from going beyond the third floor of a particularly violent, largely black housing project. Other departments similarly avoid dispatching line officers to Saturday night bar fights or domestic squabbles in certain areas or in high-risk situations.

Other (both formal and informal) police operational rules mandate the use of specialized units for particular types of confrontation.

In many cities, for example, a "man with a gun" call or "armed robbery in progress" automatically will be handled by a SWAT or other specialist team. In other cities, backup officers will be dispatched to certain categories of high-risk assignments. In Rochester, New York, crisis intervention trained officers (or civilians) will be dispatched to certain types of domestic squabbles. The following account describes a case where specialized police officers (tactical team) were able to "seal off" and "talk out" (rather than "rush") obviously frightened armed robbers.

It wasn't clear at first who was more relieved—the hostages, the robbers or the police.

Bellevue police last night arrested two gunmen, freeing two hostages unharmed and ending a brief but tense siege at a coin and jewelry shop in a small shopping center on the north side of the city.

The robbers, who had tied up the owners of the shop, had barely enough time to peek inside the two open safes before police arrived.

The panicked gunmen tried to ram their bodies through a rear window of the shop to escape. They only bounced off the double-pane glass, Conrad said.

That was when one robber's gun went off, sending a bullet crashing through a glass display case.

One of the men tried to pound a hole through the roof. It wouldn't have done him much good. Officer J. A. Rochell was on the roof with a shotgun trained on the source of the pounding.

Meanwhile, the store was being surrounded by dozens of uniformed policemen, detectives, tactical-squad officers and a canine unit.

"I told them that since they were giving themselves up, we should call the police and tell them what we were doing," Conrad the store owner said, explaining that he didn't want the officers outside the store to mistake him for a robber.

The two gunmen, frantic by this time, tried to use the phone. But they were too nervous to dial out. They had to untie Conrad so he could make the call for them, police said.

Conrad spoke with a police dispatcher, explaining that the two were ready to surrender. He said their only request was to be allowed to call their wives first.

Police agreed and the surrender came moments later.

The suspects emerged one at a time, hands high in the air.

Conrad, a former New Yorker, said he was not particularly unnerved by his experience.[30]

An important set of operational rules deals with the possession and use of weapons while off duty. In most departments, operational rules regulate carrying weapons while off duty. Many police departments require their officers to carry their firearms off duty because they are expected to enforce the law on a continuous basis (24 hours a day). Others, like Kansas City, leave the decision up to the individual officer, while advising against doing so when alcohol might be consumed. Fyfe found that more than 23 percent of shooting incidents involved off-duty officers.[31] In addition, in the 320 shooting incidents surveyed by Milton et al., in their seven-city study, 17 percent were by off-duty officers.[32] In Detroit, which accounted for 38 percent of their shootings, more than 22 percent involved off-duty officers. Fyfe has commented that off-duty armed confrontations tend to be associated with erratic officer behavior.[33] Such confrontations, he argues, are in part preventable through departmental operational rules regulating off-duty weapons. Alternatively, the carrying of off-duty weapons may be limited by operational rules to particular contexts and purposes.

The use of operational rules to lower the rate of police deadly force represents a most promising line for systematic intervention. It may well be, as Reiss has suggested, that many police uses of deadly force are averted by creating rules that make improbable an armed confrontation between a patrol officer and dangerous citizens.[34] This strategy is, of course, effective in averting only certain types of deadly force: primarily those with adequate time to call for backups and to deploy special weapons and special personnel.

It should be noted, however, that there are inherent difficulties associated with the use of operational rules. First, the idea of creating an "empirically grounded" rule to guide discretion in risk situations is alien to many "seat of the pants," "intuitive" police officers and administrators. Also, at this point, our knowledge of the mechanisms of armed confrontation is not advanced enough for the development of operational rules for any but the most obvious of situations. The next step in development might require that a department know not only how many armed robberies (of a particular type) resulted in a police use of deadly force but how many total armed robberies of that type were encountered in a particular period. Finally, completely effective use of such rules might not be possible in the context of a human interaction that has the infinite nuances of a police-citizen armed confrontation. Even a pilot may operate with considerably more circumscribed array of potential variations.

Shooting Review and the Punishment of Weapon Abuse

Perhaps the most direct administrative means of controlling police use of deadly force is the objective administrative review of all weapon discharges. Underlying the reliance on review and punishment of abuse is, of course, an assumption of the officer's belief that his conduct will be vigorously scrutinized and that the punishment will be significant. This position is stated by the chief of a large southern city department:

> Obviously, if the first effort, the effort at positive discipline within a department, is totally successful, there's never any necessity for any other activity on the part of the administrator; but experience and knowledge of human nature tells us this will not always be successful. So there must exist also within the department the negative aspects of discipline where sanctions are exercised against those officers who fail to comply, in those instances where there is not conformance with the established rules and regulations and policies of the department. In law enforcement, those sanctions go all the way from a verbal reprimand through written reprimands, disciplinary transfers, demotions, loss of pay or privileges, to suspension, and the ultimate punishment within a department is termination or separation from the service.[35]

Others have stated similar positions even more graphically. One deputy chief said emphatically that "if *any* of my guys do anything with a gun that's out of line, they know I will get their ass!" Another chief added, "There has to be credibility in that when an action involving a gun leads to wrongdoing, they [the policemen] must know that something will happen." An internal affairs officers commented, "Look, you gotta be absolutely objective, no favors to anyone. If you start saying 'Hey, he's an O.K. guy' or any of that shit you stop being an investigator and become something else."

There is at least some empirical foundation for the assertion that effective control of police use of deadly force is facilitated by sure, rapid, and certain punishment of wrongdoing. Deterrence theory from Beccaria and Bentham to Gibbs has emphasized the role of public sanctions in controlling social behavior, and psychologists have theorized about behavioral control through punishment for generations. Deterrence theory would lead one to conclude that actions that are publicly, certainly, rapidly, and severely punished will tend to be reduced. In a closed administrative system (such as a police department), the detection and punishment of wrongdoing should be, in theory at least, readily attainable.

Fyfe and Culver have related police rates of force to the frequency of police discipline following a review of force incidents. Fyfe, as we noted earlier, found a significant drop in the use of deadly force in New York following new, and more effective, shooting review policy.[36] Culver found, in a three-city comparison for use of force complaints, that the rate of sustained complaints following internal affairs investigation ranged 15 to 0 percent.[37] He also was able to relate these rates to the frequency of the use of force in these cities. Kobler observed that of 1,500 police shooting incidents he reviewed, only three resulted in criminal charges against the officers; even in cities with troublesome shooting rates, legal punishment of police shootings was practically nonexistent. The Los Angeles sheriff's office had referred but a single case for prosecution in almost eight years. More recently, Sappel found that of 77 shooting incidents in 1978–79, not one finding of wrongdoing was sustained:

> Block [the Undersheriff at that time] said discipline was not imposed in the 77 shootings between 1978 and 1979 because the deputies involved had adhered strictly to the department's shooting policy. In those 77 incidents, 27 civilians were killed and the rest suffered wounds ranging from minor to critical.[39]

Harding and Fahey were able to relate Chicago's high shooting rate to its lack of effective review of police shootings. The authors observe that in 1970–71 Chicago had the highest rate of police homicide of the five largest U.S. cities[40] (see Table 7.5). The authors attributed the city's high rate of police homicide to the often super-

TABLE 7.5   Shooting Rates in Five Cities

City	Population	Number of Officers in Police Department	Number of Civilians Killed	Annual Death Rate per 100,000 Population	Annual Death Rate per 10,000 Officers
New York	7,895,000	31,671	21	3.6	8.8
Chicago	3,367,000	12,961	32	12.6	33.7
Los Angeles	2,814,000	6,806	8	3.7	15.8
Philadelphia	1,949,000	7,780	13	8.9	22.3
Detroit	1,511,000	5,159	4	3.5	10.3

Source: R. W. Harding and R. P. Fahey, "Killings by Chicago Police, 1969–70: An Empirical Study," Southern California Law Review 46, no. 2, 1973.

ficial review of shootings performed by the department. For example, they cite a grand jury analysis of the review of the Fred Hampton (the Black Panther slain by the Chicago Police) case as an example of the failure of the Chicago police to monitor itself in terms of placing deadly force under objective administrative review:

> The performance of this branch of the Chicago Police Department . . . was so seriously deficient that it suggests purposeful malfeasance. . . . Instead of a complete investigation of any of the factual controversies raging in the press, the investigation consisted only of gathering all the police reports, soliciting cooperation from counsel for persons accused of crimes (knowing that no defense counself would permit pre-trial statements by an accused) and asking the officers involved a few simple conclusory questions in which they denied wrongdoing. No officer was given the opportunity to explain in detail what happened, and all the subordinate officers were asked only to ratify their sergeant's account—which itself was based not only on prepared questions, but suggested answers composed by a Police Department lawyer and shown to the sergeant in advance.[41]

On the other hand, claims abound of cities where a seemingly effective shooting review policy has maintained a credible deterrence in terms of police abuse of deadly force. One common element in these cities is that the review process becomes detached from the power and influence of those officers most directly involved in the shooting incident.

A publicized case of innovative shooting review reform is found in San Jose, California. When Joseph McNamara took over as chief in 1977, the city was in the midst of a controversy regarding the shooting of a man named Danny Trevino. The police had answered a disturbance call at a home on the city's predominantly Mexican-American East Side. One car found Danny Trevino sitting in his parked car with his girlfriend, Maria Duarte. The couple had been fighting, and Miss Duarte apparently was being held in the car against her will. The police officers approached the car from either side. As the woman leaped from the passenger side of the car, Trevino reportedly reached under the car seat with his right hand and then raised the hand and pointed it at an officer. A San Jose officer fired into the car, killing Trevino. Later police found Trevino had been unarmed.

McNamara responded to this controversy by taking several steps to control police abuse of firearms. Soon, eight "abusive" officers were fired; also the Internal Affairs office was both strengthened (it now reported directly to him) and moved from police headquarters to a rented office. McNamara believed this would encourage both objective appraisals of cases and a sense of trust in Internal Affairs by the Latin American community. McNamara comments:

> In San Jose a little over two years ago I was greeted with demands for a citizen review board, for transfer of certain patrol officers, and other signs of great lack of credibility on the part of some fraternities who had represented citizens against police officers, charging abuse of authority and excessive force. Today, the number of complaints against police officers, charging abuse of authority and excessive force has dropped in half. We have not had a questionable shooting in two years. The self-initiated, internally initiated, actions by supervisors have increased by 30 percent, and once again, the minority community spokesmen are the strongest supporters of the police agency.[42]

Other departments have claimed great advances in the systematic review of police shooting incidents. In Newark, all investigations are handled by a two-man shooting review team (including a black and a white officer) who report directly to the police director. They will "roll out" to the scene of a shooting immediately after the incident. (Four A.M. "roll outs" are not rare.) Efforts are made to contact civilian witnesses as well as other police officers at the scene. By bypassing the shooting officer's normal chain of command, the department believes it increases the chances of what several senior officers call an "objective appraisal of fact." The internal affairs officers are often feared but respected by line officers. Six-hour searches for a spent bullet (even a miss or a warning shot) are possible. Results from investigations are reviewed both by the internal affairs captain and by the police director. It should be noted that such objective appraisals often exonerate officers involved in controversial shootings. One officer who was involved in several previous shootings was thus cleared when two initially reluctant civilian witnesses supported his version of an ambiguous shooting incident.

Despite the evidence as to the efficacy of the stringent enforcement of shooting policies, many departments show scant interest in such measures. Often the reality of civil liability suits discourages the stringent review of police shootings. One chief articulately explained what he called the catch-22 of the internal review of police shootings:

> The reality of it is that there is a big catch-22 in the whole business. The better your shooting review is, the more likely you are to get your ass had. The quieter and vaguer you keep it [the review] the safer you are, from a legal point of view.

Police union politics also discourage the active prosecution of police wrongdoing. In several cities, police unions have vigorously defended officers charged or actually disciplined by the police department. In Los Angeles, three officers charged by the district attorney were legally as well as politically defended by Police Benevolent Association lawyers. One LAPD internal investigator commented, "They won't even talk to us if the union lawyer isn't sitting there." One former chief of a very large eastern city department stated, "Even if the guy is stone guilty, the chief couldn't do anything about it, even if he wanted to. Once I caught a guy with his trunk full of T.V. sets. After the union gets finished with the case, he almost got a medal."

Another problem lies in the extreme difficulty of defining unreasonable or even negligent conduct in police shooting decisions. Even in those cities where use of deadly force is restricted to the apprehension of armed and dangerous felons or self-defense, a wide latitude in judgment is still allowed to the officer. For example, in Los Angeles, an officer was exonerated by a shooting review board after he shot a 21-year-old white man, shortly after receiving a report that a 35-year-old black man had attacked a manager of a motel. This type of incident illustrates a core dilemma of the administrative review of police deadly force: that only grossly negligent cases of abuse can be controlled through administrative means. In situations where the officer reasonably (or apparently reasonably) believes that his life is threatened, administrative review is either difficult or impossible. The only incidents in which administrative sanctions are most commonly applied are cases in which gross professional negligence or criminal intent is readily evident. Milton et al. found that the cases in which sanctions resulted were most frequently cases in which the officer lied, was drunk, blatantly exceeded guidelines, or showed obvious erratic judgment. An example of this last type of situation is described by Milton as follows:

> Case L. An officer has parked the patrol car in order to observe a supermarket plagued by robberies and shoplifting. The officer, seeing a clerk chase some shoplifters out of the store, and knowing he can't catch the suspects, fires at them.[43]

Negligent conduct in more complex cases is far more difficult to define and document. Often the investigator must infer negligence from the position of bullets or persons rather than from the testimony of the officer himself, who in controversial cases will be immediately represented by the union attorney. One investigator thus commented, "Who (besides God) can with certainty say if an officer who confuses a raised wrench with a pistol made an unreasonable or negligent decision. We can't say and we can't prove it!" Unless there is evidence of lying or distortion of evidence, review boards rarely doubt an officer where there is even plausible evidence indicating that a reasonable man in these circumstances might have believed that his or someone else's life was in grave or mortal danger.

Whatever effect is exerted by the existence of an objective review policy may depend on an intangible factor: the belief by line police officers that their conduct will be rigorously scrutinized by the chief executive of a police agency and that wrongdoing will be punished. The case of Kenneth DiAngelis in Newark is interesting in his respect. In November 1978, DiAngelis, who had previously been involved in a series of controversial shootings, shot a young prisoner in a precinct jail cell. After a local prosecutor failed to act in the case, the police director, Hubert Williams, ordered DiAngelis arrested and charged with murder. Although the facts of the case were ambiguous (DiAngelis claimed the prisoner had attacked him with a chair leg in the cell) and the aftermath controversial (Williams's firing of the officer was sustained by a civil service commission nearly two years later), shootings by Newark police officers in the five months immediately following Williams's action dropped by nearly 60 percent.

The impact of what one police official labeled "effective heat" is similarly observed in the 70 percent drop in shooting in the four months following the Eulia Love controversy in Los Angeles and similar reductions in police use of deadly force following stern administrative actions in San Jose, Kansas City, and Atlanta. Such responses to public sanctions indicate that the subjective belief that wrongful shootings will be punished may be more important in reducing the rate of police deadly force than are the specific formal shooting review policies or procedures. As Machiavelli (perhaps sadly, but also astutely) observed, "Men react to fear more readily than kindness." This sad truth may apply to the behavior of police officers, as it did to the behavior of Machiavelli's subjects in *The Prince*. But the question remains to haunt us: How much of the diminution in shootings results from a restraint on the part of police officers to act appropriately aggressively?

CONCLUSIONS

In this chapter we have outlined several of the major difficulties implicit in the administrative control of police use of deadly force. We have surveyed existing research linking administrative policy to the rate of use of deadly force; summarized some of the theoretical issues related to the administrative control of deadly force; and speculated about the impact of administrative guidelines, training, operational rules, and review policies on the rate of police deadly force. On reconsideration, one might ask: If the administrative means exist to control police deadly force, why is it that in some cities police use of deadly force remains strangely high while shooting policies remain essentially unchanged?

Before attempting to answer this question, we present a summary and highlighting of previously discussed issues. Each of the four administrative mechanisms we have discussed makes key social and psychological assumptions about the way that police shooting behavior might be effectively controlled. These assumptions are summarized in Table 7.6. Obviously, a department's strategy of social control may include several of the administrative means we have described. Also, different departments or officers may define the assumptions of each of these mechanisms differently from the way we have characterized them. We offer the table to illustrate that the choice (or ordering of choices) of administrative mechanisms makes important assumptions regarding the definition of the problem of deadly force and, implicitly, asserts a theory of how deadly force may be controlled and how the officer makes a decision to use or not use deadly force.

Although it is conceptually and practically possible to develop a consistent and effective administrative system to control police deadly force, few departments have systematically implemented the types of administrative techniques we have described. In many departments we find tortuously ambiguous shooting guidelines, sporadic and obviously ineffective training, few efforts to define operational rules designed to minimize the risk of deadly force, and incomplete reviews of officer decisions to use deadly force.

In many cities, the chief reacts defensively to the admittedly complex dilemmas of police deadly force. Faced with countervailing union pressures, demands for proactive policing, community pressures and threat of legal actions, the chief follows (understandably) a policy of pragmatic vacillation. "We are," as one chief admits, "between a rock and a hard place on this issue. It's a no-win situation."

TABLE 7.6 Summary of Assumptions About Police Behavior

Administrative Mechanism	Implicit Assumptions About Why Avoidable Shootings Occur	Implicit Theory of the Control of Deadly Force	Implicit Assumptions of How to Control Police Decision Making
Guidelines	Avoidable shootings occur when officers lack specific guidelines defining when they may be permitted to use deadly force.	If guidelines are made more specific, then inappropriate shootings will be reduced.	Officers have difficulty implementing ambiguous abstract legal statutes and policy statements.
Training	Avoidable shootings occur because untrained officers make errors in tactical or perceptual or legal judgment.	If officers are given realistic training, the probability of panic, tactical mistakes, etc., will be reduced.	Officers can be trained to implement deadly force policies by making finer discriminations in situations and using tactics that make use of deadly force less likely.
Operational Rules	Avoidable shootings occur when officers enter situations in which risk factors are too high to avoid use of deadly force.	Avoidable shootings will be reduced if certain risk situations are avoided through use of backups, back-off procedures, etc.	Officers cannot be expected to implement deadly force decisions in certain volatile situations.
Intensive Shooting Review	Avoidable shootings occur because officers fail to use caution or act emotionally due to failure of the department to review and sanction avoidable shootings.	If level of sanctions is increased, avoidable shootings due to lack of care, experience, and emotion will be reduced.	Officers are deterred by fear from shooting abuses.

Another chief (known for his reform policies) similarly described his frustration at not being able to "go after" an officer who had been involved in "two bad shootings" during a six-month period:

> Now what can I do? The union wouldn't let my "IA" even talk to the guy. The city manager is in bed with the union and the guy's brother-

in-law is an ex-city councilman. The grand jury will smile at anything a
policeman does, providing it's not an out and out execution, and let's
face it, I've got battles going on in other areas. I have to choose my fight.

Such comments echo the key question we have raised: Why, if the
means are available to reduce deadly force, are police policies in this
direction not always implemented?

Of the many constraints facing change, perhaps the most insidi-
ous is the lack of clear legal statement on the issue of police deadly
force. To date, the U.S. Supreme Court has not expressed itself
explicitly on the topic. The legal status of many state statutes is
much like the state of educational racial codes prior to the *Brown* v.
Board of Education[44] decision or arrest laws prior to the *Escobedo*[45]
and *Miranda*[46] decisions. In California, the state "use of deadly force"
statute has been effectively ruled unconstitutional by the *Kortum*
decision.[47] A further indication of the larger legal confusion is found
in the observation that approximately half of the states still have
codified the widely criticized common law rule that allows deadly
force to be used in the arrest of any felony suspect. A somewhat different type of statute is found in the seven states that permit deadly
force as a response either to specific felonies or to a general category
of felonies. Finally, seven other states follow the Model Penal Code
provisions, which restrict the use of deadly force specifically to violent felonies.

Many critics of the existing status of deadly force law emphasize
that additional restrictions are needed on the broad discretionary
powers given to the police by the justification statutes.[48] A common
theme in these arguments is an ethical concern that flight from purely
property crimes should not result in the death of the suspect.

The failure of many legislatures to adopt the Model Penal Code
or a similar code has led to a growing number of constitutional challenges. Finch finds substantial, though not altogether convincing,
grounds for constitutional review of justification statutes under
Fourth, Eighth, and Fourteenth Amendment guarantees.[49] Particularly convincing to him are claims of Fourteenth Amendment due
process protections against unconstitutional deprivations of the right
to life and trial. Sherman argues that the common law statutes are
capricious in that they almost randomly punish fleeing felons.[50] And,
most recently, Geller and Karales looked favorably upon the federal
court decision that declared a state common law statute unconstitutional:

Indeed, the one beacon of hope for opponents of the common law any-felony rule shines dimly from the federal court house in St. Louis, which houses the U.S. Court of Appeals for the Eighth Circuit. This court, sitting *en banc*, in the 1976 split decision of *Mattis* v. *Schnarr* held that the Missouri statute which codified the any-felony doctrine violated the due process clause of the Fourteenth Amendment to the Constitution.[51]

The expression "beacon of hope" is used because constitutional challenges to deadly force laws have been rejected in other federal courts.[52]

A police administrator finds himself forced to choose between a number of shooting guidelines. As Uelman's study of police shooting policies in Los Angeles County shows, cities even in the same county may have radically different shooting policies.[53] Lacking a clear legal foundation, administrations may face a choice between expediency and idealism. One example of this tension was observed in a city (headed by a nationally known reform chief) where the city attorney advised the chief to drop all training and restrictive guidelines because state liability law (following *Peterson* v. *Long Beach*[54]) held the city liable to actions that exceeded departmental guidelines, though within state law.

It should be further emphasized that the courts have been largely silent on several major definitional issues relevant to the administrative and legal control of deadly force. One issue deals with the concept of "criminal negligence." With few exceptions like the *Somers* case,[55] which attempted to define what a reasonable belief is that a confrontation is dangerous, the courts have not given clear signals on issues as to how certain an officer must be that his or a citizen's life is in jeopardy "or how serious the threat to an officer's life must be." Two cases in Los Angeles illustrate the definitional difficulty. In one case, the district attorney prosecuted, on felony assault charges, three LAPD officers who confronted a gas station attendant with a shotgun, but there was considerable uncertainty as to the actual risk to the officers (they were acquitted). In another case, the district attorney reviewed a case where an officer fired at a crazed man who was about to throw a typewriter in the direction of the officer. The key issue in this case, according to the investigator in charge of the case, was "whether or not the threat of the typewriter could be considered a lethal threat against the officer." The dilemmas of internal affairs officers, chiefs, juries, and lawyers is that the courts have been virtually silent on such issues. One result of the ambiguity is that police chiefs, grand juries, and district attorneys have been reluctant to take action (legally or administratively) against all but the most egregiously negligent cases of the abuse of police deadly force.

Another constraint against effective reform involves the tenuous political status of the chief. One study found that the average chief enjoys a tenure of under two years. Caught between political, union, and community power blocks, the police chief of the 1980s finds himself in a constant battle for survival. The case of Boston's Robert DiGrazia is instructive. Leaving Boston, because of a refusal by the mayor to grant a long-term contract, DiGrazia accepted a job in Maryland. He was fired within a year. Professionally ostracized by law enforcement generally and virtually hounded by embittered unions, DiGrazia has not been employed as a police chief for many years. Commenting on what he called the "DiGrazia object lesson," another well-known reform chief said: "Look, who's kidding who? What happened to Bob could have happened to any of us. Don't think that when we contemplate something radical we don't think of DiGrazia and his five kids."

Another of the many constraints making the job of controlling deadly force difficult (or impossible) is the recent rise of union militancy. The age of the Boston police strike in which virtually a whole police force was fired is long gone. As one nationally prominent chief said, "The mental patients are running the asylum." In many cities, police deadly force policy has become a major union issue. In San Jose, the officers' association filed a legal action against that city's deadly force policy. In Miami, the suspension of five officers for defacing the property of blacks involved (presumably) in the recent Miami riot was reversed due to the threatened statewide strike of police officers. In Los Angeles, the Police Protective League filed a class action suit designed to rescind certain policy recommendations of the police commission. Routinely in cases involving police use of deadly force, police unions defend the officers involved and vigorously fight actions to sanction officers for the abuse of deadly force.

And the public is not willing to support what are widely considered undue restraints on police operations. In many cities, there is virtually a public obsession with the reality of street violence and crime, a concern that in many cities overwhelms other considerations. One veteran city police reporter, for example, observed: "If the guy on the street has a choice between risking getting killed by a wacko hype and a wacko cop, he'll take his chances on getting wasted by the cop, so that the cop can kill or arrest the hype." Recently, many middle-class backs have articulated similar positions. A New York

Village Voice article by an articulate black journalist, Stanley Crouch, argues that blacks have more to fear from black criminals (he uses the example of the notorious Harlem black drug dealer) than they do from violent cops. He quotes one black officer as indicating the pleasure he would take in "wasting" Nicky Barnes and similar street predators:

> A black cop, a friend of mine for years, told me this after the *Times* ran that story on Nicky Barnes. He says, "Listen, man. Let me tell you something. The white cops in Harlem, they don't give a fuck about drugs. They don't give a fuck about nothing. They think maintaining order up here is a losing proposition. They think black people will inevitably kill or maim each other or tear up each other's property. But the black cops, we take it personal. Particularly when they try to make somebody like Nicky Barnes a goddam folk hero or some motherfucker tells you how dope provides jobs for the downtrodden! If they'll sell dope or help cut dope, they need to be down and out. If one of us black cops had a chance, we would have taken Nicky Barnes somewhere when nobody was looking and put two in his head. Quick." That's the way he felt about it.
>
> "I wish they had've killed him. I wish they'd killed all of them," adds one of the others, "because they not only sell dope, they're the ones the kids get this attitude of not giving a fuck about anybody else from. This is why kids beat up people after they already done gave up their wallet, or set somebody on fire. They probably think they're being cute, like one of these goddam hustlers beating one of his bitches in the street. He's proving to the world how cold he is. Now you got kids who want to prove the same thing, or maybe they're just mad at the world. When you don't give a fuck, you'll do anything. People like that need to be behind bars or in the graveyard."[56]

Crouch predicts—we think with some justification—that this new law and order vigilantism will increase as more middle-class citizens, black and white, resettle the inner cities:

> If lots of white people start moving into Harlem, the schools will improve and so will the policing. They'll run all those dope dealers off 116th and Eighth Avenue and the other boulevards. Given the gas crisis and the fact that young, successful couples are moving into the city and looking for places to live, Harlem brownstones and refurbishable grand apartment houses concretized the grim sense of the observation. It would also add another irony to the many connected to this story, for it would mean that the criminals who have done so much damage to Harlem are now helping to change it even more. When they once made

whites afraid to go there, they might now be making it much easier for them to return.

Interestingly, Columbia University just bought three buildings at 145th and St. Nicholas, one of Harlem's most crime-infested blocks. The tenants have been removed and told they can come back. No one believes it. As the buildings are renovated, the word among the hustlers is: "It's time to clear out. They're ready to clean up this block."[59]

The reality of violent crime leads to what we might call the "administrative dilemma of the hard charger." The "hard charger," in police vernacular, is an officer who achieves many arrests through his aggressive "street attitude" and possibly at times excessive force. The dilemma posed by this type of officer was articulated by a very bright, young, and perceptive urban police force deputy chief:

Look we've got guys we *know* will get involved in shootings. The problem is they also will get involved in many arrests. The older fat officer (we got lots of these too) won't shoot anybody. They also won't arrest anybody either. Ten percent of our guys will get involved in 80 percent of our shootings and make 90 percent of our best felony arrests.

The observations made by this deputy chief were supported by a sergeant who was commissioned by his chief to do a study of "officer shooting risk." The sergeant commented that the major finding "was that most of the shooters had won medals." He went on to observe that the more surprising thing was that "the chief threw his study in a wastebasket as soon as he saw it." He said, "We couldn't fire those guys," and, "If the lawyers found out we knew how dangerous those guys were, they would murder us if they could prove we knew."

Klockars has recently written on what he calls the "Dirty Harry problem"—the juxtaposition of good ends and dirty means. In a traditional example, Inspector Harry ("Dirty Harry") Callahan stands on a kidnapper's mangled leg to torture him so that he reveals the location of the kidnapped girl. Klockars phrases the dilemma as follows: "The Dirty Harry problem asks when and to what extent does the morally good end warrant or justify an ethically, politically, or legally dangerous means to its achievement?"[58] Transferring the issue to deadly force, what should our moral or practical position be if we know that "hard chargers" (Dirty Harrys?) may at times use excessive force, but are the best cops in the sense of getting violent criminals off the streets?

Another constraint against the effective administrative control of police deadly force involves the very myth of police deadly force itself. As we observed in Chapter Three, while the early urban police were not armed (the first reported shooting in New York occurred amid much controversy in 1858), policing has become perhaps irreversibly intertwined with the mystique of the revolver. The early western marshals often were selected because of their prowess with a six-shooter.[59] Media police officers such as Starsky and Hutch, Popeye Doyle, Kojak, and Bullitt, as well as Dirty Harry, seemingly use their guns as frequently as they use their forks and knives if one were to believe the movies.

Any effort to disarm (or even control) an armed police force violates the public (and police) conception of the essence of policing—even though this conception may have little foundation in reality. For a police chief to demand control of his officers' weapons will appear to some almost un-American—a violation of a frontier myth in which one's security is measured by the speed of one's draw and the power of one's .44.

Such constraints should make the seemingly ineffective efforts by many police chiefs at least understandable if not blameless. The typical police chief is (as one fellow chief puts it) almost by necessity (if he is to survive) a political animal. Torn between his (possible) humanistic ideals and such diverse groups as a local Urban League chapter, Civil Liberties Union, police union, law and order citizen, and politicized courts and district attorneys, the line of least resistance (a tempting one, we might add) is a pragmatic course of action. Such a choice may maximize one's career chances in an (at best) extraordinarily difficult political role. It cannot, however, confront the realities of the effective control of police use of deadly force.

NOTES

1. G. Berkley, *Democratic Policeman* (Boston: Beacon Press, 1969), p. 1.

2. K. J. Matulia, *A Balance of Forces* (Gaithersburg, Md.: International Association of Chiefs of Police, 1982).

3. L. Brown, "Police Use of Deadly Force," in *A Community Concern: Police Use of Deadly Force* (Washington, D.C.: National Institute of Justice, 1978).

4. J. J. Fyfe, "Shots Fired: An Examination of New York City Police Firearms Discharges," Ph.D. dissertation, State University of New York at Albany, 1978.

5. A. Etzioni, *A Comparative Analysis of Complex Organizations* (New York: Free Press, 1961).

6. D. M. McGregor, "The Human Side of Enterprise," in *The Planning of Change*, ed. W. G. Bennis, K. D. Benne, and R. Chin (New York: Holt, Rinehart and Winston, 1961).

7. C. Argyris, *From Theory to Practice* (San Francisco: Jossey-Bass, 1974).

8. J. Q. Wilson, *Varieties of Police Behavior: The Management of Law and Order in Eight Communities* (Cambridge, Mass.: Harvard University Press, 1968).

9. G. F. Uelman, "Varieties of Police Policy: A Study of Police Policy Regarding the Use of Deadly Force in Los Angeles County," *Loyola of Los Angeles Law Review* 6 (January 1973): 1–65.

10. H. Williams, "A Chief Speaks on Deadly Force," paper presented to the American Society of Criminology, Philadelphia, 1979.

11. S. G. Chapman, *Police Patrol Readings* (Springfield, Ill.: Charles C. Thomas, 1971).

12. Matulia, *Balance of Forces*.

13. Los Angeles Police Department Manual, Section 1/556.40.

14. S. G. Chapman, "Police Policy on the Use of Firearms," *The Police Chief*, July 1967, p. 16.

15. Charlotte, North Carolina, General Order, 1980.

16. Report of the Board of Police Commissioners Concerning the Shooting of Eulia Love and the Use of Deadly Force, Part IV, Officer Involved Shootings, Los Angeles Police Department, 1979.

17. Ibid., p. 15.

18. J. J. Fyfe, "Administrative Interventions on Police Shooting Discretion: An Empirical Examination," *Journal of Criminal Justice* 7, no. 4 (Winter 1978): 322.

19. J. Rubinstein, *City Police* (New York: Farrar, Straus and Giroux, 1973).

20. R. J. Gioliotti, "Guidelines for the Use of Deadly Force," *Law and Order*, March 25, 1977, pp. 48–58.

21. Ibid., p. 54.

22. Gerald Kaplan, "Review of Los Angeles District Attorney's 'Roll Out' Program" (Washington, D.C.: Law Enforcement Assistance Administration, 1980).

23. *Peterson* v. *City of Long Beach*, 24 Cal. 3d 238 (1979).

24. P. Scharf, "Shooting: Moral Judgments Related to the Police Use of Deadly Force," in *Criminology Yearbook* (Santa Monica, Calif.: Sage Publications, 1980).

25. Rubinstein, *City Police*, p. 304.

26. New York City Police, Tactical Training Manual, 1979, p. 19.

27. M. Bard, "Family Intervention," *Journal of Criminal Law, Criminology and Police Science* 60 (1969): 247–50.

28. J. Schwartz, *Crisis Intervention Training Manual* (San Jose, Calif.: Liebman and Schwartz Associates, 1980).

29. A. J. Reiss, Jr., "Controlling Police Use of Deadly Force," *Annals of the American Academy of Political and Social Science* 452 (November 1980): 122–34.

30. *Seattle Post-Intelligence*, "Police Corner Robbers," December 21, 1980.

31. Fyfe, "Shots Fired."

32. C. H. Milton, J. W. Halleck, J. Lardner, and G. L. Abrecht, *Police Use of Deadly Force* (Washington, D.C.: Police Foundation, 1977).

33. J. J. Fyfe, "Always Prepared: Police Off-Duty Guns," *Annals of the American Academy of Political and Social Science* 452 (November 1980): 72–81.

34. Reiss, "Controlling Police Use of Deadly Force."

35. G. King, speech to National Institute of Justice Conference on the Police Use of Deadly Force, Dallas Police Memorandum, Dallas, 1978.

36. Fyfe, "Shots Fired."

37. D. Culver, "Police Discipline Practices," *Law Enforcement Newsletter* 3 (1975): 14–23.

38. A. Kobler, "Police Homicide in a Democracy," *Journal of Social Issues* 31, no. 1 (Winter 1975): 163–84.

39. J. Sappel, "Police Review Policies in Question," *Los Angeles Herald Examiner*, March 26, 1980, p. 1.

40. R. W. Harding and R. P. Fahey, "Killings by Chicago Police, 1969–70: An Empirical Study," *Southern California Law Review* 46, n. 2 (March 1973): 285.

41. Ibid., p. 297.

42. J. McNamara, speech to Community Reconciliation Service Meeting on Deadly Force, Silver Spring, Md., December 10, 1979.

43. Milton et al., *Police Use of Deadly Force*, p. 46.

44. *Brown* v. *Board of Education*, 347 U.S. 483 (1954).

45. *Escobedo* v. *Illinois*, 378 U.S. 478 (1964).

46. *Miranda* v. *Arizona*, 384 U.S. 436 (1966).

47. *Kortum* v. *Alkire*, 69 Cal. App. 3d 325 (1977).

48. See, for example, F. R. Finch, "Deadly Force to Arrest: Triggering Constitutional Review," *Harvard Civil Rights–Civil Liberties Law Review* 11, no. 2 (Spring 1976): 361–89; and L. W. Sherman, "Execution Without Trial: Police Homicide and the Constitution," *Vanderbilt Law Review* 33, no. 1 (January 1980): 71–100.

49. Finch, "Deadly Force to Arrest."

50. Sherman, "Execution Without Trial."

51. W. A. Geller and K. J. Karales, *Split-Second Decisions: Shootings of and by Chicago Police* (Chicago: Chicago Law Enforcement Study Group, 1981), p. 43.

52. *Wiley* v. *Memphis Police Department*, 548 F. 2d 1247 (1977); *Beech* v. *Melancon*, 465 F. 2d 425 (1972); and *Jones* v. *Marshall*, 528 F. 2d 132 (1975).

53. Uelman, "Varieties of Police Policy."

54. *Peterson* v. *City of Long Beach*.

55. *Somers* v. *Superior Court (Sacramento)*, 32 Cal. App. 3d 961, 1973.

56. S. Crouch, "Crime Moves Uptown," *Village Voice*, March 23, 1980, p. 4.

57. Ibid.

58. C. B. Klockars, "The Dirty Harry Problem," *Annals of the American Academy of Political and Social Science* 452 (November 1980): 35.

59. F. R. Prassel, *The Western Peace Officer* (Norman: University of Oklahoma Press, 1972), p. 9.

8 Where Do We Go From Here?

THE SOCIAL COSTS

During a five-week period early in 1980, four police officers were shot to death in New York City.[1] A patrol officer was killed while stopping a motorist for a routine check; the driver rapidly sped away after shooting the officer. A second officer was shot by a man in a scuffle that followed the man's attempt to avoid paying a 50-cent subway fare. Another officer was killed on a streetcorner in Harlem after he and his partner approached a man who seemed to be carrying a gun; the man turned rapidly and opened fire. Finally, a firearms instructor was shot in Brooklyn in the process of trying to stop a holdup in a bar.

A female officer on the Nashville police force, responding to a robbery in progress at a food market, shot three innocent persons—the manager of the store and two customers.[2] The manager died instantly and the two customers were wounded; all three were fleeing from the robber and shot as they left the store. In New Orleans, an officer who reportedly had been drinking, became involved in a scuffle with a band chaperone, fired his gun, and wounded a nearby student in a high school band.[3] In Philadelphia, an officer was charged with murder for fatally shooting a 17-year-old unarmed boy who was stopped by the officer for driving a stolen car.[4] When the youngster ran from the car, the officer struck him at least twice on the head with his service revolver, producing skull fractures and

231

leading to the discharge of the weapon and the shooting of the young-ster. Finally, in Miami in 1982, a police officer's use of force in killing a young black man in a video arcade touched off a costly disturbance and further damaged police–community relationships in that city.

All these incidents illustrate the tragedy that can result from armed confrontations. The modern response calls for a balancing of risk between officer and citizen—in distinct opposition to the former orientation in American law enforcement on officer survival. It repre-sents a position somewhere between those of officer protection at any cost and foolproof protection of all citizens whatever their his-tories of violence.

Before discussing approaches that we feel will advance that balance of risk, let us restate and highlight certain other possible con-sequences of failures in the realm of deadly force. First, of course, are the riots that frequently result from a controversial shooting. These have been mentioned at various points throughout the book, but as a further example, violence recently broke out on the streets of Philadelphia after the shooting of the 17-year-old described above. Streetlights and windows were broken, a police car was stoned, an officer was injured with a brick, and three news photographers (white in a black neighborhood) were attacked by a crowd.

Then there is the issue of civil suits and the resulting cost to society. Two officers and the city of Houston have been directed by a court to pay the parents of a victim of police shooting $1.4 million.[5] The victim had stolen a van and been chased by the police in speeds up to 100 mph before the armed confrontation. The officers claimed the victim had come out of the van firing, but the investigation indi-cated that a "throw-away" gun was placed near the body by the offi-cers. In another case, the widow of a man shot by an officer in Idaho was awarded $44,040 by a jury.[6] In an altercation outside a bar between officer and victim, the two exchanged blows with the weapons, flashlight and beer bottle, and then fought with fists. Even-tually, two shots from the officer's gun ended the altercation and one life. A 29-year-old man in New York City, paralyzed from the waist down by a police shooting, was awarded $7,014,000 in dam-ages by a jury in Brooklyn State Supreme Court.[7] Yet the officer who shot the plaintiff had been commended for "meritorious police duty" in the same incident for which the award was made. Moreover, in his previous 12 years in the police department, the officer had earned 19 commendations and a medal of valor. The award came five and a half years after the shooting.

Virtually every police shooting that leads to injury or death can be expected to lead to a civil suit in the 1980s, no matter how justified the action may seem to the outside observer. Whether or not a given suit is successful, the process is very expensive for society. We have firsthand knowledge of the reality of recent litigation patterns from the number of times one or the other of us has been asked to be an expert witness in a civil action resulting from a police shooting.

Third, there is the intense psychological distress to many minority citizens when one of their members is shot by a police officer, presumably, but not necessarily, without adequate justification. It is a symbol of derogation, a sign of the small regard they conceive the police have for their members. Whether or not the reaction is justified (as we indicated earlier, people often find it difficult to place themselves in the shoes of the officer at the time a shooting decision must be made—they react to the outcome only), the resulting emotions are painful.

Another cost exacted in the general arena of police use of deadly force involves police morale and the implications of that morale for crime control. We observed that the officers in Newark and Birmingham reacted with extreme caution and restraint in law enforcement when they felt that the administration was unreasonably heavy-handed in policy formation or in the imposition of sanctions. To illustrate, in an article entitled "Keeping Order in Dodge City East," a Newark newspaper recounted the enormous numbers of murders, muggings, burglaries, and assorted other crimes in that city.[8] An interview with the president of the Fraternal Order of Police by the writer of the article brought the following response:

> The police feel that if they take action, they'll go to jail. There seems to be a move by the police director to have them curtail pursuing crime for fear of sparking a riot. . . . It's demoralizing. The majority of police will go out and do a hell of a job, but they are afraid they are going to be left holding the bag and end up being prosecuted.[9]

Perhaps, as many would argue, that statement represents an advocacy position rather than a real cost to society. That issue is admittedly less than clear, but surely there is no question that the morale of the police is affected by administrative (and legal) decisions regarding deadly force and that there could be spillover to crime control. The importance of police morale for the community has been discussed by Toch.[10]

Finally, there is the psychological damage to many officers that results from shootings that lead to death or serious injury. A reporter for the *Los Angeles Herald Examiner* sued for confidential records of officers who became psychologically disabled by police shootings and eventually obtained the records in an out-of-court settlement.[11] In his lead article, "Police Casualties: The Deep Wounds of Man Behind Gun," he described one officer, S., as "a once healthy, happy investigator" who had become a paranoid schizophrenic as a result of shootings: "A number of officers have suffered psychological trauma after civilian shootings, but [S.'s] case is one of the most severe in LAPD history. His case is tragic proof that police can be devastated by their own bullets."[12] Another officer, B., became psychologically unfit for duty after a shooting:

> As another psychiatrist put it, [B.] is . . . psychiatrically impaired to the point where he is unable to perform either restricted or unrestricted duties.
>
> The doctor further wrote: "He has chronic difficulties sleeping, with nightmares consisting of usually being chased. He becomes shaky when he drives by a police station. . . . His sex life has decreased because of a lack of desire. He is irritable, requiring a great deal of effort to avoid outbursts."[13]

THOUGHTS ABOUT IMPROVING MATTERS

Commitment and Training

The pluralism of values related to deadly force raises several practical questions for police administrators. It appears that the process of policy socialization is far less complete than many or most police executives believe. Also, there is evidence that police officers may be more responsive to values gleaned from line supervisors or from peers in operational units than from administrative policy statements. In an area with such irreversible stakes as the police use of deadly force, it seems desirable to have far more uniform standards within police departments than seem evident. Just as two offenders with similar records and charges who receive very different sentences may complain about the injustice of the system, so too police departments should be concerned about widely different policy and legal interpretations.

It would seem desirable for police chiefs to articulate carefully their personal commitment to departmental policy and guidelines.

That is clearly a problem when a departmental policy statement has been forced on a chief and his department by a political process. The chief could (as a good public servant must) then verbalize support for the policy, though deep-down commitment is certainly not there. As part of this package, we, therefore, think it desirable for sensitive responsiveness by politicians to the police perspective, even in turbulent times where a large segment of the public is demanding radical change. There should be negotiation and compromise, even if it means gradual implementation of change. The effort could minimize the type of phenomenon found most dramatically in Birmingham (see Chapter Two) after the imposition of a markedly more restrictive shooting policy by its mayor, with resulting intense and severe conflict between the mayor and the police. For reasons of concern for safety (the police interpretation) or of deliberate slowdown to express animosity (the political interpretation), the resulting decrease in police action—though possibly short-lived—surely exacted a price from the public.

It would seem, further, that the effort to achieve uniformity in knowledge and attitude among officers in regard to deadly force calls for greater emphasis in formal training. Cases should be reviewed and discussed that emphasize ambiguous or marginal areas in deadly force policy. Where possible, police officers should walk through real-life simulations dealing with legally, as well as tactically, ambiguous policy areas.

It also appears useful to offer more advanced legal training to line supervisors on the topic of deadly force. Line supervisors should be trained in communicating restrained attitudes toward the use of deadly force even in highly charged situations. The ability to operationalize deadly force policy should be tested in promotional exams. Finally, there should be efforts to rotate officers periodically through different types of assignments to avoid highly cynical "Fort Apache" type police unit subcultures from developing within high contact units in large police departments. Care also should be taken to place highly mature and restrained officers in such units.

The Use of Operational Rules

As discussed in the last chapter, high-risk contact with armed, or potentially armed, people must be controlled by carefully formulated operational rules. The position is consistent with our sequential model of police officer decision making and our most general hypothesis that decisions early in an armed confrontation make an eventual use of deadly force more or less probable.

Where time and tactical considerations allow, patrol officers should call for backup officers (specially trained in coping with armed persons) rather than attempt to confront the opponent themselves. Sealing off an opponent and seeking cover, while calling for backup, should be emphasized in policy manuals. Other operational rules should be generated from data collected by individual departments on both actual and averted uses of deadly force. Such data would establish the efficacy and risks of particular operational rules.

It is surely clear that one can far more readily generate rational, minimum-risk alternatives for particular armed confrontations in a laboratory setting than one can in the heat of rapidly developing street scenes. And human beings need structuring when anxiety, fear, intimidation, a "need to look good," and quick decision making are present in complex interactions. The concept to do a specific such-and-such, like call for backup, provides that type of structuring. Moreover, where a choice of that sort is necessary rather than merely a remote possible alternative, the officer has no conflict with his need to act courageously or with bravado rather than dependently.

There are other gains from this approach. First, there would be an increased likelihood that officers with the greatest skill would actually confront armed persons wherever possible. In addition, the evaluation of such operational rules and their impact upon the rate of deadly force would greatly contribute to our conception of the types of tactics likely to avoid unnecessary uses of deadly force. Finally, in implementing such rules a police department would further articulate to its officers its commitment to restraint in the use of deadly force.

Avoidance of Unrealistic Conceptions of Threat

As stated in the last chapter, some training approaches in the area of deadly force seem oriented toward producing paranoia. Clearly there is much danger associated with police work, and clearly there is need for appropriate training to cope with that danger. But there is a considerable gap between appropriate training and training that produces paranoid fear. It is clear that the rate of use of deadly force is directly related to violent crime rate.[14] And there is marked fluctuation in a single city over time, though there is no regular periodic pattern, seasonal or otherwise. For example, in Oakland in 1979, the rate of deadly force increased by 600 percent, then rapidly subsided. In Newark, the summer of 1980 and winter of 1977 saw marked increases in deadly force incidents.

We conjecture that at least some of the surges are caused by a climate of agitation, fear, or animosity created by violent crime or perceived risk on the part of the officers. We note, for example, that there is occasionally a blip of increased shootings following the killing or wounding of an officer by a civilian. The shootings that led to the abrupt termination of James Parsons as chief in New Orleans provide another dramatic example.[15] Those shootings directly and rapidly followed the slaying of a New Orleans officer.

Several experienced officers have suggested that many questionable uses of deadly force occur during these cycles of increased perceived danger. The shooting of Eulia Love occurred during a period of both high crime and increased shootings by officers during the winter of 1978–79 in Los Angeles. A shooting of an innocent man in Newark in the winter of 1977 occurred during a month in which no fewer than 11 officers fired their weapons compared with an average of four per month during 1977 as a whole.

For those precipitative circumstances that make it possible, police departments should attempt amelioration. In the process, reports of dramatic crimes and arrests should be used in a balanced manner, to make police officers aware of possible dangers, but not to create a climate of irrational danger. Informal briefings by line supervisors should seek to place in realistic proportion, perceptions of danger to the police officer. This type of briefing style requires both maturity and skill. Techniques should be developed to train line supervisors in techniques to prepare line "high-contact" police officers to interpret, in a balanced manner, the dangers they might encounter during duty on the streets.

There is evidence that personal perceptions are critical in terms of officers responding to citizens in an overly reactive manner. In many shooting incidents there was an initial perception of risk seemingly greater than would be warranted by the objective circumstances of the incident. Also, as we have observed elsewhere,[16] in such tragic incidents as the shooting of Bonita Carter in Birmingham, the police perception of community violence seemed to play a significant role.

The issue of reaction to the shooting of an officer is particularly difficult. The immediate feeling of outrage and the need to invoke control are unquestionably related to perceived threat in the long run (as well as to other factors). All the leadership ability of the chief and the command staff is, therefore, necessary for amelioration. At this stage, we simply point out the need for alertness on the part of the chief. Future research can perhaps lead to specific strategies for implementation.

Community Tensions and Police "Community-Conflict" Teams

We have discussed earlier in this chapter the extraordinary sensitivity of minority citizens to police actions that can be interpreted as derogatory. And, of course, that sensitivity at times leads to violent expression. To help ameliorate such perceptions, it seems highly desirable for police departments to initiate community relations teams (probably made up of persons from a variety of racial and ethnic groups and including civilians as well as police officers). These persons should be multilingual, as needed, and comfortable in communicating with citizens from a variety of economic backgrounds and political persuasions. They would also include people with aptitudes and training relevant to working with juveniles.

The team would be sophisticated in the distinction between a reasonable or unreasonable decision, on the one hand, and a correct or incorrect decision, on the other. It would act to further understanding between groups that too often distrust each other vehemently, but would have no fact-finding authority. Investigation, the formation of explanatory constructs, and corrective action should properly remain with units having the necessary expertise—internal affairs, homicide, the prosecuting attorney, the U.S. attorney, and so on.

The underlying theme of the team would be that the police-citizen encounter is a transaction involving fallible human beings. Errors may occur in either direction—the citizen may unexpectedly remove a toy pistol from his pocket or make a gesture that is easily interpreted as threatening; the officer may unholster his gun prematurely or misperceive an entirely innocent gesture or motion on the part of the citizen. Immediate understanding would hopefully lead to change in the longer run.

Monitoring the Behavior of Officers

It seems clear that police departments should more carefully track the shooting behavior of officers. Keeping records is not enough; an alerting or triggering mechanism should be built into the system. Several writers have pointed out that the prediction of violent behavior is scientifically, ethically, and legally hazardous.[17] In seeking to incarcerate persons predicted as dangerous, for example, one runs the risk of incorrectly imprisoning many people who in fact are no risk to society. In terms of the prediction of police officer behavior, one faces similar dangers. Moreover, police unions and civil rights advocates have pointed out that the use of such predictive technology may violate some fundamental rights of officers.

The one area where such objections are not so clearly compelling is that of force complaints and prior shooting behavior as predictive data. Although a police officer might complain that his divorce or hair color or weight is illegitimate in terms of assignment or restriction decisions (regardless of previous empirical findings), it is difficult to argue that police departments should not be permitted to keep detailed records on the use of force or that reassignment should not be based on such data. A false positive does not have serious consequences of the order of longer incarceration, and the relationship of predictive behavior to outcome behavior is quite direct.

As discussed in Chapter Six, shooting histories indicate intriguing commonalities in officer shooting behavior. One Newark officer with three shootings fired all his shots from cars. Another officer with eight shootings in ten years fired seven times in off-duty confrontations. Another officer's confrontations resembled "wild west" duels. Still another officer's confrontations all followed hand-to-hand fights with Puerto Rican males. Such data may be useful to supervisors in keeping officers away from situations, which, for one reason or other, may lead them to become involved in shootings. For example, the officer who had had a series of duels was assigned to a traffic squad where he has avoided a use of deadly force incident during the past three years.

In monitoring officer shooting behavior, the department should be careful to consider the contact rate of the particular officer in assessing his behavior. As we noted in Chapter Six, knowing the number of shootings encountered by a police officer is not particularly useful unless one can reasonably estimate (perhaps by his assignment history or armed arrest rate) the number of encounters in which he might have used deadly force.

Psychological Services for Officers

It would seem highly desirable for police departments to require one or two interviews with a psychologist for all officers who kill or seriously wound someone in a deadly force encounter. As pointed out at various points in this book, one finds a full range of responses to a killing or wounding, from the officer who sneers that the "bastard deserved it" and states slight satisfaction as the only lasting after-effect to the officer who needs psychiatric services, perhaps hospitalization, and disability release from sworn duties.

Officers frequently report a lack of social support from superiors and other officers following a trauma. That was particularly the case for B., described earlier in this chapter. They may even be separated from other officers who were involved in the incident in order that investigators may gain independent descriptions of the episode. Many officers similarly report feeling abandoned by a police administration committed to objectively (and possibly punitively) scrutinizing their actions.

A promising model to cope with officer psychological trauma following such traumatic events was found in the Rochester, New York, Police Department. Officers who themselves had been involved in use of deadly force episodes were trained in peer-counseling techniques and dispatched to counsel other officers involved in a shooting incident. Often these officer-counselors met with the officer-participants within hours of the shooting episode. And the Dallas Police Department has a full-time clinical psychologist with two (M.A.-level) aides who are sworn officers.

It seems desirable for the initial visit(s) to a psychologist to be mandatory rather than voluntary because of the implication, for some, that a need for psychological services indicates weakness or a lack of vigorous masculinity. Service for the officer, as well as his family, beyond the required contact would be at the option of the officer and his family.

Although the principal gains of this approach are obvious enough, a subsidiary gain is the open recognition that police officers (as well as citizens) become active victims (sometimes physically, other times psychologically) of armed confrontations. It is not fully appreciated that many officers find the necessity of wielding (and occasionally using) deadly force at best a distasteful and possibly debilitating obligation. It is our opinion that recognition of that fact would enhance the reputation of the police in most communities.

Decision Making in Armed Confrontation

As we pointed out in earlier chapters, the state of the art of training in deadly force is not at a high level of sophistication. The following provides an overview of particular problems:

1. Existing training curricula focus either on the mechanics of shooting or decision making in the final frame of an armed confrontation (the Motorola "Shoot/Don't Shoot" program).
2. Training in shooting decision making rarely reflects the most frequent types of encounters actually confronted by police officers.
3. The affective context of the shooting training environment is totally different from the types of pressures that might be exerted upon the officer in a real-life armed confrontation.

In terms of our sequential mode of thinking about armed confrontation up to the point of shooting or nonshooting, it is clearly essential to provide armed confrontation decision problems at each phase of the armed encounter. Officers, for example, might be trained in developing sets toward information received from dispatchers, in various alternatives in seeking an advantageous position (in addition to the usual stress on the importance of cover) prior to encountering the opponent, and in different modes of communicating with opponents in the confrontation.

It is useful, too, to train in specific decision matrices to be followed during the confrontation. For example, officers should be trained to back off in certain confrontations in which the risk of a shooting becomes unacceptably high. It is important to teach officers techniques of assessing risks in opponents based on prior information as well as observations on the scene. Also, officers should be taught the importance of planning and coordinating actions with other officers wherever possible.

Training examples rarely reflect the types of incidents police officers face in street encounters with citizens, including lighting, time of day, type of physical surrounding, time frame, number of opponents, characteristics of opponents, and so on. Training examples should, in short, be geared to model types of encounters experienced by police officers in a particular area, not simply shootings. By gearing training only to shooting cases (especially dramatic and atypical shootings), officers may develop unrealistic cognitive sets toward armed encounters. A scene in the Motorola "Shoot/Don't Shoot" series in which a 12-year-old boy on a bike suddenly draws on a police officer provides an example of how the use of an atypical (or possibly nonexistent) case may contribute to the creation of unrealistic conceptions of danger on the part of police trainees.

It is also suggested that effective training attempts to simulate (impossible to accomplish fully) some of the affective dimensions of police-citizen armed encounters. By including partners, bystanders, and other social actors in the simulated police-citizen confrontation, as well as some of the fear and uncertainty in such episodes, one may begin to approximate the real-life demands of such incidents.

It seems that considerable emphasis should be given in training programs to coping with unarmed, though threatening citizens and with people who have weapons that are not guns. The training should emphasize communication skills and the use of "less than lethal" weapons (described in Chapter Seven). In devising the program, some thought must be given to the concept of "balancing the risks" in terms of identifying and reacting to threat. In several instances, shooting a person who did not have a weapon or who had a weapon that was not a firearm created a major community incident (consider, for example, the shooting of Eulia Love in Los Angeles). And, in many situations, the police officer may tactically retreat and avoid immediate peril.

CONCLUDING STATEMENT

Given the history of violence in the United States, and its continued widespread expression, it is clear that police shootings and police killings will not be substantially reduced over a short period of time, no matter what is done. The research of Geller and Karales on shooting by the Chicago Police Department is illustrative of that point.[18] They, in the concluding chapter of their report, recommend the following as the policy statement that should adopted by American police departments: "A police officer is justified in using deadly force only when such force is intended to defeat a present threat to the officer's or another person's life."[19]

That is indeed a restrictive statement, as any citizen has the right of defense of life, and a more restrictive one is not possible. It is at the other end of a continuum that is anchored at one end by the common law—any fleeing felon policy (or law). But, if that policy of Geller and Karales had been in effect in Chicago during the years they covered in their research, their data indicate that the police shootings in Chicago would have been reduced no more than 25 percent. It will take sincere cooperation between police and minority communities to reduce mutual paranoia while efforts are made within the police domain to reduce the number of shootings to the minimum number a balance of risk policy allows. And that balance of risk, as we repeatedly emphasized throughout the book, refers to innocent citizens, police officers, and offenders.

Given the level of crime, particularly violent crime, in inner cities, where minority citizens tend to live, it would seem reasonable to expect them to be ambivalent about the police—suspicious about police motivations but needing whatever protection they afford. And the positive side of that ambivalence is being shown more and more in such forms as letters to newspapers by blacks supporting the police and by the formation of police-citizen liaison committees. To illustrate more specifically, in a recent meeting in Newark between the new captain of the West Precinct (the precinct of the 1967 riot) and the local community, the black audience demanded in very strong terms that the police *do* something about the criminals hanging out on the block: the robbers, the rollers, the drug addicts. As a police officer at the meeting remarked: "These are the same people who 15 years ago were screaming 'pig' at us and throwing bottles. Now they want us to do things we aren't prepared to do."

Perhaps tolerance for a broader margin of error in the police use of deadly force will result from the increasing acceptance of the need for police services. That could lead to meeting the police halfway in the latter's shift from an officer survival perspective to one demanding a balance of risk (to injury or death) between police and citizens. That may be easier when more people realize that the surprise of our observations over these past several years is not that there are unjustified and unnecessary shootings (as indeed there are) but that, given the numbers of citizens who are armed and the frequency of police-citizen armed confrontation, so relatively few shots are fired by the police and so relatively few people are killed by their bullets.

NOTES

1. *Los Angeles Times*, March 1, 1980, Part I, p. 3.
2. *New York Times*, August 31, 1980, p. A10.
3. *New York Times*, April 18, 1981, p. A12.
4. *Los Angeles Times*, August 30, 1980, Part I, p. 18.
5. *Webster* v. *City of Houston* (USDC 1980).
6. *Dilka* v. *Haynes* (USDC, Idaho 1981).
7. *New York Times*, December 19, 1981, p. 1.
8. *Star-Ledger* (Newark), August 25, 1980, pp. N1, N4.

9. Ibid., p. N4.

10. H. Toch, "Police Morale: Living with Discontent," *Journal of Police Science and Administration* 6, no. 3 (September 1978): 249–52.

11. *Los Angeles Herald Examiner*, March 16, 1980, p. A-1.

12. Ibid.

13. *Los Angeles Herald Examiner*, March 17, 1980, p. A-10.

14. See, in particular, J. J. Fyfe, "Shots Fired: An Examination of New York City Police Firearms Discharges," Ph.D. dissertation, State University of New York at Albany, 1978; and A. Binder and P. Scharf, "Deadly Force in Law Enforcement," *Crime & Delinquency* 28, no. 1 (January 1982): 1–23.

15. *New York Times*, November 20, 1980, p. A18.

16. Binder and Scharf, "Deadly Force in Law Enforcement."

17. F. A. Wenk, J. O. Robison, and G. W. Smith, "Can Violence Be Predicted?" *Crime & Delinquency* 18, no. 4 (October 1972): 393–402; S. Halleck, *Psychiatry and the Dilemmas of Crime* (Berkeley: University of California Press, 1971).

18. W. A. Geller and K. J. Karales, *Split-Second Decisions: Shootings of and by Chicago Police* (Chicago: Chicago Law Enforcement Study Group, 1981).

19. Ibid., p. 183.

Index

[armed confrontations]
  positioning in, 121–122
  postshooting relationships
      in, 132–134
  premise of, 22
  real life, 55–58
  records of, 62–63
  reflexive shooting in, 128–
      129
  and risk assignments, 86
  and social influence upon
      decision making in, 116
  space in, 89–91
  thematic portrayal of, 65–66
  tragedy of, 232
  training for, 91–92
  with unarmed citizen, 61
  "undermanned," 87–88
  and urban police, 60–61
armed confrontations, decision-
      making phases of, 111–
      112
  aftermath, 115–116, 132–
      134
  anticipation, 112, 116, 118–
      120
  entry and initial contact,
      113, 120–124
  final decision, 114–115, 123–
      130
  information exchange, 113–
      114, 125–128
Arrington, Richard, 16
averted shootings:
  in "Christmas Eve in the
      Ghetto," 19–22
  incidents of, 20
  statistics of, 97–98
Avery, Mike, 14

Bard, M., 159, 164, 208

"Barney Miller," 38
Berkeley, G. E., 34, 183
Binder, A., 71–72, 135
Birmingham (Alabama), 14–16
Bitner, E., 38
Black Marble, The, 35
Boston police strike, 225
  See also police unions
Brown, Lee, 187–192
Brown vs Board of Education,
      223
Bullitt, 37
Burns, Walter Noble, 37

Carter, Bonita:
  citizen's panel for, 16
  killing of, 14–16
  parents of, 16
  police review panel for, 16
  testimonies in killing of, 15
Chapman, S. G., 17–18, 47,
      195, 199
Charlotte (North Carolina) Po-
      lice Department, 199
Chicago Police Department,
      217, 242
Choir Boys, The, 33, 161–164
"Christmas Eve in the Ghetto"
      incident, 19–22
  See also averted shootings
cities, political unrest in, 10
citizens:
  body language of, in armed
      confrontations, 126–
      127
  communication of, with po-
      lice in armed confronta-
      tions, 125–126
  intimidation of, by police,
      45–46
  See also armed confronta-
      tions; guns; police

246

Klockars, C. B., 227
Knoohuizen, R., 71–72
Kobler, A. L., 42, 71–72, 216
Kohlberg, L., 170
    See also morality, stages of
"Kojak," 37
Kreskin, 201

Lake, Stuart N., 37
Langworthy, R. H., 10–11
Law and Order, 33
Lefkowitz, J., 40
Lewis, Ronald, 105
literature:
    depression-era, 37
    pulp novels, 37
Lofland, J., 112
Los Angeles Commission
        Reports, 103
Los Angeles narcotics search
        warrant raid, 85–86
Los Angeles Police Depart-
        ment, 42, 65, 110,
        196, 208
Love, Eulia:
    and criteria of reasonableness
        in use of deadly force,
        24
    daughter of, *see* Love, Sheila
    personal history of, 110
Love, Eulia, shooting of, 103–
        106, 237
    and conflict with gas com-
        pany, 103–104
    and decision making in armed
        confrontations, 112–
        116
    "majority report" in, 105
    witnesses to, 104–105
        See also O'Callaghan, L. W.;
        Jones, Mrs.; Ramirez,

[Love, Eulia, shooting of]
        John; Hopson, E. M.
Love, Sheila, 105

McDuffie, Arthur, killing of, 17
McNamara, Joseph, 217–218
"Man with Ax" incident, 11–13
Margarita, M., 17–18
Melekian, Barney, 95–98
media, and mythology of urban
        police, 37
    See also films; literature;
        television
Miami:
    killing of Arthur McDuffie
        in, 17
    riots in, 10, 225, 232
Milton, C. H., 71–72, 159,
        214, 219
Miranda vs *Arizona*, 223
Model Penal Code, 223
morality:
    of shooting, 167, 170
    stages of, according to Kohl-
        berg, 170–172
    stages of, according to Scharf,
        172–176
    study of, by Scharf, 172–176
Motorola Films, 203
murders, statistics of, 42
Muir, Paul, 110, 147, 159
Myer, M. W., 65, 71–72, 200

Nashville, 13, 231
Newark:
    averted shootings in, survey
        of, 98
    booking precinct in, 2
    deadly force in, police use of,
        7
    and Guardian Angel incident,
        13

About the Authors

PETER SCHARF was born in New York City and attended the University of Rochester and Harvard University, where he received his doctorate in 1973. He has published five books including *Readings in Moral Education* (1978), *Growing up Moral* (1979), and *Toward a Just Correctional System* (1980). He, along with Arnold Binder, has served as co-principal investigator for the National Institute of Justice on a grant regarding the police use of deadly force. He is currently director of the corrections program at Seattle University and serves as a consultant to the Seattle Police Department.

ARNOLD BINDER is a Professor of Social Ecology and Psychiatry and Human Behavior at the University of California, Irvine. He has held visiting professorships at the University of California, Los Angeles; University College, Dublin, Ireland; and the University of Colorado. Professor Binder was the founder and first director of the Program in Social Ecology, and the founder of the UCI Youth Service Program, a youth diversion project. He serves as consulting editor to a number of scholarly journals and is the author of numerous articles and several books including *Methods of Research in Criminology and Criminal Justice* (with Gilbert Geis) and *Modern Therapies* (with V. Binder and R. Rimland, editors). He received his A.B. and his Ph.D. from Stanford University in Psychology and Mathematics.